INDIA AT TURNING POINT

T.S.R. Subramanian retired as the Cabinet Secretary to the Government of India. He has since become a forceful advocate of governance reform. The PIL, TSR Subramanian & Ors v. Union of India, has led to the 2013 Supreme Court decision, hailed for bringing about genuine civil service reform.

Subramanian has a master's degree in public administration from Harvard University, and has previously published *Journeys Through Babudom and Netaland: Governance in India*.

Praise for the book

'In the context of current public anger and debate in India about deficiencies in public governance even after more than six decades since independence, TSR's book will provide ample food for thought to the policymakers as well as students of public administration.'
—T.S. Krishnamurthy, Former Chief Election Commissioner

'In this incisive analysis…TSR has combined his rich and varied experience of the system with his immense analytical skills, to critically appraise the complex political, social and development challenges facing the nation today.'
—Vinod Rai, Former Comptroller & Auditor General

'I cannot think of a more engaging work than this one by T.S.R. Subramanian for all those who are interested in figuring out what is wrong with India's political and administrative machinery and how best to set them right.'
—Dipankar Gupta, Sociologist

INDIA AT TURNING POINT

The Road to Good Governance

T.S.R. SUBRAMANIAN

Published by
Rupa Publications India Pvt. Ltd 2014
7/16, Ansari Road, Daryaganj
New Delhi 110002

Sales centres:
Allahabad Bengaluru Chennai
Hyderabad Jaipur Kathmandu
Kolkata Mumbai

Copyright © TSR Subramanian 2014

First published in RAINLIGHT/hardcover in 2014

All rights reserved.
No part of this publication may be reproduced, transmitted,
or stored in a retrieval system, in any form or by any means,
electronic, mechanical, photocopying, recording or otherwise,
without the prior permission of the publisher.

ISBN: 978-81-291-3556-8

First impression 2014

10 9 8 7 6 5 4 3 2 1

The moral right of the author has been asserted.

Typeset by RECTO Graphics, Delhi

Printed at Replika Press Pvt. Ltd, India

This book is sold subject to the condition that it shall not, by way
of trade or otherwise, be lent, resold, hired out, or otherwise circulated,
without the publisher's prior consent, in any form of binding or cover
other than that in which it is published.

For
THE POOR CITIZEN OF INDIA

who continues to pay for the sins and poor governance by the ruling classes of this 'democracy'; where everything is done in his name, but he is left holding the sack, continuing to remain in the most miserable condition, tolerating what elsewhere would have led to a bloody revolution decades back. Surely he deserves the opportunity to blossom.

CONTENTS

Acknowledgements		ix
Preface		xi
1.	Activity as Substitute for Action?	1
2.	Should Growth Be the Only Criterion for Economic Policy?	17
3.	Placebo Governance	38
4.	Has the Media Become More Shrill, But More Effective?	51
5.	What Is Modernity—Is It Rejection of Tradition?	66
6.	Public Health—The Huge Cost of Neglect?	76
7.	Education—Imperative Need for a Revamp?	86
8.	The Neglect of Physical Infrastructure— The Heavy Price?	101
9.	Strategic Issues—Are We a Soft State?	117
10.	Does Parliament Represent the People Anymore?— Reforming Politics And Politicians	130
11.	The CBI Needs Fixing (Also How It Tried to 'Fix' Me)	148
12.	How Can Government Ensure Improved Delivery of Services?	159
13.	Direction of Civil Service Reforms?	171

14.	Who Wants Corruption Eliminated—Except the Citizen?	192
15.	Can Coalition Governments Give Good Governance?	208
16.	Do We Recognize the Glory of Our Classical Arts?	229
17.	Cricket is Religion—Others Don't Exist?	237
18.	Those Carefree School and College Days	252

At the End   273

ACKNOWLEDGEMENTS

Vinay Sitapati helped me from the beginning, commenting on the structure and contents, often with some brutal honesty (well justified); he has probably made a very poor draft passable! I am very grateful to him. Shankar and Amy Sitapati read through the draft, and made valuable suggestions.

Ambassador R.L. Narayanan has done much high quality research work on the coalition governments of 1996-98, based on contemporary documentation and media reports. Much of Chapter 15 incorporates his conclusions, with some comments from me. I gratefully acknowledge his contribution.

Chander Lekh spent a lot of his spare time helping me with the draft of this publication. My thanks to him.

The poor ground conditions, accompanied by some carelessness from me, were responsible for an Achilles tendon tear in my leg, confining me to my residence for a couple of months, and providing me the time to write the book. My thanks to the grounds committee of the Noida Golf Club!

PREFACE

Sudiksha is a 13-year-old child studying at VidyaGyan School in a village not far from Delhi. VidyaGyan is a remarkable school. It admits bright 10/11-year olds from poor village schools, including the most backward districts, and gives them a free education of high quality. When Sudiksha came to VidyaGyan three years ago, she hardly knew any English, was shy and diffident. After just three years of exposure to trained teachers, resources, and nutritious food, she can outperform the most privileged children from Delhi's elite private schools. It's a simple lesson: Indians have the ability to compete with the best, if only we give them the opportunity.

It is this opportunity that we have failed to provide our citizens. The reality in 2013 is far removed from the promise of our Constitution, given by us to ourselves in 1950. At that turning point in our history, we simply took the wrong turn. In every index of human development—education, health, even peace and harmony—India ranks near the bottom of the world. For example, practically every other country in the world provides electric power without break; we are unable to provide our citizens with this basic service. As a result business suffers, households are hurt, farmers are seriously handicapped, and millions of our poor children are unable to study at night.

We cannot blame our past; most countries in Asia who started on their development path after we did, are now far ahead of us. We also cannot blame our people. It is not they who have failed us, it is our government which has failed its people. Poor governance is the one factor that has to take responsibility for this state of affairs. If we are able to fix our governance problems, then every village school can become like VidyaGyan, every child in India can become tomorrow's leader.

I have been in the Indian government for 37 years. I have seen public service at the village, district, divisional, departmental and state secretariat levels. I have also had the privilege of functioning, during an eventful period as the official head of the largest Indian state, Uttar Pradesh. I have worked in central ministries, and was privileged to be the official head of the central administration for two years. I can truly call myself an 'insider'.

But since retirement 15 years ago, I have become an outspoken 'outsider'. I have not held any official post. Instead, I have been associated with public service outside of government. Through writing and television appearances, I am a consistent voice of governance reform—and don't hesitate to take on the powers that be. I should also add that my post-retirement experience has led me to review and revisit a number of opinions I held strongly in service life; perhaps I didn't know enough then to take a broader view. One of my books, *Journeys through Babudom and Netaland: Governance in India*, has been well received, and is quoted even now. I have been associated with the corporate sector, and have served on many boards. However, what makes me happiest is my close association with a number of charity programmes such as VidyaGyan. As an insider-outsider, I can see both sides of the link between governmental activities and public welfare. I can relate to the interface between the government and the 'governed'.

The essays in this book deal with this relationship between the governed and the government. Why are places in India, like those in which Sudiksha grew up, so lacking in basic facilities? What has gone wrong with our governance—and how do we fix it? While I have written this book more to please myself, I feel I am qualified to call myself an 'outsider' as well as an 'insider' in governance. I owe it to myself to share my thoughts, for whatever little it may be worth. This book is also a personal retrospective. I have weaved in my experiences, incidents from my life, mainly with a view to bring attention to public policy and implementation issues, rather than recount them for their own sake.

Except for one early chapter and the last one, which are in the nature of reminiscences, most other references to my experiences are intended to highlight structural weaknesses in the system, and lead to reforms. In the process, perhaps there has been repetition of a few incidents from my earlier books. I have not edited them out, as they flowed naturally. This book is not an autobiography, even though I have dealt with many incidents and events in my life. My closest thoughts and most important experiences, I have kept to myself—this book is not a vehicle for that. I expect these will depart with me, unrecorded. This book relates to my experience with public policy issues and implementation measures.

Each chapter is conceived as a self-contained essay, on one theme each. I have also interspersed the discussion with personal experiences that could have relevance to the theme. I have tried to suggest reform measures in each chapter; these need to be developed into concrete actionable policies and programmes. The last three chapters are more or less personal reminiscences, perhaps not fully relatable to policy issues. The reader interested in public policy could skip those—or forgive an old man his indulgences.

Six decades after Independence, we are at another turning point. We failed to make use of earlier opportunities—the Constitution guarantees dignity and self-respect to the citizen, but how many Indians live such lives? Our governance has not permitted our citizens to reach even these minimal goals. The general elections are due in 2014, and there is change in the air. India is now a young country, and one can distinctly discern restlessness for change and better governance. But will we lose our way once again? This book is a cry for reform; a prayer that the right leader will emerge and take us on the right path. If some of these ideas or reforms, based on commonsense, are listened to, we may end up taking the right turn this time around.

Post-Script: The book was written in Summer 2013, well before the election campaign of late 2013, and the historic developments of early 2014, which brought a new government into place with a massive majority scripted by Narendra Modi, who became Prime Minister in May 2014. This is a new beginning. The nation's hopes are pinned on him to lead it forward to meet the aspirations mentioned in the last para of the book.

1

ACTIVITY AS SUBSTITUTE FOR ACTION?

Things are not always what they seem—Plato

If Plato were to write his book in India in the early 21st century, he would have rephrased his comment to 'Things are always not what they seem', with reference to governance standards these days. The classic injunction to an administrator has always been that he should not only do the right thing, but should always appear to be doing it—this has now transformed to include only the second part—only appearances matter, substance is of little relevance. Action is not really required; what is essential is the illusion that action is taking place—activity is of the essence. The attempt of course is to fool all the people all the time and there has been a large measure of success over the past 70 years; never mind if one is found out—brazen it out. Tell a lie a thousand times, the majority starts believing it. It is convenient to blur the interface between policy and implementation. It is important to acquire power without responsibility and accountability. These represent evolution in the art or science of governance, Indian style.

There are three main pillars in our governance structure, as envisaged in the Constitution—the legislature, the executive and the judiciary, each having distinct areas of responsibility, with corresponding powers and obligations. The Executive, responsible for administration is headed by the political executive, representing the people, supported by the permanent executive—the bureaucracy; both are public servants. The political executive and the permanent executive are really two sides of the same coin, the former primarily for forming policy and the latter for its implementation with this variant that the senior bureaucracy in the secretariat assists the political head closely, and is part of policy formulation. In our administrative structure, both in the Centre and in the states, administration is done through policy decisions taken in the secretariat and their implementation done through field agencies. At the secretariat, divided into line departments, the minister is the elected head of each department. He is supported by a phalanx of officers, headed by the secretary, who supervises the other officials in the team. The head of department in each ministry supervises the field machinery at the district level, where the District Magistrate as the chief representative of the government coordinates the work of the district heads of departments, who are responsible for field level implementation. For good governance, it is imperative that while there should be close coordination and cooperation between all concerned, the lines of activity and responsibility should not be crossed, and each person or group should confine his work to the task envisaged and assigned to him. If wires are crossed in a large system there is great danger of confusion and mal-administration. In this chapter, we look at issues relating to action versus activity and confusion between the roles of the administration, and the general harm routinely done to the administrative structure during the implementation process.

The policy-implementation continuum

The inability to distinguish between policy issues and supervising their implementation is illustrated by the extraordinary story of the then Cabinet Secretary, going on a secret visit in 2010, accompanying a couple of senior ministers, to meet Swami Ramdev at the airport, and to escort him 'through the backdoor', to a hotel for private discussions. Presumably, the 'government' team was keen to persuade Ramdev, through use of inducements, threats and cajolement—the entire gamut of साम दान बेद दण्ड (*Sama-Dana-Beda-Danda or the progressive use of force only after all persuasion fails*)—to dissuade him from a fast for creating a Lokpal (ombudsman). Recall that this was the time when Anna Hazare had shaken up the system with his demand for a Lokpal and demonstrated massive public support for it, in the aftermath of the 2-G Supreme Court ruling. The government had not yet become totally and shamelessly brazen as it became later; and it was keen to pre-empt Ramdev from opening one more 'front'. The astonishing thing was that the then Cabinet Secretary found it necessary, convenient and acceptable to join this political delegation to meet Ramdev informally in this context. Under the scheme of things, the Cabinet Secretary has no role to play in field level politics, indeed in politics of any sort. Was the Cabinet Secretary a secret agent? Did he have a formal 'written' mandate? Did he have a Cabinet sanction? Was he a political functionary? Wasn't it fully indecorous of him to join this infamous delegation, and lend it dignity? If the highest bureaucrat in the country were to dabble in politics, working closely with professional politicians, with what moral justification can we demand that the district or block or village official should not bring politics into his administrative function and should operate independently without fear or favour?

One has learnt on reliable authority that the Director Enforcement and the Chairman of the Central Board of Direct Taxes (CBDT) also met Ramdev, not once but at least twice, separately in Delhi at some secret unspecified locations, to dissuade him from the proposed fast. One cannot see the propriety of senior government officials intervening in purely political issues. Clearly these meetings were with the full knowledge, indeed tacit concurrence of the then finance minister. In a properly functioning system, those officers might have been charge-sheeted for indiscipline and for violating conduct rules (indulging in political matters). Was the Enforcement Director threatening Ramdev with charges of violating the Foreign Exchange Management Act (FEMA)—true or trumped up? Did he and the Chairman CBDT meet the Swamy in their personal capacity to seek his spiritual blessings? Or did they meet him to threaten him with severe punitive action? Or to sweeten him with a promise of 'dropped charges'? When the attempt failed, the Swamy was slapped with FEMA charges. Were they and the Cabinet Secretary not morally, ethically, procedurally and even legally in the wrong? Shouldn't the senior officers be ashamed of themselves for bringing the system to disrepute. Should they not have been discharged from service with dishonour?

One can recall, that in the early 1990s, the then Cabinet Secretary, Rajgopal had accompanied the then minister of state for home affairs, Rajesh Pilot in an open jeep, traversing the streets of old Delhi to 'restore calm' after some riots. Was the Cabinet Secretary the Superintendent of Police of Delhi? Is he a field functionary? Should the Army Chief go to a trench in Ladakh to fight enemy fire, leaving aside his leadership role in Delhi? Isn't there abdication of leadership exhibited here in favour of populism and cheap publicity? The spectacle was like a show of force by the District Magistrate (DM) and the Superintendent of Police (SP) in a troubled district town. Is this what national governance has come down to? On another occasion a few years back, when the government was facing a critical close vote of confidence in Parliament, the then Petroleum Secretary and a very senior official from the Prime Minister's Office (PMO) went to meet the leader of a political party and his cohort (now defunct politically), ostensibly to explain the 'petroleum policy', but actually to cadge the faction's political support, with heaven knows what inducements. In a recent Supreme Court monitored case (the Coalgate scam), two senior officials from the PMO and the coal ministry were conspiring in the Central Bureau of Investigation (CBI) office to alter substantially, presumably to suppress the emergence of facts, the status report to be submitted by the CBI before the apex court. This fact has been established through an affidavit by the CBI Director. If these do not amount to gross violation of discipline, and possibility of dismissal, what does? Has the dividing line between politicians, the political executive and civil servants been erased? Have the 'civil servants conduct rules' been rescinded? These are only some of the glaring failures brought to public notice—sadly these are not exceptions, they are the norm at the Centre and in the states. We can see the roots of the collapse of governance in these episodes.

These are extreme cases of total lack of grasp in differentiating between policy and implementation issues, seen at all levels, at the

Centre, in state capitals and in district towns. Ministers constantly deal with issues relating to transfers and postings, as well clearing individual cases—clearly for a consideration—with policy matters 'relegated' to be dealt with by the officials. This is a total role reversal of their envisaged functions. I recall asking a Revenue Secretary in Uttar Pradesh in the 1970s about the distribution of work between him and his minister. His reply: 'The minister looks after the important work of transfers and postings of tehsildars and naib tehsildars—I look after revenue policy.' Clearly there is deterioration in standards in this regard, which is progressively worsening sharply in each decade.

The only justifiable exception I recall from the early days relates to the then Cabinet Secretary—was it Dharma Vira?—going successfully to Srinagar in the 1960s to 'recover' the stolen hair of the Prophet at Hazratbal. The circumstances were peculiar— perhaps the then prime minister could not trust a local politician or the local administration in Jammu and Kashmir for a variety of reasons. The full story of how the 'success' was achieved and how 'authentic' the success was, was never told. This intervention in extremely sensitive aspects, with potential emotional overtones is perhaps not unique. Many stories, some perhaps true, may be told about similar crisis management relating to, say Ayodhya's Ram Lalla, or others, which are possibly in circulation, though some have been quietly buried. However, apart from this incident referred to, one does not recall any instance where the Cabinet Secretary or a Secretary to the Government of India directly got involved in managing or implementing operational issues, however pesky or inconvenient, and descended to ground-level political contacts to achieve political objectives.

However, such instances now abound. Recall the Commonwealth Games (CWG) mismanagement panic in 2010, when about six weeks before the event it was discovered that preparations were in a terrible mess. Astonishingly the prime minister created a team, headed by the Cabinet Secretary, with membership including a large number of 'bright' young joint secretaries, to literally 'clean-up' and prepare for the Games—which the team successfully accomplished. Was this proper? Was this not a complete and total derogation of the approved scheme of things—an abuse of governance processes? Were the senior secretaries responsible for creating policy or for functioning like a municipal clean-up team? Could the PM have asked his Cabinet Secretary and his central team to take the broom and clean up, if the Commonwealth Games were being held, say, in Bangalore or Kolkata or Rajkot instead of New Delhi? Are we short of quality manpower in our state and central systems, as well as in our municipalities and corporations? Little comment has been made on how and why the last minute induction of a Cabinet Secretary and his team was required to complete the construction and ground level jobs. If there had been a failure, clearly this team would have been held responsible—the ministers and the CWG authorities, who had massively mismanaged and looted the system would have pinned all the blame on the Cabinet Secretary and his team. The spectacle was disgusting. In the Louisiana Typhoon in the US, would you be seeing the Chief of Staff of the White House and a team of secretaries from the US government taking the broom to clean up the toilets, and restoring electricity connections? We seem to have totally lost direction with respect to the basic principles of governance.

Image versus reality

The need for publicity and image projection for a politician is so great that every single opportunity is utilized for it. Thus, for example, the decision to construct Delhi Metro took place in 1996; all policy and major operational decisions were taken during that time, including arranging finance. When the work concluded and the metro was inaugurated five years later, the faces shown were of the then persons in power in the state and central governments, who had nothing whatever to do with the conception, planning and implementation of the project. This can be multiplied a hundred times, and will apply to nearly every public photo-opportunity.

In May 2013, the Lok Ayukta indicted the Delhi chief minister for improperly utilizing public advertisements of the state's achievements, to project her own self. In a landmark finding, the Lok Ayukta asked for return of 50 per cent of the expenditure by her personally or by her party. This is a very welcome trend. Every day, in nearly every newspaper, one sees full page splash claims of this or that achievement, with the main credit implicitly going to some politician or the other. This is clearly private gain from public expenditure. Why should the public exchequer pay to publicize and project the political interests of this or that politician? There will be no harm if any party spends as much as it wants to advertise as many faces as it wants to back—this is the party's business—provided of course its finances are transparent, audited and available for public scrutiny through the Right to Information (RTI) Act. However, there is no justification for private aggrandizement using public expenditure. I recall that in 1997 as Cabinet Secretary I had issued a circular to all departments that no official advertisements should exceed a quarter page, they should be confined to the details of the schemes which were sought to be publicized, and at any rate no pictures of any political or administrative leaders should be projected. As far as I know this has not been rescinded; however we carry on as if these instructions do not exist.

Apart from looking after the most important work of postings and transfers, the main job of politicians, particularly ministers, is to be available at every photo opportunity. Thus, one sees all the familiar faces at important funerals, marriages and other happy and unhappy occasions, usually surrounded by black-cats or obtrusive security personnel. The regular ritual of chief ministers, and union ministers visiting drought or flood areas, is an annual feature. For each VIP, such shots, taken with sympathy and consideration, are on the files and are released to the general public each time, to show how public-spirited they are, and how much sympathy and shared sorrow they want to exhibit to the victims and the world at large.

Insiders will know that if there were a competition for the 'most-ineffective' home minister ever, Shivraj Patil would win the cup. In fact he has had fairly severe competition, including from the present incumbent Sushil Shinde. Indeed Shivraj Patil's main contribution, when he was home minister, was to give the facility of the official plane to the Congress President to make 'sympathy' visits to troubled spots. On departure from Delhi, it would be the home minister in his plane, with the Congress President accompanying him; but on landing at the venue, it was the Congress President who hogged the limelight, and claimed sympathy vote—the home minister would not even be seen in the frames of television shots. The theme is that appearances count—substance be damned. Apparently in recent times, the home minister's role has been taken over by the PM himself—perhaps P. Chidambaram or Sushil Kumar Shinde were not sufficiently flexible! The visit of the prime minister, the Congress president, as well as Rahul Gandhi, the Congress vice-president, to Raipur in May 2013 is hierarchically an indication of the 'gravity' of the event. This was again reconfirmed as the photo opportunity provided by the Muzaffarnagar tragedy (September 2013) was utilized by this trio—the Congress president and the prime minister condoling the locals, with Rahul Gandhi dutifully in tow.

It is usually forgotten that the presence of VVIPs in hordes at a place of a disaster severely disrupts relief and rescue operations. The local administration head, the District Magistrate or the local commissioner or police chief as the case may be, will have to give greater attention to the visiting VVIPs. If he attends to his primary job of handling the disaster and is not around to be seen boosting the egos of the visiting VVIPs, he runs the risk of being labeled 'inefficient', and is liable to get transferred immediately in disgrace. It may be recalled that during the 9/11 disaster in New York many years back, President Bush did not visit the site for seven days; indeed the New York's Mayor was in full charge. Soon thereafter in a major tornado damage in Miami, Vice-President Al Gore was refused permission, rightly, by the local governor from visiting the troubled area on the ground that relief work would get disrupted. In India it is standard pattern for the chief minister or the Union home minister or other heavy-weight dignitary to land by helicopter within hours, sometimes even before the local authorities can reach with ambulances and medical assistance by road, heavily disrupting relief measures. There clearly ought to be standard operating procedures, forbidding VIPs from visiting disaster areas within specified time periods; just like there should be a standard dispassionate inquiry procedure to look into the quality, promptness and efficacy of relief measures undertaken by local senior authorities.

***

George Fernandez, the then defence minister, during his 3-year tenure, visited Siachen 18 times—some newspapers referred to 32 visits—each visit naturally by helicopter. What work did he have which made him travel to the same army outpost, nearly every month? Was he doing research on high-altitude warfare? Was it just macho to show the army, or the people of India or Pakistan, or even to himself how seriously he was defending our borders? Or, perhaps whenever he got bored at his desk at South Block, he took a flight to Siachen, to view the Himalayan sights. Did he visit Nathu La, Tangdar or other border posts with equal regularity and assiduity—did he have no work in Delhi? One recalls that during the early 1980s, the then commerce minister Pranab Mukherjee used to visit the Middle East at short notice whenever he found an item coming up before the Cabinet which he wanted to avoid thus placing our envoys in Dubai and Abu Dhabi at great inconvenience in finding something for him to do in those 'salubrious' countries. I wonder how the local commander in Siachen 'entertained' the defence minister on these visits—were there new tourist-spots to thrill the visitor with, or were there great new exploits against enemy outposts across the valley, to impress the boss with? Substance be damned—so long as the administrator shows that he is very active, that's enough—no real action is required.

If we find the repeated visit of the defence minister to Siachen perplexing, one can cite a number of other instances, which may not be as mysterious. Indeed, till recently, there was this railway sales outpost at Badrinath which reportedly was the 'most inspected' office of the railway system. This two-man office had 650 'inquisitorial' in depth examinations of its performance over a 5-year period, clearly by senior railway officers who were keen to ensure that their offices performed efficiently! To quote another instance, a respected and genuinely effective Chairman of the State Bank of India decades back, made over 100 visits to Pondicherry during a 5-year tenure, ostensibly to inspect the SBI branch there; 'coincidentally', the Aurobindo Ashram, Auroville is located there, and he was an ardent devotee—by all accounts he was an outstandingly effective chief executive, though he was apparently axed prematurely for his special relationship with this branch. The reality was that he was asked to go because he fell foul of the prime minister of the day, failing to oblige the system in a critical matter. I recall the then chief minister of Uttar Pradesh, Narayan Dutt Tiwari finding it necessary to go very frequently to Pant Nagar University. The efficient administrator that he was, was it his passion for agriculture or he wanted to go regularly to the proximity of the Almora mountains? In any case, the entire guest house had to be vacated for the night and the area sanitized for his regular, frequent, incognito visits. Surely important public work of national importance was getting transacted in the guest house. One of my younger colleagues in the Foreign Service also mentioned to me that N.D. Tiwari was extremely conscientious in performing his duties as external affairs minister. He would find every opportunity to visit Bangkok, so critical to India's external interests, where after a busy day he would invariably dismiss his security detail, no doubt to contemplate important policy issues of a pressing nature. Finally, I recall that M.A. Qureshi, one of the first ICS officers I met in my career, who was then the Agriculture Production Commissioner in Uttar Pradesh found the need to inspect a village in Ballia every 15 days. The village had to be within a 30-minute drive from his ancestral house in Ballia town—the farthest district from Lucknow. Every fortnight, as his vehicle whizzed past Ghazipur where I was posted, the local planning officer would ensure the planting of red flags, somewhat like the flags that are placed on golf-holes, about 100-yards on either side of the road, at every half-mile interval. Each flag was supposed to represent a 'kachcha well', part of the 'million wells programme'—except that there was no well, only the red flag. When I chided the planning officer for this deception, he innocently told me, 'Sir, don't worry, APC sahib never gets out of his car to inspect any well—there is no danger.' In these instances as in the so many others that one has witnessed, one could discern a pattern or divine a possible reason; I dare anyone to explain 32 visits to Siachen.

Ceremony and substance

I left Uttar Pradesh in late 1970s, for assignments in Delhi and abroad, and returned to Lucknow only in the early 1990s. Soon thereafter, I had to make an official visit to the state-run cement plants in Churk in district Mirzapur; I made the trip by state helicopter. On arrival, I had forgotten that I had become 'senior', and the practice to receive senior officers is by giving them a 'guard of honour'. Suddenly on alighting from the helicopter, I found myself inspecting a small column of uniformed policemen, standing at attention in front of them, with their leader shouting something in Hindi, presumably telling me that the guard was ready for inspection, and that would I kindly do so. I felt quite silly, didn't know how to react or what action to take or what to say—I had totally forgotten how to handle this unexpected situation. As I stood silent, the column waited for my command. I could sense some of the policemen laughing silently to themselves at the specimen who they were fated to salute. The column was waiting for me to say something; the officer accompanying me whispered to me that I should say *visarjan* (disperse), which I did. The ordeal was over.

I wonder how Mayawati or Mulayam Singh Yadav feel while they are inspecting guards of honour, which presumably they do every day. Indeed when Mulayam is surrounded by his black cats, who do their brand of dance around him, it is quite an amusing sight. The other day I saw the spectacle of defence minister A.K. Antony, looking puny, with a simpering smile, wearing a funny non-descript cap, clad in a shawl draped around his khadi shirt, surrounded by generals and jawans, each a foot and half taller than him, saluting him formally, and he returning the salute 'picking-your-nose-with-a-finger-style', an incongruous sight indeed. I do not know if this practice needs to continue. This is a throw-back on the British days, when generally even the civilians had a military background, with a dress-code while taking the salute—there was then no significantly apparent size difference between the saluters and the saluted. One wonders whether the practice should continue in the changed circumstances. No doubt in a democracy, the armed forces and the police function under civilian control; but is this the proper way to demonstrate to the people in India as to who is in command? Indeed such ludicrous sights may create a feeling of ridicule for authority, not only among the general public but also in the armed units. The time surely has come to revisit this practice. Can't we have an Indian version of 'salam' or 'namaste'? I am unable to speculate—perhaps more competent people can suggest alternatives which will be in better taste.

Talking of guards of honour or salutes, a reference must be made to the welcome given to a visting Head of State and Head of Government in Rashtrapati Bhawan's courtyard in New Delhi. The office of the Cabinet Secretary overlooks this venue; the Cabinet Secretary is always an invitee, with the Indian Head of State or Government, as may be, being the host. There is usually an inter-service guard of honour, with an elegant band in attendance, with the visiting dignitary taking the salute and inspecting the guard. I do not know if this function gets televised or not; I have always found this of high standard, very pleasing and quite dignified. While the 'Beating the Retreat' function of Independence Day is among the pleasantest and sweetest public performances presented by the armed forces, my vote for quality would go to these formal welcome occasions to visiting dignitaries.

Things are not what they seem

In India, if you wear a dark suit and tie, you become respectable. You may be the biggest crook, but somehow society takes you to be a gentleman. You wear khadi, with Nehru jacket and suddenly you are transformed and you become a demi-god. People go out of the way to give you respect, strangers say namaskar to you and bow before you. These are short-cuts for fame, success and even protection in Indian conditions. If you wear a dhoti, south Indian style like P. Chidambaram or A.K. Antony, you may at best be ignored or at worst ridiculed in the market place or a commercial business office. But at FICCI or ASSOCHAM or CII's plenary, in a seven-star hotel, where everyone is tie-woolen-suited in mid-summer, you will surely get respect, also reverence—indeed abject fawning, prostration and surrender from the billionaire business magnate since he sees you as the lynch-pin on which his windfall profit depends. I know of a person who embezzled two million dollars from the accounts of a private company in Nairobi owned by an Indian. When he was discovered, he ran away to UP, just slipping away from the local police. Despite a 'wanted' notice and an international look-out, he 'became' a politician in UP, got himself photographed along with the chief minister on public occasions and made sure that the photograph was well publicized. This was insurance that no local policeman or magistrate would dare to apprehend him and send him to face 'due process' in Kenya. Being a politician in India has great pre-emptive advantages.

If one is a civil servant, as soon as a 'prima facie' case emerges, with or without allegations, the person gets suspended and gets reinstated only when the inquiry is concluded in his favour or if he is charge-sheeted, only when the court procedure declares him innocent. However, for the political public servant, the rules are fully different. He insists on staying in office till he is proven guilty. Holding of public office is treated as a fundamental right and one can be dislodged only after following all the processes of law to establish guilt. This differential treatment for a permanent civil servant and an elected official is totally indefensible. Indeed the concept of Lokpal was introduced to meet this gap in our system. The Lokpal was to act as an umpire of first examination, whether to ask someone to step-down pending an inquiry or investigation. The Lokpal was not designed to dispense final justice by declaring guilt or innocence, only to give a prima facie finding. Thus, a Cabinet minister could get away without resigning, even when his own nephew, who lives in his house, is caught taking a hefty bribe for enabling a promotion (which is actually ordered by the signature of the minister himself) on the grounds that there is no proof of the minister's direct involvement. Even the suggestion that he should step down during the investigation is seen as unreasonable. Likewise the President of the Board of Cricket Control of India (BCCI), who presides over the activities of a game which is treated as the highest religion in India, and who has obvious conflict of interest by also being the sponsor of a competitive team, steadfastly refuses to step down pending investigation; indeed even after his own son-in-law, described as the principal/owner of the team has been charge-sheeted for heavy betting in games where his own team is involved. What is the justification of a team continuing to be allowed to play competitive support, when its own owner is betting on its fortunes illegally? The continuation of the BCCI President cannot be explained by any logical set of arguments. These are inexplicable positions taken by those in authority in India. The standard expression is 'the law will take its own course' or 'the guilty, when found, will be strongly punished'. The real meaning here being that the law will be engineered to be derailed, and that no one will ever be caught.

Businessmen, even the more sophisticated and suave among them, hold bureaucrats in general contempt. A Calcutta-based jute magnate met me in the textile ministry in Delhi and asked me to intervene to solve some problem confronting his company, with respect to some license etc.—I forget the details. What he asked me appeared reasonable. I called for the file and got the proper orders issued. When he came home to thank me, with a small gift, I asked him casually why he didn't go to the minister and ask him to intervene— 'you are so friendly and close to him', I said. He laughed, and told me that in this kind of a matter, 'If I went to the minister, it would have cost me Rs10 lakh or more, for getting exactly the same thing that you did for me in a day—I was not asking anything special, except what was due to me—now I got the same work done at the cost of a small gift.' I was quite pained that this gesture—goodwill gift—was not just that, nor was it token thanks for facilitating an approval—it was an inexpensive 'bribe', however unpleasant the thought may be. Sadly we have reached the stage even when something is to be done legitimately, there is the concept of a quid-pro-quo. No citizen or businessman can now routinely assume that any transaction or dealing with the government can be done without a 'consideration'—a painful thought indeed.

As Cabinet Secretary, I frequently got visits by the highest level business magnates in the country, usually accompanied by their personal hangers-on, frequently also by a foreign business group negotiating a joint venture. Typically this would be with an appointment, the Indian tycoon entering my room accompanied by his team, including the foreigners. In that five-minute meeting, he would explain the proposed approval sought from the government, mention the stage in which it was and ask that this may be cleared early. As the group got up, shook hands and left the room, just at the door after the others had left, the tycoon would close the door from inside, turn back to me and say 'just one more thing', exchange some minor pleasantry about the weather or cricket or something, and then leave the room. The purpose of spending that extra minute alone with me was to convey a message to the foreigners presumably about the 'deal' struck with me and to impress them about how 'well-connected' he was. The first time one of the Hinduja brothers did this in my room, I caught on to the game. In all future visits by business delegations, I would ensure that all conversation took place in the presence of the entire delegation. The games our businessmen play to create 'impressions' are astonishingly inventive.

Who says there is no humour in our public life? The public gaffe of 2012 for me was the speech read out by our then foreign minister, S.M. Krishna in New York at the plenary of the United Nations. This was, as usual, a prepared text, outlining India's position on some subject or the other—prepared in six pages—double-spaced for ease of reading. It is a practice that formal speeches delivered in the session by national representatives are soon thereafter duplicated and the copies placed at the desk of each participating delegation so that so much 'collective wisdom' can be at the disposal of each delegation every day! On this occasion, the Portuguese foreign minister had spoken just before our representative and a copy of his speech was placed before our foreign minister. Krishna, when he was asked to make his comments picked up the Portuguese minister's speech and started reading it slowly—not surprisingly not one soul, including the minister realized the snafu. The Indian minister profusely thanked the Chairman, on behalf 'of the people and government of Portugal' for the kindness and opportunity given! It was only after he had read more than a page that the realization came of the blunder that had been made; the minister picked up his own speech and read it again from the beginning. Our PR to the United Nations Hardeep Puri was sitting next to the minister. Much later when I asked him as to how he permitted the minister to make such a blunder, he laughed and said that immediately after the second or third line, he had realized what was happening, tugged the minister's jacket a couple of times but the minister shrugged it off and continued with the Portuguese speech. Hardeep Puri then had to snatch the Portuguese speech away from the minister's hands and replace it with the Indian speech and the minister promptly started from page 1 line 1, thanking all for the opportunity given to the government and people of India etc. etc. The Peter Principle does work, everyone is kicked upstairs till he reaches his level of incompetence.

Talking of humour in public life, George Bush always referred to his 'noucular policy', which is not understandable, considering his Princeton background; though Mulayam Singh's 'nuyêclear' is perfectly excusable. Our present President, in an earlier avatar, presenting his last budget, referred to 'volatic' cells, presumably he was referring to Volta, one of the pioneers in the field of electricity. Appreciating his budget speech, Prime Minister Manmohan Singh praised him publicly for a 'good jab done'! Manish Tiwari the minister, who used to be Congress spokesman would refer to others who would 'obsufucate', which he would 'retriate' is a 'travesty'—he would term every other presentation by others as 'eronous'. I have even heard the redoubtable Arnab Goswami of Times Now referring to 'renumeration' in the context of public salaries. Who said there is no humour in our public space? When long ago, I was rushing to an Indian restaurant in Second Avenue in New York to take out a carry-home meal, I heard an American crossing me in front of the restaurant describing me as a 'curry in a hurry'.

2

SHOULD GROWTH BE THE ONLY CRITERION FOR ECONOMIC POLICY?

Democracy must be something more than two wolves and a sheep voting on what to have for dinner—James Bovard
The only criterion for policy making in a poor country is how it will ultimately impact the poorest man—Mahatma Gandhi

Over the past ten years or so, the only mantra for development has been 'growth'. No attention has been given to equity considerations. In one of the largest countries with about 70 per cent of the population suffering from abject poverty, this is a recipe for structural instability.

All attention has been on narrow 'finance sector' reforms, and that too focusing on a tiny sub-sector thereof—foreign direct investment (FDI). While the situation is crying for reforms in diverse sectors, it is the ineptitude, lack of relevant experience and ignorance about Indian conditions that has led to this paralysis in policymaking. The national development machinery is in the hands of people who have little idea about how to go about managing the change.

During the past decade, the economic management of the country has been entrusted to three 'renowned' economists—Manmohan Singh, Rangarajan and Montek Ahluwalia, all three macroeconomists—with little feel or understanding of microeconomic processes. The entire approach appears to have been that the country's economy can be handled essentially through the macroeconomic instruments available. It is a pity that there has been insufficient understanding of the inter-relationship between micro and macro factors in the management of the economy. It is indeed the micro-processes that aggregate to generate macro parameters. Apart from direct and indirect taxation issues, there has equally been little understanding among our policymakers of the critical importance of ground level activities in diverse fields such as agriculture, education, health, small industries and a wide range of other sectors, which aggregate to bring up the macro-economy. This has been a tragedy— the price is now being paid by the nation, in the last year of the current government.

Are three 'blind' men leading India?

In the autumn of 2012, Prime Minister Manmohan Singh announced in the context of the Planning Commission's 12th Plan (2012–13 to 2016–17) that in the following year he aimed for a 8.2 per cent growth of the gross domestic product (GDP). In June 2013, the previous year's growth figures were officially announced by the Reserve Bank of India (RBI) at 4.8 per cent. It is going to be a tall order for any government of the day, to 'double' the rate of growth, in the following year—the international climate, the near-desperate domestic situation, the chaos, confusion and policy paralysis in a pre-election year will all ensure that growth, if any, will be limited. If even the 5 per cent rate of growth is maintained, that will be an achievement of sorts.

It is very sad to note in a poor country, that the prime minister talks only of growth. He is perhaps not aware of the widespread poverty, distress and desperation prevalent in the country. In the summer of 2013, the Centre went in for a 'food guarantee scheme', which will assure minimum food grain distribution at highly subsidized rates, to about 75 per cent of the rural and 50 per cent of the urban population. This is clearly a tacit admission that a vast majority of Indians are living in great poverty. It is tragic to note that nearly 70 years after independence, nearly three-quarters of the population is in desperate straits. After the figures of poverty identified by Arjun Sengupta and N.C. Saxena a decade back had been widely pooh-poohed by the Planning Commission, the Central Government is now de-facto admitting that these actually represent current poverty levels in India. It is catastrophic to note that the number of poor people in India today is double the total population of the country at independence. What greater commentary is required to describe the massive failure of governance?

Repeated pronouncements, nearly every week or month, by the prime minister or the Deputy Chairman of the Planning Commission, Montek Ahluwalia, or the Chairman of the Prime Minister's Advisory Council Rangarajan concentrate exclusively on 'growth rates'. One rarely hears any reference to income distribution, removal of poverty, social advancement and other such issues. These three worthies to whom our economy, indeed our fate, has been surrendered, clearly have no idea of what inflation, want, poverty, hunger deaths, illiteracy, malnutrition and such-like words mean to the populace—these are the conditions of life attendant on 75 per cent of the population. Those who have lived exclusively crunching numbers, particularly in the corridors of academia in the US and Europe, are sadly in-charge of the lives of nearly a billion hapless Indians. The maximum concession that 'a problem exists' is the occasional reference to 'inclusive' growth.

Talking of 'inclusive growth' is like rubbing salt to the wound. It is a highly insulting, arrogant concept translated to mean that the elite, the ruling classes, the upper classes, the business classes and the politicians have a right to grow. In that process, any leftovers also may be partly distributed to the abject poor. It is the right of the elite to grow; they have no objection if a little bit trickles down to the poorest. In a democracy, the top 5 per cent 'concede' that the bottom 75 per cent could possibly be entitled to the lowest form of animal life, through a 'trickle-down' approach—though nothing presumably needs to be done proactively. There is now near-unanimity that the 'trickle-down' theory has been proven to be invalid—that nothing will 'trickle-down' without active facilitation. It is astonishing that this pejorative reference to the poorer classes of India has not been adversely commented upon—this is the official policy, the mantra is 'growth'—that is practiced and articulated shamelessly. The theory learnt in London and Harvard is that 'the cake has to be bigger'—which is not untrue; but the other side of the coin is that if it is not distributed properly to mitigate poverty and insecurity, the cake will disintegrate, however big it is. None is against growth—more the better but the minimum needs of people must be met as a priority. Stable growth is possible only if this minimum condition is met.

As the economy was tumbling in the summer of 2013 with high inflation, a rapidly depreciating rupee and an uncontrollable current account deficit, the World Wealth Report 2013 announced that 120 new Indian entrants had entered the rank of ultra-high-net-worth (UHNW) individuals, in the previous period. Indeed the collective net worth of this Richie Rich club of 8,000 or so individuals amounts to nearly half of India's GDP (Mail Today 12 September 2013). Skewing the income distribution patterns in a country where 75 per cent of the people are in great poverty, surely is a recipe for social instability.

In the summer of 2013, the Planning Commission of India proudly announced that 'poverty' had been 'drastically reduced' in the previous eight years rule of the government—a statement seen with incredulity and ridicule, as well as anger by most Indians. The benchmark for minimum income to qualify for poverty level was fixed at ₹27 per day (less than half-dollar a day) when all over the world, anything under $2 a day per capita is seen as crushing poverty. While there may be some merit in the claim that poverty has been reduced purely based on serial statistical data, the claim may not inspire any satisfaction. The official percentage of the poor may have gone down, but the numbers of those in poverty clearly have not decreased. In Indian conditions, the level fixed may not even meet just the daily cereal requirements, not to speak of the cooking medium, fuel and vegetables. Clearly the poor people in India do not need any vitamins, no medicines, no clothing and no footwear. They can survive year-in and year-out on just a daily cupful of cereals, garnished perhaps with one chilli—even onion is out of range. How out of touch with reality can one be! The same government, as an election sop, wants to give 75 per cent of its citizens nearly-free food grains, while declaring that only 21 per cent of the people are 'below the poverty-line'. To what absurd lengths can governance descend?

Leap in the Dark—Desperate measures

Looking back over the past ten years, the only reform of substance was the enactment of the Right to Information (RTI) Act. It should be added that the origin of the act comes from 1997, as mentioned in another chapter. This indeed has been the only 'achievement' of the present government—even this is now negated by a proposed legislation to take political parties outside the ambit of RTI, a clear denial of the fundamental principles behind the RTI Act.

Other so-called 'reform steps' are devoid of content. The Right to Education Act is an empty shell, a motherhood statement, with no impact on the ground. The nuclear policy is surrender to foreign interests; the approval for FDI in retail, permitting marketing MNCs to enter and become predators in our rural areas is a potential time bomb. The MNREGA is essentially a subsidy programme, and has already proven that it has not generated employment in rural areas. The illusory Food Guarantee programme has been touched upon elsewhere. Reform has been narrowly defined as opening up foreign direct investment (FDI)—a short-term measure to tackle crisis of current account deficit. Inflation has been rampant resulting in untold limitless misery for a vast majority. Thanks to this list of measures, the growth rate has plummeted. We will see later that so many vital sectors are in urgent need of reforms; these have not been mentioned in public discourse. In short, economic governance has been non-existent over the past ten years. Those in-charge of the economy and society have failed us miserably. We have not only lost ten vital years of development, we have slid seriously on a downward skidding path.

As the economy nose-dived in 2013, we now need scapegoats for the failure of governance in the economic sector. The favourite theory trotted out is that the international economy has been on a skid since 2008, and practically all our economic woes stem from international origins—domestic policy has been 'perfect'. This is the standard excuse heard from all levels and all spokesmen of the ruling party. To a very small extent, this may be true. Economies in the US, Europe and Japan have not been in good health in recent years, and this has had an impact on our economy. I would probably attribute 20 per cent of our failure to this factor but 80 per cent due to policy paralysis within the country; this is my own assessment. Firstly, India is not fully 'integrated' with the world economy in the sense that the US and European economies and markets are freely exposed to each other; we still have many controls in place with much regulation, well or ill. Classic economic theory says that the larger the international exposure, the higher are the chances of 'catching a cold from outside'; in this respect India has not dismantled all its barriers. Another factor is noteworthy. The smaller the country, the larger is the impact on it through outside forces. Conversely, the larger the country, the less the impact from outside. Thus US has the largest economy—surely it will be affected by international economic factors but not as much as, say, Italy or Spain or Greece, which are much smaller economies. India is a large country so applying this principle, external factors will surely influence our economy. However, because of the size and scale of domestic activity, the proportion of our external economy to our total economy is relatively small compared to others so the impact will be that much less. The continuous wail that our failure is due to external factors is hogwash. Indeed this explanation has recently been replaced by the theory that the economic decline is all due to the actions of one CAG–Vinod Rai; how absurd can one become—'shoot the messenger' is the operating formula!

Clearly as of summer 2013 when this book is being written, the government has suddenly become desperate to usher in 'reforms' as the elections are staring it in the face, and having failed to bring in substantial reforms in the previous nine years. The education and health sectors, infrastructure (including power) and so many other areas are crying for reforms. The desperation is evident in the whistling in the dark cry that "we are embarking on a process of reforms". For example, the Biotechnology Regulatory Authority of India (BRAI) Act, which needs to be looked at with great care because of massive potential consequences, is being rushed through to show the world (to Monsanto and the US?) that we are 'good boys'.

One suspects that the concerned senior bureaucrats in the various ministries—science and technology, agriculture, food, etc.—have not really applied their mind to the potential disastrous consequences of even a small slip. One can understand, but cannot condone, the political urgency; Can we forgive our bureaucrats? The examples can be multiplied.

***

P. Chidambaram, another high priest in our economic pantheon, who has a better understanding of Indian conditions, but whose background and education have come from the same western universities, is also part of the same decision-making process, destined in effect not to remove poverty, and which will not bring prosperity to the country. Sometime back he spoke, sarcastically, of India's '5000 years of poverty', and wondered as to how it can be removed so quickly. Perhaps he was expressing the thought that he and his party should be in power for 500 years more for poverty to be removed. His facts are not valid. For two-thirds of human history, India was the leading, most prosperous country in the world. The accurate descriptions in *Ramayana*, rendered originally in Sanskrit, and in at least 30 Indian languages, speak of contented citizens, plentiful availability of milk and honey and high quality governance. Much of the poverty referred to is of relatively recent origins. Be that as it may, surely one does not require a century to provide basic minimum needs to the citizens, particularly in a democracy where a citizen is supposed to be supreme. Nearly every Asian country started much worse economically, structurally and institutionally than India. Nearly every Asian country has overtaken India in practically every index of development. Japan has had a history of development from the Meiji era; however, in recent years, South Korea, Taiwan, Malaysia, have all vaulted to the top. Sri Lanka and Pakistan beat India in nearly every human index indicator. Even Bangladesh, treated earlier as a basket case has better quality education and primary health services, including nutrition, than India. The 2013 Global Peace Index ranks India in the bottom 10 per cent of the nations of the world, in the same league as Iraq and South Sudan among others, in terms of peaceful living conditions.

There is clearly a strong linkage with the Human Development Index and the Poverty Index, in all of which India rests close to the bottom of the pile. Clearly there is a strong connection between the economic health of the country and public safety. One heard recently with sadness that India ranks the highest in terms of being 'most unsafe' for women; we seem to be getting all the un-required dubious accolades! The 2012 'farmer suicides' figures depressingly indicate no reduction in numbers—indeed an increase is seen. On the contrary states are taking clear steps to 'suppress' these numbers through non-reportage. Surely, Chidambaram cannot be serious in making his comment.

In another context, Chidambaram also mentioned how difficult it was to provide services to every corner of such a large and diverse country. His solution was that we should urbanize and 90 per cent of the population should now be located in a limited number of urban complexes so delivery of services will be easier. This is as unrealistic a view as is possible. We are essentially an agrarian country with 80 per cent of the population dependent on agriculture and allied rural service sectors. Practically the only resource that most families have is a few square yards of farmland; can one imagine the trauma of a poor villager losing even this petty possession, becoming a vagrant or a daily wage labourer in cities. Can there be a surer prescription for bringing the entire nation to its knees? Even now, we have 'jobless' growth—the average age of the citizenry is among the lowest in the world—the gap between new-job creation and entrants to the job field is growing alarmingly. In the next 10 years, job-generation will be a most serious issue. Does anyone need say any more about how impractical these ideas are? With advance of technology, many services relating to education, health and a host of other areas can now be brought to the deepest rural areas much easier than before. Sadly our highest policymakers do not have their feet on the ground. Other decision-makers are busy, venally enjoying their perks and privileges and a nation of sheep is slowly but surely led to slaughter.

I recall Chidambaram's brilliant performance as the finance minister in the coalition governments of 1996–97. He held a tight leash on the critical macroeconomic indices. I recall his great concern for keeping inflation under check, as this is the most significant single factor affecting the poor common man. I also recall that he kept a sharp eye on the budget and current deficits and managed the economy with much panache. One wonders what new factors he has had to face in his two avatars as finance minister in 2004–13.

In the summer of 2013, while visiting the US to 'attract' investment in India, finance minister Chidambaram made two notable public announcements. The first was a clear statement that China has 'abolished' poverty, while poverty is widely prevalent in India. This was in the context of 'threatening' USA that if there is poverty anywhere in the world it is not conducive to international peace! Incidentally, if there is widespread poverty in India, it may or may not threaten USA, but it is surely highly threatening to India's stability. However, what Chidambaram said in the US is surely factually correct, though this is the first time I have heard a senior functionary making such a statement in explicit terms. It also shows the level of mal-governance in India that has led to the continuation, indeed expansion, of poverty levels in the country.

The other notable statement was that India is now ready to 'open-up' for foreign investment, and is ready to 'dismantle all barriers'. This is a fantastic statement; one wonders from where the finance minister obtained this mandate. In every international forum, at GATT, IMF etc., India has been taking the position that the developed countries should lower their barriers, while the developing countries need to protect their nascent and emerging economic entities, which cannot withstand unprotected the onslaught of major predatory MNCs. What Chidambaram announced in Washington has not been debated in India. Besides where is the need to take a begging bowl to US business? If the conditions are right in India, investments will flow automatically. Recall that three decades back, when China opened up, it ensured that its agriculture and rural sector was fully protected, primary and secondary education was universal, minimum health conditions among the citizenry prevailed, and finally the system was prepared for absorbing massive FDI. Besides, the investments were mostly restricted to special zones, like near Shanghai and other areas, and much of the rural countryside was insulated. FDI really flowed because of the very cheap labour provided by the Chinese authorities to MNCs to shift their manufacturing operations to China. Chinese progress has been well thought out and well executed. The loose comments mentioned earlier by senior Indian functionaries reflect the worst form of economic governance, impinging on the quality of life of our citizens. The catastrophic failure of our governance over the past seven decades has been due to thoughtless economic management.

***

The other high priest of our economy is Montek Singh Ahluwalia, who learnt his basic economics from the experience of the 1940s and 1950s in post-war Europe and America. Economics taught at LSE and US universities, and having been applied in the World Bank and IMF, institutions created for economic subjugation of the 'third world', are now being applied with no thought, no need for transformation or adaptation, mindlessly to Indian conditions which are totally different. The land-capital-labour ratios, the basic parameters of any economic system of the US and Europe, are as different as they can be from Indian conditions. However, the basic postulates learnt there have become our fundamentals; while some can be applied in India, many others are totally inappropriate in our conditions. The 'markets' in western countries may not be perfect and the population there surely is not fully homogeneous. On these two factors, however, the Indian situation is infinitely worse. The inter-state, intra-state, inter-community, intra-society differentials with respect to income, education, understanding and every other relevant factor are quite different than what obtains in western countries. It is tragic that the 'axioms' applicable in the west, which may have no relevance in India, are applied here thus opening up our farmers and rural markets to MNCs, whose main objective is to make money and not develop our infrastructure; this is tantamount to throwing our rural population to the wolves. It is a tragedy that people who have no understanding of Indian rural society and living conditions are allowed to become the main decision-makers to determine the destiny of rural India.

If onions are too expensive, no problem; we will make them available, at double the price, through imports—why not try shallots?

If Indians cannot get bread, let them eat cake! This is the ruling philosophy. Now that (summer 2013) the economy has plunged, one does not hear the pontifications and prescriptions and the prognoses one is used to from Montek Ahluwalia. Nearly every month, the oracular pronouncement would be 'the signs are good—GDP will rise to 12%, 10%, 8% ... 7.9% ... 6% next year'. Inflation is under control, it will now get reduced to '12%, 10% ... 12% ... 14%'. Every month the message was an optimistic one about the future. We have lived in a dream world for the past seven decades—or is nightmare the right word? No reference whatever is ever made in the monthly pronouncements about 80 per cent of the population living below the $2—Rs 60-a-day—'purchase parity' income levels in India.

***

To illustrate again as to how people who are thoroughly unqualified to make policy find themselves influencing major issues of governance, let me cite the example of our Panchayati Raj (local decentralized administration) policy. I recall that the new Panchayati Raj Act was drafted in the Government of India, and under a provision of the Constitution the Centre asked all the states to adopt this draft and have it enacted as law in the states. This was in 1993, when Mulayam Singh was the chief minister in Uttar Pradesh, and I happened to be the Chief Secretary. Mulayam who always had his feet firmly on the ground, had a good and close look at the Government of India draft, went into choicest expletives (Agra-Etawah belt language, as expressive as anywhere in India) against the person who had drafted the model law announcing to his Cabinet that that person had no clue whatever about rural India, of Indian villages and that the draft law was thoroughly absurd; predicted that it had no chance of success. Time has proved him right. All over India, the Panchayati Raj Act has failed; sensible decentralization has not taken place and the country is the greatest loser.

However, I knew that the author of the Act was my good friend Mani Shankar Aiyar, a former Indian Foreign Service officer, whose knowledge of Indian rural conditions was as much as I know about living conditions in the Antarctica. I did not disclose to Mulayam Singh that I knew the author! Mani's claim for undertaking this major task was the important fact that he was a schoolmate of the then Prime Minister Rajiv Gandhi—whose own understanding of India was nearly non-existent. Clearly the claim to expertise stems from who you are close to, rather than what you know. Naturally, with Montek in-charge of our economy, what can one expect? By the way, Mani is as brilliant and versatile as anyone I know—I do hope I have not lost a friend!

***

No doubt the disastrous policies which have cost the country heavily in the past decade or so have been under the watch—I would hesitate to call it leadership, since there was none—of Manmohan Singh. In the late 1980s, Manmohan Singh held the assignment of Secretary General of the South Commission in Geneva, chaired by Julius Nyerere, who had earlier been Prime Minister of Tanzania. This Commission was the secretariat, representing the interests of the developing countries. It was to help developing countries take up issues of interest in the various UN and other international fora and conduct research on themes which needed to be projected by developing countries. By definition, it had an orientation directly opposed and inimical to the economic interests of the west. The daily, weekly and monthly research papers it churned out had to be critical of the west, western institutions and had to eternally lament the lack of consideration from the west about the interests of development in developing countries. Thus the World Bank, IMF, GATT (now called WTO) and western governments as well as the EU Secretariat would come in for intense and sustained criticism by this body. Manmohan Singh was the head priest of this organization. His job was to orchestrate the attack by developing countries on the west; this posture was held by him till a month or so prior to his becoming the finance minister in Narasimha Rao's Cabinet.

One has often wondered why Manmohan has allowed himself to become the butt of so many jokes and much ridicule and a delight for lampooning cartoonists. Why didn't he throw it all off at some stage and call it quits? The temptation must have been very heavy, at least a hundred times. One theory has it that he sees himself as the 'messiah' who 'rescued' India in the early 1990s and is willing to put up with much public anger and ridicule, make enormous 'sacrifices', just so that he will have the chance to 'save' India again—Superman, Spiderman or Ben Ten style. However, this theory will not wash. The nuclear deal and liability act with benefits to 'flow' 20 years later, or 'FDI in retail' are the only acts of 'courage'—hardly enough to shore up a tottering governance structure, hardly earth-shaking. Besides, was he the one who really 'saved' India in the early 1990s? Actually it was Narasimha Rao.

Grapevine has it that Manmohan was the second choice for the finance minister's post at that time—I. G. Patel was the first choice. He could not or would not take up the assignment due possibly to poor health. Among the very first things that the new finance minister had to do was to orchestrate the prime minister's policy to 'open up' the economy. The 'liberalization' of the early 1990s was credited to Manmohan Singh. Actually the policies were dictated by international financial agencies using the threat of declaring India a financial 'defaulter', arising out of the very poor state of the then economy. Insiders have mentioned that the decision to 'liberalize' had already been taken by Narasimha Rao, before Manmohan joined him as finance minister. The decision was a purely political one and had to be fully attributed to both circumstances, and the political will displayed by Narasimha Rao. The finance minister's role was merely to pass on to the machinery the implementation of the political directions given by Narasimha Rao. Recent history has inaccurately attributed to Manmohan the initiative to liberalize—an oxymoron, since the ability to take any initiative is alien to him as has been amply demonstrated in the past decade. This is also extremely convenient, as it is the current policy to debunk or downplay the role of Narasimha Rao in our recent history.

It may appear strange that Manmohan was able to make a 180 degree shift in his attitude to the west within a couple of months. He had now become a great devotee, once again, of the Bretton Woods institutions, and had converted from the venom spewed against the west to one of total admiration, indeed cringing servitude of the west—US in particular, and all it represents. Strange as this may seem, those familiar with Manmohan Singh's career would not have been surprised at all.

I recall once seeing Narasimha Rao in 1992 after his return from the US, where he was a special invitee at the US President Clinton's personal retreat. Those days, as Textile Secretary, I had occasion to meet him often. I had met him in Buenos Aires in 1983 when he was foreign minister. I had gone there for the Group of 77 preparatory meeting for UNCTAD VI and it so happened that Narasimha Rao had a lot of spare time, part of which was spent with me, and which he remembered much later when he became the prime minister. After the US visit, where he was 'feted' and 'celebrated' by the then US president, arguably the most powerful person in the world, Rao had stars in his eyes for a long time and became a devotee of the US. However, practical and highly balanced that he was, he never lost his footing, never went overboard, had enough Indianness, background and experience to feel and think with India's long-term interests in mind. His reactions, despite the dancing stars in his eyes, were sober, practical and measured.

I guess much the same thing happened to Manmohan Singh, when President Bush invited him to his personal ranch and gave him the 'treatment' that US presidents can turn on at will on a visiting dignitary when they want to 'bring him in'. I guess Manmohan Singh fell for the charm. I could see his body language on those television shots, and told myself that they have done the same to Manmohan as they did to Narasimha Rao. This perception of mine has been amply reconfirmed, at least to my satisfaction, by events in the following years. The blind support, even nearly placing his job on the line for the nuclear deal and the Nuclear Liability Act, and later in the matter of 'FDI in retail', which was trumped up as a 'nation-saver' and not recognized to be the long-term high value time-bomb that it will turn out to be, are examples. The Hydro-Fluro-Chloride (HFC) issue, relating to domination over the refrigeration industry is another instance of capitulation in the teeth of total opposition by all Government of India line-ministries, by our senior decision-makers to US corporate interests, as demonstrated at the G-20 Summit in St. Petersburg in September 2013. My extensive contacts with senior officials in many ministries, especially economic ministries, has reconfirmed my suspicion that Manmohan Singh also has 'stars in his eyes'—whenever US interests are projected, he is unable to resort to rational thinking. However, he does not have the mitigating 'feet-on-the-ground' balance possessed by Narasimha Rao—he was nudging every department to push pro-US policies. One often wonders whose side our senior policymakers are batting for—for India or for commercial interests abroad? Is it just 'stars-in-the-eye', or something that does not meet the eye?

I recall a conversation with the then Deputy Secretary in the finance ministry, who attended the junior 'lunch club' in North Block in the early 1970s. At that time Manmohan Singh as Deputy Economic Advisor to the finance ministry used to attend the same lunch club every day and the participants would exchange gossip and notes about the goings-on in the ministry. My friend, the then Deputy Secretary told me much later that the lunch club knew even then that Manmohan was destined for 'greatness' and that he would go 'far'. They had assessed that Manmohan would quickly and shrewdly grasp what the boss wanted—the Additional Secretary or the Finance Secretary or the minister as the case may be—prepare a case for 'approval' by the boss of exactly what he (the boss) wanted even before he articulated it, couch it with arguments replete with economic theory, make it sound profound and put it up for the boss's approval, finally announcing the policy as emerging from the boss, which indeed it actually did. This assessment of Manmohan as a young man, made at that time, was highly prescient—we have seen ample demonstrations in the past decade or so.

Clearly Manmohan is the ultimate demonstration of the Peter Principle, as evident not only over the past ten years or so, but throughout his illustrious career. He must be a special case variant of the Peter principle, as explained later. When he moved on to the South Commission as Secretary General, he had already reached his 'level of incompetence', and had been 'kicked upstairs', to this post where he could do no harm. Till now this is classic Peter Principle. However, when an incompetent person is kicked back into a position of substance and authority, a new variant of the principle kicks-in; when he had spent some time in this position, he was kicked upstairs to the post of the prime minister of India and here the Peter Principle variant postulates, or at least ought to, that in such circumstances, he demeans the position itself and renders it insignificant and inconsequential. Alas, this is exactly what has happened to the highest executive post in India. A cardinal principle in administration is that a person should leave the post that he has held in at least as good a condition, if not better, than when he took over the post; this is one measure of performance in a post. Clearly the post of the prime minister has been highly diminished. If the leader of the country cannot change the direction, and give it new momentum in key areas, clearly this is a sign of major failure.

India abounds with many economists, who have studied abroad, learnt their basic economics based on western experiences in western conditions, in schools in the US and Europe. A number of them have taken the political route and have played highly influential roles in determining India's development path over the past six decades. Most of them can be classified as 'Political economists', written with a huge P and an infinitesimally small e. This will surely fit the description of Manmohan Singh. Montek comes in the same category as far as economics is concerned, but surely not as high in politics. Both have 'envying' reputations as 'economists'. One has looked around for papers or theses or research findings or theories in the field of economics attributable to them without success. I couldn't find any – perhaps they are hidden somewhere!

Abdul Kalam once upon a time may have been a fine scientist. However, over time he became a Scientific Administrator, gradually outliving his science credentials, moving on to becoming a pure administrator, and in course of time entering the political arena—retaining the enviable position of being a politician among scientists, and a scientist among politicians. This cross-fertilizing career development model has been emulated by many illustrious leaders in India; Montek and Manmohan are prime examples. The unfortunate aspect of this for India has been that we need decision-makers and leaders with sound commonsense, with feet on the ground, aware of Indian conditions and with a modern outlook, to lead us. Our polity is not well developed enough to throw up such people to the helm of affairs. This we have not seen so far—however, we need not lose hope. Narasimha Rao learnt his politics at the ground level. He understood India and Indians well, and our rural areas thoroughly. He understood the Indian psychology in the sense that Gandhiji (I refer of course to the Mahatma) understood it. The real salvation for the country will come only when our senior-most leader understands the smallest part of India, and Indianness well. One hopes that the day is not far off.

To be (PM), or not to be

Before I conclude this chapter, a reference may be made to the impending elections in 2014 and the possibility of a new leadership emerging to take the country forward—indeed backward as the case may be. It does appear that if the present ruling dispensation continues, there is the possibility of the scion of the nation's first family being projected to become the captain of the ship. So far, 'thrice was he offered the crown, and thrice did he refuse'—as Marc Antony referred to Julius Caesar; who knows, our budding Caesar may accept it the fourth time.

We need to carefully ensure that any leader we select knows India well. Mahatma Gandhi and Sardar Patel knew the country well. However, Nehru was more westernized, a product of a liberal England, and had enormous empathy for the Indian, coupled with intellect, without detailed knowledge of the Indian mentality, as possessed by say, Patel. One is entitled to one's views—many great traditions and achievements that we now have, could be attributed to Jawaharlal Nehru. However, most of our major persistent problems today have stemmed from his attitude, his lack of knowledge and prescience, and his inaction at critical times. Without flogging the point, it is not in our interest to have a top leader who does not possess hard ground-level administrative management and political experience. Indira Gandhi was a special case, she had understood India better than her father. However, she did her bit to destroy many sacred institutions, for which we pay the price today. Rajiv Gandhi could have solved many outstanding issues, cleared the overhanging baggage, and cleaned the Aegean stables, sadly he did not have the grounding and field level experience and so could not capitalize on the massive mandate given to him through a two-third majority in Parliament—a luxury no future leader is likely to enjoy in the foreseeable future. This is the potential danger of having a young person, with little field experience, with no management and administrative successes in his belt, having the key to the country—we will be taking a huge chance.

Rahul Gandhi is reported in the media as having mentioned in some context that 'poverty is a state of mind'. I do not know how true the reportage is, whether he actually said it or not—I go by the newspaper reference. If he actually said so, indeed this is in some senses true for the nouveau riche. There is a saying in Tamil, transliterated 'even when someone overcomes poverty, the poverty in his mind remains'—meaning that those who make it big financially often remain cheap in their thinking, mentality and miserliness. The Hindu philosophy does not automatically link 'happiness' with 'riches'. Our revered sages, the Buddha Bhikkhus command more respect than emperors. I recall a couplet from the Tamil *Kamban Ramayana* describing the arrival of the sage Vishwamitra in the court of Dashrath: the emperor was in a hassle of reverence to receive the honoured visitor and left his throne and ran towards the entrance to prostrate before the incoming rishi. Even today, in the Chamundi hills near Mysore, when the Mysore Maharaja goes for darshan of Devi, he climbs the last 30 or so stair-steps just in front of the sanctum sanctorum not walking but crawling—an attitude of great humility. When I have the occasional massage or go in a taxi, or chat with the paanwalah and when the subject of great men is discussed, the reference invariably is to Mahatma Gandhi, or Ramakrishna, or Vivekananda or Kabir, or Sai Baba—one even talked of Ramana Maharishi—there is never a reverential reference to Birla or Tata or Ambani. 'Goodness is better than greatness'—this is the essence of the philosophy which is our heritage. When I deliberately named a politician to elicit a response, one of them told me, in original high-voltage Rajasthani abusive words, dripping with contempt, to the effect 'they are all the same, all like dogs—jostling, putting their heads down to eat from the same plate'. However, it will be not just an insult, it is contemptuous to suggest that 70 per cent of Indians, who are in poverty, should feel happy in their misery and hunger and disease and squalor. This will be the limit of heartlessness. The first qualification for any Indian leader has to be 'compassion'.

Wikileaks has revealed a conversation between our 'Prince in waiting' and the US Ambassador of the day in New Delhi, at a dinner with the former reportedly saying: 'Hindu terrorism is even more serious than "cross-border" terrorism'. Since this public revelation has not been contradicted or denied, one can reasonably assume that it could possibly be a correct quote. If it is true, it is astonishingly naïve. Certainly there are terrorist groups in India, many supported from across the border, who are bent on contributing their bit to destabilizing the country. It is quite possible, even likely, that some fringe elements consisting of rabid Hindu elements could have formed localized groups to indulge in terrorist activities. However, no sane person in India could identify such groups as the most powerful or potentially dangerous elements, out to destroy the country. Normally any person in authority, or one who aspires to high office ought to be careful in what he says, particularly so when foreigners are involved; especially when that person is an official accredited representative in India of another country. Any responsible person ought to be guarded in speaking in such circumstances. The Wikileaks cable mentioned shows extreme disregard for minimum standards to be displayed by those aspiring to public office.

Mahatma Gandhi took pains to understand the country by extensive travel, in third class railway compartments, covering nearly every district, and getting to know every bit of India. One of my childhood memories, when I was eight years or so, was a 'whistle-stop' visit by him to the suburbs of Tanjore, close to our residence, a few months before independence—probably in 1946. The special train for him (imagine today's government providing a special train to Anna Hazare, or Swami Ramdev or even Advani or Narendra Modi) stopped adjacent to the playground at the edge of our colony. There was no station there so a temporary wooden platform was raised to the level of the door of the compartment. Gandhi, in his loin cloth, at the crack of dawn on a summer day, probably it was 4.30 am, walked on to the platform, stood in silence for about three minutes and the train whistled off to the next destination.

I had climbed up a tree to get a better view. The brief darshan left a lifelong impression on me. I could see as I came down from the tree, so many people in silent tears. Many will recall Richard Attenborough's movie *Gandhi*, showing a similar scene. I can vouch that it was authentic, and could well have been shot in Tanjore as anywhere else; incidentally it required a foreigner to bring out an authentic film portrait of Gandhi—was no Indian film producer or director up to the job? Again on the subject, I recall seeing the movie *Gandhi* in Buenos Aires in 1984, a 9 pm show. As the 6 pm show audience was streaming out of the hall, one could see nearly everyone, including the most hardened grownups, with streaming tears in their eyes—these were Argentinians. I also recall an Indian newspaper cartoon—was it Laxman?—of a conversation between two politicians, both MPs, after seeing the movie, 'a wonderful movie, a great man, I am told this is based on a real-life story'!

Instant greatness is sought to be obtained in India through contrived Bharat darshans. Many would recall the 'inside' series by John Gunther—Inside Africa, Inside Indonesia, Inside India, Inside Asia and so on. An apocryphal version of his modus operandi described Gunther as taking a week off from his normal routine in the US, taking a flight to his target destination, say China. On the plane he would read up some portions of a couple of books on China; on arrival he would find out 'all' about the country from the taxi driver taking him from airport to the hotel. He would 'extensively' interview the attendant in his hotel room, the clerk in the front office and the waiter at the bar-restaurant on all aspects of Chinese social, cultural and spiritual, economic and political life. During his three-day stay in the capital, he would meet as many people as possible at tourist spots and 'interview' them—never mind if these were Indians or Japanese or Americans. He would spend the next three days dictating his first draft of the book 'inside China', fine tune it on the return flight home—his new incisive, definitive, informative and authentic 'Inside' book would be in the market within a month, and would be a best seller for its remarkable insights! Many of our politicians, who fly in and out by helicopter, surrounded by hundreds of hangers-on each moment of the one-and-half-days' field visit, out of which six-hours of the night are spent in a 'dalit' home, acquire extensive knowledge of local conditions. Of course to make up for the two-day strain of the trouble taken to get to know our rural areas and our peoples, a 15-day holiday in Paris or another salubrious venue is called for! Our nation is full of such specialists in Delhi, holding authority, with immense power, who are 'experts' on the living conditions in rural areas. One wonders if our railway minister has ever traveled anywhere in India by train (on the few occasions, when he has not used the state plane, or heaven forbid, the commercial flight); even then not using his special private coach—has he even traveled once by AC First Class, not to speak even of ordinary first class. Don't mention third class sleeper, or unreserved third class as these are meant only for 'ordinary' Indians, not for us special people who 'run' the country, or are preparing to do so.

Delhi is full of bright young brilliant budding journalists and politicians, aspiring to be public figures, wanting to chart the course for our billion-plus population. Many have taken the trouble to study for a year or two in prestigious foreign universities, live in five-star conditions in the capital, make a one-or-two-day 'incisive' and 'intensive' visits to 'rural' areas like Lucknow or Madurai or Rajkot, meet activists, social workers and NGOs at the local club or bar and have animated discussions on local, national and international issues. They return 'enriched', full of information, knowledge, and indeed 'experience'. They consider themselves ready to write extensively on any subject, and give their opinions and solutions on TV on how to mitigate or remove rural problems or agricultural distress. You throw a stone anywhere in central Delhi and chances are 2:1 that you will hit a brilliant, young budding 'leader'. Clearly in India, leadership is nurtured in capital cities so why waste time learning useless 'reality' by staying long periods in our rural areas? Usually their strong point is command over the English language! There is little else to commend them. Our prince may not qualify on this ignoble count.

3

PLACEBO GOVERNANCE

All the world's a stage—As you like it

During my childhood Tanjore days, we had *athai*, aunty for you. She was an aunty for everyone in the ashram, from age 2 to age 70. She was of indeterminate age. During those childhood days, probably anyone over 30 was 'old' in my eyes; *athai* clearly was super-old. She was the custodian of the kitchen and all miscellaneous arrangements. One day, she was bitten by a scorpion in one of the rooms adjoining the kitchen. She was writhing on the floor, moaning and proclaiming loudly that she was dying. My uncle, a medical doctor from Palghat who was visiting, quickly came to the scene to take charge. Very ostentatiously, and gesticulating rapidly, he called urgently for hot water, opened his medical suitcase, took out his injection kit, and injected her with distilled water except that he loudly proclaimed to all present, that is the entire household of 30 or so, that the medicine being injected was the latest invention, specifically prepared for snake and scorpion bites, guaranteed to completely cure, and remove all pain within exactly one minute. He also added that if within 30 seconds it did not take hold, that was a dangerous sign, but in his experience of 40 years, it had never failed once! Actually he quietly showed me the phial which had only distilled water. For 30 seconds after the injection, he kept quiet; then asked *athai* if she was still alive—the moment she nodded her head, he turned to all of us triumphantly to proclaim that 'the injection is successful'—

actually this was meant for aunty's consumption. Sure enough within a minute thereafter, aunty was on her feet and within half-an-hour she was going about her normal activities. This is an early lesson that I learnt in life that the cure administered may not necessarily be directly related to the issue at hand; that if sufficient drama is created, with enough hoopla—the victim feels that there is sufficient recognition of his trauma by the general public—a placebo treatment may work in most situations.

Governments frequently produce schemes which they know will not work, to appear to be acting, to appease segments of the citizenry. Frequently amendment to laws are resorted to as a proxy for addressing the real issue of reforming the implementation apparatus. Policies and programmes to lift people from poverty, expanding rural activities and generate jobs and ushering in development are often not meant seriously. Thus, subsidy schemes to act as palliatives are often resorted to, knowing full well that these only address some of the symptoms and surely will not result in cure. More often than not, these populist but ineffective programmes are announced with great fanfare before elections, clearly with an eye on the ballot-box and with no other objectives in mind. Surely some money can be thrown back at the poor in the country, in subsidy schemes, considering that this is only a small fraction of the massive transfer of resources from the rural/agri sector to the urban industrial sector. There are many games that are played to lull the population into thinking that serious attention is being given to basic problems, frequently through 'placebo schemes'. I have given some illustrations in the chapter, though the inventiveness of the system in throwing dust into peoples' eyes is very high, honed by decades of experience.

***

Usually the official reasons given for a decision or a course of action is totally different from the real purpose for which the exercise was undertaken – frequently diametrically different. Some random examples follow.

Sometime in 2012, there was massive public outrage in Delhi, echoed in many other cities, at the brutal gang rape in a moving bus right in the middle of Delhi city, of an unfortunate girl, given the name 'Nirbhaya'. While crime against women is rampant all over the country, and most of these go unreported, unrecorded, uninvestigated and unpunished, the attack on this poor girl generated a massive outcry. It was a revelation to see people of all ages, particularly boys and girls, marching peacefully, protesting the helplessness of women in India and confronting the atmosphere of crime against womanhood. The establishment was taken aback; there was no standard operating procedure (SOP) to address such large outpouring of anger and sympathy.

As is standard practice, the government had apparently no desire to do anything serious or worthwhile in response. The objective was to contain the anger, buy time, divert the attention of the agitators and finally 'yield' nothing. This ignoble objective has been successfully accomplished. The government established a committee under the chairmanship of an ex-chief justice, with the main terms of reference relating to changes in rape-related laws. It was quite obvious at that point that the government had no desire or will to do anything substantive in the matter. The other major action was to get the Nirbhaya case hearing expedited; so after nine months of court hearings, four of the accused were handed the death sentence. Thus addressing one instance of the malaise in an aggressively ostentatious manner, the illusion was created that the government had successfully addressed the question of women's safety in India.

No society can advance till there is a basic level of security. Not that the existing laws are perfect, but the real issue relates to implementation of laws and processing the punishment of law-breakers. Having a law with near-zero enforcement is completely meaningless. The issue with offences against women, indeed the issue relating to crime in India stems from a fundamental weakness of the machinery to undertake seriously and effectively any of the necessary steps involved. Thus, registering a FIR, a fair and quick investigation, providing comfort to witnesses that they will not be harassed or attacked, mounting a credible prosecution swiftly and ensuring that the case goes to court with a strong chance of success are fundamentals of the 'process'. Sadly every part of these gets vitiated, as a rule. There is corruption at every level, collusion, FIRs are auctioned, investigations influenced heavily by money and political power, prosecution procedures are suborned, where for a consideration the prosecuting agency colludes with the accused—these are basic evils permeating the system. These problems have been examined repeatedly and many recommendations are forthcoming. The government has clearly no desire for any reforms. In the event mentioned earlier, they resorted to the convenient and superficial process of 'amending' the rape laws. This was done with great speed, as if by sleight of the hand—presto, the government had 'handled' the crisis—it could now coast till the next outcry surfaces. Who is being fooled? Can anyone expect the slightest change in ground conditions? Can a woman feel safer, one wee bit more? The answer, sadly, is a resounding 'No'.

***

The government has promulgated a food guarantee scheme, another programme to hood-wink the public. This programme, which will provide heavily subsidized food grains to about 70 per cent of the population is a tacit admission that real poverty is of the order of 70 per cent in the country, as opposed to the 30-odd or so per cent hitherto claimed by the government. Essentially, an agrarian country is now going to be on food-dole for most of the population—what a tragic irony, seven decades after independence! This also means that we accept that most of the farmers do not produce enough food grains for themselves; that creating infrastructure (power, roads and irrigation) in rural areas has been so tardy that it has not contributed to agricultural growth, or stimulated new energies to be unleashed in this sector. The ultimate impact of this programme will be to inhibit growth of agriculture, and contributing to greater poverty.

Of the four elements in the 'revolutionary' new scheme, three are already being implemented, wholly or substantially. Even heavy-subsidy food distribution schemes have been in existence for a while. The programme is clearly an eye-wash, a sleight-of-hand trick to conjure up votes.

***

The much vaunted Right to Education programme is another shell project, long on slogan and very short on substance. It promises the moon to a citizen and delivers absolutely nothing. It is akin to a 'motherhood' statement—a self-evident proposition, nobody can object to it—the entire issue is its implementation. The programme has not been funded; the states, already strained for resources are left to their own devices to implement the 'right', without being given the wherewithal. Having made this grandiose announcement, the Centre is sure to blame the states for 'non-implementation', as this is a 'State subject' under the Constitution—the kind of shallow reasoning resorted to by the Centre in every instance of national failure.

***

The official purpose of the million wells scheme of the mid-1960s—the precursor to the much later MNREGA—was to improve irrigation and the availability of drinking water by constructing kachcha wells. In the event, less than 10 per cent of these wells were actually dug. In general, two adjacent pits were dug and the mud transferred from one to the other. The real purpose was to grease the palms of party functionaries at the field level and show great concern for generating 'employment opportunities' and show commitment to 'development'. MNREGA is not much different. The latest National Sample Survey Organisation's surveys comparing 2009–10 with 2011–12 indicate that there was actually *loss* of women's jobs in rural areas during this period. Regular jobs were lost in a significant way, with a marginal gain in temporary jobs. This has been the net impact of MNREGA, apart from creating a large number of new millionaires among Panchayat secretaries.

The aim of course is to show lip-service to development, simultaneously spending money on doles with a view to improving electoral prospects. MNREGA actually does not produce new jobs, nor is it designed to create permanent assets in rural areas—it is tantamount to a free subsidy. While none can seriously object to money being passed on to the needy, one should recognize it as such. The old adage 'it is better to teach a person to fish, than to give him a fish to eat' is valid in this case. A recent government sponsored study has brought out that MNREGA has not generated new rural jobs—a shattering indictment of the philosophy of the scheme. During British days, the 'test works' programme used to be introduced at times of severe drought or agricultural failure to provide immediate relief by organizing local agricultural work in rural areas. This was a device resorted to only in crisis situations to test the level of agrarian distress. With MNREGA, it is now clear that agricultural distress is permanent, widespread, endemic and has affected every part of the country. Can there be a stronger indictment of our governance model?

***

Dalit memorials in Noida and Lucknow: the ostensible noble purpose was to give expression to 'Dalit pride'—the celebration of the emergence of Dalits from the shadows of society to one of equal partnership with other communities. In reality, as the Lok Ayukta has formally pointed out, the exercise was mainly geared to generate illicit money—at least 40 per cent of the expenditure was siphoned off to private pockets. The allegations are that some senior ministers and other officials have used the massive constructions to corner large leakages for personal benefits.

***

Communal riots take place in many states with a fair degree of regularity. Whereas historically communities have lived in peace and harmony, in the past four or five decades, with the perception of communities as 'vote banks', much politics is devoted to engineering or sponsoring or creating riots so that waters can be muddied, and fishing may be resorted to—if one may be forgiven for saying so. Usually there is a clear indication in advance about the build-up to a riot and generally adequate time is available to pre-empt it, or cool down the situation. No doubt a small local event may develop into a disturbance but a vigilant local administration can douse the fire and not let the conflagration spread. However, sadly some state governments, with their own political logic, foster and create a tinderbox atmosphere. When a minor event inevitably occurs, it explodes into a major riot. Generally in these situations, the local authorities—the DM, SP, SSP, DIG and Commissioner have all been given, very subtly and indirectly, instructions as to which community or group to support, in the build-up to a vitiated atmosphere. In other words the state government and the politics of the day is the main, though possibly not the proximate, cause for the conflagration.

When an inevitable large explosion takes place, with significant loss of life, injuries to many, damage to property and general public distress, the 'placebo' reaction of the authorities is predictable. All the ten or 12 local authorities are immediately transferred. This is the first activity designed to show how vigilant the state government is. They are replaced by new incumbents, who do not know the local area, who take over at a time of much confusion. They are supposed to 'hit the deck running', and 'control' the situation. Very soon a state VIP visit takes place, disrupting the local machinery, the law and order apparatus as well as refugee management—to provide a photo-opportunity, to exhibit 'grief' and to announce 'financial relief'. The chief minister usually orders an 'inquiry', with the main objective of showing to be keen to 'get to the bottom' of the issue, but really to send the matter into limbo. This is soon followed by further visitations from officials in the Government of India—depending on the scale, the home minister or PM/party president or others visits the spot and does his share in disrupting local operations; depending on the complexion of the state government, either condemns the state or praises it for good handling of a 'situation' created by 'opposition' forces. These are played to a script well laid out, well rehearsed and practiced over decades of experience. The basics are never addressed—fostering communal harmony, giving independence, authority and responsibility without interference to the local police and magistracy, as well as punishing them for failure. We can see this pattern, with many variations and innovations depending on the circumstances, in nearly every riot anywhere in India. This is in general the anatomy of an Indian riot and the standard ineffective response to it.

***

'Transfers and postings' are officially done in 'public interest'. In reality most postings away from the district and in the secretariat are on the demand of one or the other local mafias, who find a particular official 'inconvenient'. Ashok Khemka in Haryana has been transferred 43 times in 21 years' of service. He has an excellent 'service record', he has been approved on merit to be a Joint Secretary in the Government of India. If he is really competent, why should he be transferred so frequently? If he is incompetent, why hasn't he been dismissed or given adverse annual remarks? The situation stinks and requires major corrections. In many states, the minister has understood well that money is to be made in transfers and postings.

In mid-2013, two notable instances of abuse of the transfer and disciplinary powers of state governments came to light in the way in which Khemka in Haryana and Durga Nagpal in Uttar Pradesh were shabbily treated. Both of them were merely doing the work assigned to them. However, their official actions were extremely inconvenient to the powers that be, in that they were interfering in the free-run given to local mafias who are often the benefactors and associates of the parties in power. It should be noted that just as in the Nirbhaya case, the Khemka and Nagpal cases are merely instances of widespread abuse of powers for managing the services by the state governments. The central government is not too different, as seen later in this chapter.

The other purpose of effecting a transfer or starting a disciplinary proceeding is to divert attention from the real issues. Thus, for example, Durga Nagpal aggressively confronted the sand mafia in her district and became highly inconvenient for a powerful local politician. She had to be transferred out, obviously 'in public interest'. In the event a false charge was leveled against her on a totally unconnected issue. The government successfully diverted attention from the nefarious activities of the mafia, as the media focused on the injustice to Durga Nagpal. This is part of the government's standard armory for manufacturing a new issue with the primary purpose of diverting attention from inconvenient situations.

***

It is well-known that parties in power in states regularly treat certain communities or castes or groups as vote banks. The local administration is given the signal that a particular caste or community needs to be treated with 'kid-gloves'—in every situation, they should be given preferred treatment. Very often, when local incidents take place, the DM or SP is reluctant to discourage the wrong-doers if they come from the preferred group and they frequently resort to excessively enthusiastic action against those from the non-preferred group. Every now and then this results in a riot, sometimes quite serious as the Muzaffarnagar riots of summer 2013. Usually the army and the para-military forces are called in, 'peace is restored' (after engineering the destruction of peace in the first place). Then 'action' is taken. Generally this means that the Commissioner (who incidentally has absolutely no role in law and order matters), the DM, SP and the DIG of Police are transferred, ostensibly in 'public interest'. Local officials pay for the sins of the party in power. At the end of it all, the party chief sanctimoniously proclaims that 'the security forces and administration reacted with great sensitivity and promptness; the situation is well under control; our response has been prompt and swift', or words to that effect. These are charades which are regularly played. However, many of them are quite deadly.

***

While the next example does not exactly fit into the mould of the theme of this chapter, it is illustrative of the rot that has set in the system. In April 2013, the nation was shocked to know that the nephew of Pawan Bansal, the Union railway minister, was caught taking a bribe from a Member of the Railway Board. Enough evidence had emerged that the nephew was close to the minister, used to hang out in the room of the minister's private secretary much of the time and that there was a direct connection with the promise made to the officer of promotion for cash! The minister promptly 'denied' any knowledge, loudly proclaimed his own 'honesty', protested that he was innocent and refused to resign. That he was forced to, was a result of a public outcry. If one wants to be charitable to the minister, one can argue that he was the biggest idiot in the world, unfit to hold the lowest level job in the Ministry of Railways, since he did not know what was happening under his very nose; or as the overwhelming probability is, he was corrupt to the core—take your pick. The real point is that a direct cash connection with transfers and postings had apparently reached the highest level of governance—a Railway Board Member has the rank of a Secretary to the government. Even if one cannot accept it, one can grudgingly comprehend cash-related postings and transfers at the block or tehsil clerk or industry inspector level, or to accept that some thanas get 'auctioned'; It is a shattering thought that the disease has reached the highest levels of the Government of India.

***

Much like illusory action is taken by governments in India, ostensibly trying to show how helpful they are to the citizenry, the same kind of skullduggery is indulged in by developed countries, which want to demonstrate their 'concern' for developing countries by bilateral aid and through multilateral UN and other agencies. Most of the bilateral aid is actually tied directly to the business generated in the country of the donor, with hardly any altruism. Likewise most UN agencies like UNCTAD and UNIDO are shell institutions, designed to 'demonstrate' the goodwill of developed countries towards their poorer cousins. Much like the central government in India throws crumbs to the rural agriculture sector, developed countries make a big show of support for development of the 'third-world' through these agencies. Even these are ultimately designed to benefit the 'donors' in various ways. While in the commerce ministry, dealing with the Trade Policy Division, I got to know from the inside how the developed countries exploit the 'treaty organizations' to further their own interests. In the following paragraphs I recount my personal experience in this regard.

It was 1981, I had already worked for two years as Joint Secretary in the Ministry of Commerce. I do not know how I came to the notice of the Commonwealth Secretariat in London but out of the blue I had a semi-formal message from them, whether I would be willing to go to Lesotho on a three-year assignment as Trade Advisor. I quietly researched as to where Lesotho was, and to find some details about this landlocked country within South Africa. I discovered that the 'country' was not much bigger than an average Indian district, with a similar population. It, however, had about 20-odd five-star hotels, a large number of golf courses and was a 'holiday' destination for South African males to let themselves go on a binge from time to time, away from the more strait-laced conditions prevailing at home. I was inclined to accept the offer, particularly as the salary suggested was far in excess of what I was getting paid by the government. In addition every middle-level government servant covets an 'international' assignment, as it signifies recognition, and status!

P.K. Kaul, one of the ablest, finest administrators I have ever come across was my boss as Commerce Secretary. Presumably he knew how pigheaded and obstinate I was in most matters. One afternoon, walking into his office room, I was surprised to see my wife sitting in the visitor's chair. She was getting a lecture from Kaul Saheb as to how inadvisable it was for me to go to Lesotho at this stage of my career. He wanted her to convince me against the move by putting her foot down. He realized that it would have been of no avail if he had spoken to me directly. His ploy worked—Lalitha 'convinced' me not to go, and the matter was forgotten.

Apparently Kaul had told her that I stood out among the joint secretaries in the ministry and that sooner or later I would be selected for a 'better' foreign assignment. Sure enough, within a year I was selected for the post of Indian Ambassador to GATT (now WTO) in Geneva. Kaul had left the commerce ministry to go to the defence ministry well before then. In due course, that posting to Geneva for me fell through, details of which I have written elsewhere. I had taken all steps to go for that assignment, including undergoing a security briefing, authorization for tickets. The move was so imminent that one of the Hinduja brothers, usually resident in Geneva, called on me, offered me 'all facilities', including accommodation, a vehicle etc. 'till I settled down' in Geneva; presumably the Hinduja family was dedicated to pursuing the 'interests' of the Government of India even in foreign shores! Much later I discovered, in another context, as to how an Indian business family, with a branch in Geneva kept a strong watching brief on India's negotiations on various issues in WTO GATT and lent their 'good offices' to 'mediate' between Washington and New Delhi in ensuring that India took the 'right posture' in Geneva international trade negotiations. Who said our multinationals are not 'patriotic'?!

Curiously, as my assignment in the commerce ministry was coming to an end in 1984, I received two offers during the course of one day: one to go to ESCAP in Bangkok and the other to International Trade Centre (ITC) UNCTAD GATT in Geneva. Again I did furious research. The advice I received was that ESCAP was a 'defunct' toothless organization, with no useful contribution to anyone or any country, except to the welfare of its own employees. That ITC was at least a 'business-like' organization, where one can learn something new, and may be able to contribute to its work. In the event, I naturally chose to go to Geneva, where I spent six years.

At the end of it all, I learnt that nearly all the international organizations that I came across from fairly close quarters, were mainly established to look after their own interests. The *raison-d'être* of their creation is to benefit the developed countries; while the ostensible reason is to provide development assistance, the main preoccupation of the employees of these prestigious agencies is to draw substantial salaries, plan their holidays meticulously and generally appear to be busy while doing nothing. Their unwritten motto is 'self before service'. While this comment may be unfair to a few, most of the employees who had been selected were close to or related to senior government personnel in developed and developing countries—the assignment was as quid-pro-quo for some favour done, in an elaborate scheme of mutual back-scratching. As one Indian colleague pointed out, the salary levels in these organizations is of the order of a 100-times that of working for the government, while the work, responsibility and accountability was 100-times less than in government. These postings were really rewards for some good done decades earlier by the ancestors of these fortunate deputationists. I discovered that nearly all the agencies like UNIDO, UNCTAD, WFP and ILO fit the same description that was given for ESCAP earlier. These agencies may have been relevant four or five decades earlier, but now are mere appendices, irrelevancies and parasites on the international system, serving no purpose except the welfare of their employees. These, including the Bretton-Woods Institutions—IMF, the World Bank and GATT—were originally established by developed countries in a post-second-world war era, ostensibly to support 'developing countries', but in reality to create a fora for continuing and expanding the superiority of developed countries and extending their reach over their economies. They were part of the neocolonial instruments for exercising control over poor countries, at a cheap price. By now this ought to have been abundantly evident to all decision-makers in developing countries.

It is astonishing how out-of-date our national perception on such matters is, when India still hankers to be a permanent member of the Security Council of the UN, and is willing to make sacrifices for it. It merely requires China to hint that it may not oppose India's membership to the Security Council, for us to down-pedal any major issue that we have against that country. Too much of the energy in our external interface is wasted in working for this objective. The surest way to be recognized as a major power in the world is to become one through strong domestic development—education, health, infrastructure, industry and society without social tensions. The shortcut of permanent membership of the UN Security Council may avail us of very little, though it may have to be purchased at a high cost.

One comment on the utility and value of UN organizations. I would be untrue to my salt if I did not mention that I got to study for my master's degree in public administration at Harvard only due to a fellowship by UNDP, for which one is grateful. I recall that calculations showed 90 per cent of 'development aid', in some form or the other, gets spent to benefit developed economies. Aid is thus, per se not altruistic, even not accounting for the other major indirect benefits to the 'donor'!

The annual pension that I earned for working for five years in Geneva, was higher than the Government of India pension for 33 years of work in India. This was the main reason why on return, I had no sense of personal monetary insecurity, and could stand up in higher reaches of the government, holding my own and not needing to buckle down to pressures. This is the psychological advantage that the foreign posting allowed me to have. In the final analysis, is this the only benefit received by developing countries from such international organizations?

4

HAS THE MEDIA BECOME MORE SHRILL, BUT MORE EFFECTIVE?

If you do not see the TV, you are uninformed; if you see the TV, you are misinformed—apologies to Mark Twain

Before the advent of television as a medium of information, the information requirements of most households was met by the daily newspaper, commentary and analysis through weekly or monthly magazines, in English or vernacular along with, of course, the gossip that one indulged in at cards in the club, or by meeting others during the *Ramayana* or *Bhagwat* discourse in the evening. Decades back, Marshall McLuhan, at the infancy of the television medium had understood its intrusive character. It is now a part of daily life all over the world, increasingly in India. Much as a latter-day mobile phone has become ubiquitous and indispensable, the constant blare of the television set in most homes is a proximate cause for early deafness of most middle-aged householders. My grandson long back asked me how my grandfather could have lived without electricity—I had no credible answer. Indeed, he could well have asked me how could I grow up without the help of television, or even the computer or the cell phone, all of which are now indispensable for 'normal life'. I even saw a couple talking to each other on their cell phones during their evening walk. Clearly we are a civilization 'infotaining' ourselves to oblivion.

Indian television, both English and vernacular, which started off mostly to entertain has now become increasingly didactic, stridently so. It perceives its role as one of 'engineering change'. While many anchors pursue their own hobby-horses, the compulsion to 'convert' the audience to their own perspective is increasingly evident. While TRPs is the operative mantra, it is subtly intertwined with the anchor's desire to project loudly a particular point of view. Complex cross-holdings of controlling interests in channels and media outlets are a matter of public interest—where agendas of individuals or business houses can impinge seriously on national life. Considering that the ownership of each channel generally vests, however indirectly, with a political party, or a large business house, the channel becomes an important vehicle for pursuing a political or corporate strategy, well hidden through much camouflage—the message has to come through, very subtly and quietly, but definitely. McLuhan had surely anticipated all this.

The main English language channels have limited access, in the sense that they are watched by a particular class of people in urban areas and towns—the educated middle and upper classes. Clearly this group has limited impact on electoral politics. However, it has a disproportionately large impact on what the media in general has to say. It moulds the opinion of the middle class, which impacts the overall approach of a society. Thus, the English media has a much greater overall reach in terms of impact, than what its viewership warrants.

Most of the anchors on the main channel at prime time are highly self-assured, brash to the point of arrogance and think of themselves as 'messiahs of change'. They pick up a point, flog it quite aggressively, till they are assured that everyone is convinced. However, this objective is inherently contradictory to the need of having a 'balanced debate' with competing perspectives stressed by knowledgeable persons. By the very nature of the medium, a well argued, knowledgeable programme with competing points of view expressed sharply, but politely, with thrust and counter-thrust is not the recipe for success in Indian television channels. Perhaps experience has shown that this does not help with TRPs. Accordingly what is finally produced and dished-out is a kind of combination of kick-boxing, fixed WWF wrestling and 20-20 cricket, as the format for throwing light on a complex issue. The anchor sees the need to have fireworks (not just polite differences), personal attacks (not graceful sharp thrusts) and outright hostility (not polite disagreement). All these are indispensable elements in the soap-opera that the evening news-hour delivers.

Most anchors are rudely inquisitorial, and pillory the guests, particularly spokesmen of political parties with great aggression. A casual observer may feel that an intimidating attack has been mounted. Indeed I have even heard some anchors tell the guest, 'you are a liar', sometimes repeatedly so within one programme. Astonishingly, the party representative swallows even this unparliamentary language—he must have much compulsion to stay on in the programme; it should be added that the abusive attack is most often not unjustified. Usually there is a mixture of politicians of different colours (all of whom are agreed that there should be no change in the larger sense, as they are the main beneficiaries) and two or three 'experts' whose views are generally highly predictable. Usually about eight to ten guests are invited to a one-hour programme, of which about 25 minutes are taken up by advertisements, another 25 minutes through exposition, analysis, discourse and long-winded questions and interruptions by the anchor; the guests get about one minute each to speak during the hour, about 30 seconds in each spell, to cover a complex matter in great detail! Since the 'guest' is conscious of the very limited time given to him, and is not sure at what instant the anchor will lose interest and 'switch' him off, his comments are made in a breathless manner with often short-hand language, barely comprehensible, in great hurry. By contrast, when a politician is 'batting' an inconvenient point, he expansively digresses, filibusters shamelessly, is ready to resort to leisurely banalities and objects strongly when 'interrupted' and asked to come to the point, complaining bitterly that he is not given sufficient 'space'. It all makes for interesting theatre. In politically contentious matters, where two parties or politicians get into a dog-fight, much heat gets generated, and even less light is thrown on the subject. All in all, it is good entertainment for all, if you consider WWE to be fun.

There is one other significant trend that needs to be noticed in such shows over the past decade or so. Earlier, a minister or the high dignitary in a senior position was treated by the anchor with kid-gloves, with a hint of deference and allowed his say without much interruption. Thank goodness the TV talk-shows and the anchors have come of age. The VIP, minister and the 'spokesman' are treated with aggression, questioned often viciously and frequently treated with disbelief and a hint of disdain. This is an extremely welcome trend. The VIP/minister, who hitherto had been kept on a pedestal, and who used to 'talk-down' to ordinary people, anchors and fellow guests not exempted, are rightly often brought down to ground level; occasionally even floored brutally—much of it well deserved. Most anchors, insufferable as they may often be, need to be felicitated for treating the VIP/minister as he deserves to be—with incredulity, disbelief and distrust, with a hint of disdain.

Most anchors have to be, or at least pose to be 'larger than life'. In the situation in which they are placed, almost certainly they make themselves the centre of focus and attention, even if large issues relating to an earthquake or war or Naxal terror or collapse of the currency are discussed. The main focus is the anchor and not the event. Let me illustrate this through an example from a totally different sphere, where the observer becomes more important than the person observed—much like the TV anchors assume for themselves greater importance than the events discussed, or the experts discussing them. I was walking down the Marina Beach in Chennai one morning recently. The entire walk is adorned with statues of great men and women down the ages—Mahatma Gandhi, Avvayyar, Tiruvalluvar and other giants who have contributed to Tamil culture, literature or society. Near Triplicane, opposite the cricket ground where I recall having played at least three league cricket matches, is the statue of Netaji Subhash Chandra Bose—an imposing figure, in the elegant and impressive uniform that we have always seen him in. I read the legend at the base of the statue. It mentioned the name of S.C. Bose. Below that it also named the person who unveiled the statue along with the date—Mu. Karunanidhi, the then chief minister of Tamil Nadu. What was remarkable was that the letters describing the name of the person unveiling the statue were written in a huge font, three-times bigger than the letters of S.C. Bose, whose statue it was. Clearly the reporter is much bigger than the event reported; the war correspondent is more important than the war itself. Christian Amanpour IS the news, what she reports is of lesser importance! Thucydides was a bigger character than the wars that were lost—Sanjaya was more important than the events of the *Mahabharata* war, indeed than the *Bhagwat Gita*. Our anchors are 100-times larger than life, bigger than any event on which they are acting as coordinators for the discussion.

Despite the indifferent quality of the material dished out, one important aspect needs to be highlighted. In the past decade or so, one has seen a sharp deterioration in the quality of governance. The venality of the executive, at the Centre and in the states, has seen exponentially higher manifestation. The performance and contribution of the legislature to governance, which has never been seen in good light for the past six decades has sharply gone down in the last decade or so. The judiciary, willy-nilly, has become more active, due to force of circumstances, to fill up the vacuum so to speak. Some constitutional and other agencies have also risen up to fill the void. The main phenomenon has been the rise of television as a medium to take on a high-profile role in policy and in implementation areas.

Let me illustrate this with a couple of examples. Some websites can give you the annual list of scams over the past three decades; it is a mind-boggling collection of grand-thuggery. The system has got away with hardly any heads rolling or people taken to account. In 2010, when the Commonwealth Games scam broke out with the damning report from CAG, Times Now channel took it up with great vigour—Arnab Goswami, the anchor, went to town on the subject. I was a guest on one of the sessions blasting the CWG organizers, and baying for their blood. When asked my opinion, I had condemned the obvious wrong-doing roundly but had predicted that in three-months' time it will all die out, there will be new scams taking up the place of old. The second part of my comment has been proved right, repeatedly so. Happily, I have been proved wrong on the first part. For the first time, the crusading approach of television channels has actually resulted in orchestrating and raising to a high-decibel national consciousness, the enormity of the crimes and the venality of the perpetrators. Soon thereafter was the 2-G scam, whose fuse was lit by CAG, the flame was fanned furiously by the media, and finally the explosion came through the landmark verdict of the Supreme Court; a Union minister actually going to jail, and a whole bunch of licenses cancelled. How did this happen? Firstly, there was CAG, who finally stood up to his constitutional role as a critic of public expenditure, recognizing that he was a servant of the people, of the Constitution and had an adversarial—not cozy, crony-relationship—with the executive. This had happened many times before but for the very vigorous highlighting of the massive fraud by an aggressive media, this would have been swept under the carpet. The apex court also, as the saviour it has been in the past, played its role. Are we now seeing a new paradigm in public affairs? That scams and wrong-doings which are discovered in public space, will not be allowed to be washed out, swept under the carpet, brazenly ignored and waited out? Enough cannot be said in praise of the media, particularly television media, in rising to the occasion. The print media has always played its traditional role of being a critic when required. The television media has carved a new niche for itself.

The tone set by Times Now has now become the standard, followed by other English channels and now increasingly by Hindi channels. The Antrix-Devas deal, which was in a sense the forerunner of the 2-G scam, got aborted, as the evil design was highlighted by the media. I recall that at the time when the Coalgate report was getting finalized, and had not hit the headlines, I had come informally to know of its potential reach and depth and had played a small part in highlighting the issues, initially on Times Now, well before it became public knowledge. In older times, clearly this would have been thrown in the dustbin. The Adarsh Housing scam and the Vadra expose are instances of the publicity glare that the media has been able to mount on wrong-doings. The Anna Hazare Lok Pal movement, highlighted by the media, had played its role—however a wily political class had in a multi-party conspiracy mode, managed to scuttle the establishment of the Lok Pal—which politician wants an umpire, when the political class can be the player, the fixer, the bowler, the batsman, the opponent and its own umpire as well as its own board of control? The Constitution had inadvertently created for the political class no checks and balances; 120 crore people may want a Lok Pal, but 1,000 politicians will not permit it. However, to the credit of the media, it pursued large national issues, possibly for TRP reasons, but it has been on the side of the angels, not the devilish politicians.

I, as much as nearly anyone else, am aware of the weaknesses of the visual media, how the financing structures of the major houses are controlled through remote mechanisms, the compulsions of the programmers and anchors to follow certain directions and the blackmailing potential of the press in general. I have also heard criticism from a number of middle class arm-chair critics, who sneer at the 'arrogance', self-importance and one-track approach of the anchors, all of it partly or mostly true. However, the signal contribution of the television media to recent attempts for system-change cannot be underestimated.

Of course, each anchor has his own pet theories and approaches—perhaps in many instances he has been given a brief. Thus, in a programme 'who was the best PM in the past 50 years', the staff of the channel would call me for my views, ostensibly in preparation for a 'balanced' guest list. I was not be invited to the show if I had views totally differing from that of the channel. In the live programme itself, if I referred strongly to a particular ex-PM, not favoured by the anchor, he or she would cut me off—pleasantly in the beginning, and roughly if I persisted. I would not be given another chance to express my opinion in the whole hour. If it were a recorded programme, normally I would be allowed to have my say, but when one saw the final version broadcast, one could see heavy editing and interposition of my comments in such a manner that it would have least impact! It is interesting to see the many games that are played in this manner. In general, the channel has assessed me carefully and has brought me in as an 'expert', not so much to express my own expert views, but to get my views to buttress the theme that is to be projected.

There are many hardy perennials in nearly every channel, whose political leanings, affiliations and commitments are well known, masquerading as 'independent' experts. Professional journalists as they mostly are, they have built strong constituencies in political and other fields and cannot go too much out of line in any programme. They have carefully built many bridges in the past, and are anxious not to destroy any of them. It is often interesting to see the specious arguments and interposition of 'facts' that they trot out, appearing to be neutral but in fact to mount predetermined support or to defend or attack this or that point of view. Their sophistry in finding arguments to buttress prespecified points of view, in contradiction to all known facts, often deserve rueful admiration. Highly articulate as many of them are, nearly everyone has a biased point of view on every issue, perhaps based on their political leanings and support base. Sadly even so-called independent, expert views are highly skewed.

It is interesting to see how each such public affairs chat show has its own character, depending on the anchor, participants, issues and the relative political temperature in which it is discussed. Some debates are dominated by emotion, some by facts, others by logic or reason—however, partisanship is the permanent flavour. Thus, commonly, when you have someone like Shashi Tharoor, a Union minister, you can hear Oxford or Cambridge English, too sophisticated even for the British Parliament, in possibly the kind of language that Keats or Shakespeare would have used if they were on the television show today, with impeccable diction—however totally devoid of any content whatever. As Eliza Doolittle would say 'words, words, nothing but words …'; a latter-day Disraeli or Gladstone but without substance. Like Tharoor, one sees a number of 'debaters' permanently sporting a superior supercilious smile, implying that all others in the programme are idiots (not always untrue!), coming out with pithy one-liners, which sound quite impressive but mean little in the context. One can also see very high powered lawyers, in their profession engaged in defending skullduggery by top corporates, appearing as 'independent' experts on legal matters to criticize public policy, obviously propounding theories designed to project partisan views—there are at least three on view of this variety. They appear extremely logical, public-spirited and appearing to voice public interest perspectives, but quietly slip in a couple of references supporting their professional interests—this could be less objectionable if at least they declared their direct interest in particular clients. At least an eminent lawyer like Abhishek Singhvi gets introduced as a party spokesman—he could be as partisan as he wished, which he generally is in the most outrageous manner, but usually with a smile. In most hour-long talk shows, it usually takes about 15 minutes for the participants to 'warm-up' and then the fireworks start; 'Guests' accusing and abusing each other, statements made simultaneously by three or four—each at the top of the voice, gasping for breath—till a 'climax' is reached. Then a new round starts!

It is equally interesting to note how the nature of coverage by the media, both visual and written, subtly changes with perceptions of changing political fortunes of parties and personalities. Thus, for example, in the late summer of 2013, as the conventional assessment is that the stars of the Congress party are waning, die-hard vocal and strident supporters are slowly muting their voices, reducing the 'volume', making their comments increasingly ambivalent, and bracing themselves for an eventuality where they can make the volte-face in a slow graduated manner, so that they are not 'found-out'. As an outsider with a good look inside, I can see with much amusement the trauma and the uncertainties suffered by professional commentators!

The other criticism of the media can be that it focuses on items which instantly titillate. Major issues like education, health, poverty and Naxalism which are all of significant national interest are addressed only in the context of specific events or episodes. There is hardly any sustained coverage of large national issues, except when an 'explosion' takes place. Clearly the eye is on TRPs—the 'ratings'—perhaps greater sustained attention to national issues would be warranted. With respect to the visual media, one more comment may be made. It may be recalled that the Jessica Lal murder case, the Nirbhaya rape, the Arushi murder and the Durga Nagpal suspension case all received major sustained focus on television media. The common factor is that all these episodes took place in or in the vicinity of Delhi. These symbolize the violence done to the rule of law, in a routine manner across India; however, Delhi events were the ones that highlighted the atrocities. Perhaps this is natural, since television centres are focused in the metros but it is still not fully explained why similar incidents in Mumbai, Chennai or Bangalore do not hit focused and sustained television coverage, as these events did.

Another aspect needs to be highlighted. One often finds that an important story, which has gained currency and attracted much public attention, suddenly gets killed. One would never know how and in what manner that all media suddenly drops a topic, as if it never happened. In the US, it is a common phenomenon that where a subject is seen as affecting 'national interest' adversely, the media itself avoids touching it, or stops voluntarily addressing the matter on a prompting from the White House. The Indian press or media clearly does not have that level of discipline or even the concept of impact on 'national interest'. However, we still see the phenomenon of stories suddenly disappearing. The conclusion is inescapable that the media is susceptible to be influenced by a 'hidden hand'! Indeed the alleged Vadra shenanigans, in collaboration with DLF and the Government of Haryana were reported in the press as early as 2010. Despite its explosive nature, it dropped out of sight magically, till it was revived by the media some time in 2013, again mysteriously. It is also curious to note that in late August 2013 there was a brief news item that the new CAG had ordered discontinuation of an inquiry on the subject already started by the previous CAG—as explosive a news item as any; curiously no newspaper or TV picked it up for analysis or discussion. One wonders why! I have time and again seen sensitive stories, where the correspondent has interviewed me or taken a byte from me not surfacing. When I ask the correspondent as to what happened, he would give a sheepish smile and say: 'don't ask me, the story has been killed.'

***

A picture may be worth a thousand words, however, the written word still carries weight compared to the spoken. I write a regular column in a major English language newspaper, which is carried in other papers as well. From the response that I receive from readers, I see the reach and impact that this media has. No doubt English language newspapers reach a limited segment of society, but this readership is quite aware of the issues in detail. Many responses I receive from readers are of high quality, with significant thought content. I should also add that many letters are critical, and now and then are abusive in nature. Despite the sharply growing reach of the visual media, the daily newspapers still have a strong presence in opinion making.

Vernacular newspapers have a far greater reach and readership in India. According to the All India Readership Survey 2012, *Dainik Jagran* and *Dainik Bhaskar* between them have an 'average issue readership' of about 31 million daily; compare this to the English newspaper the *Times of India*, the largest selling English newspaper in the world—yes, world—with a corresponding figure of 7.6 million. This is a measure of the reach of our vernacular press. Add to this the circulation of the other language newspapers, Tamil, Gujarati, Bengali etc., and one can get a picture of the widespread readership. While many newspapers are frequently partisan in their approach, there are still highly respected vernacular papers, which are fiercely independent in their outlook. The ones with larger circulations and better reputations are quite outspoken and do not take sides—a tribute to the readership they cater to. For example, *Dinamani*, the Tamil newspaper that often carries my pieces, is totally independent and expresses its views openly and fearlessly and this in a market with other Tamil Newspapers functioning as mouth-pieces of rival political parties. It is my experience that vernacular papers in general reflect the concerns of 'real' India much better. They focus on local issues, with feet on the ground much firmer, while invariably covering fairly accurately regional and national issues. By and large, I have noticed that the vernacular press reflects the concerns of 'Bharat' better than the English newspapers, which have a strong metropolitan bias and are geared to the tastes of the urban reader. I get this strong impression based on the responses to my articles in language papers, where the comments are much larger in number and more emotional in content—mofussil readers are strongly involved in the issues, more than their metropolitan counterparts.

***

The question of regulating the media, visual as well as print, crops up from time to time. Our experience of Indian institutions is that no group of people or profession is able to regulate itself—create its own 'guild'—for effective self-regulation. The media is no exception. However, the danger of any regulation from outside is that 'big brother' will act as a censor, which will be inimical to public interest. This is a very delicate and complex issue, and no readymade solution is available. There is no doubt that the clout of the media, especially the visual media is sharply on the increase; television is now slowly becoming a bulwark for the protection of liberty and democracy, much like an active higher judiciary is playing a magnificent role in saving our democracy. A vigilant and active media, along with reawakened constitutional institutions, along with an emergent enlightened social media, supported by the Right to Information Act are now emerging as saviours of our democracy. In the circumstances, one would be chary of suggesting any outside control mechanism over the media in the present stage, till the media itself over-reaches its self-appointed mandate.

One quick word on the Press Council of India, currently chaired by the garrulous Markandey Katju. While the body itself is toothless, its chairman regularly fires, like a loose cannon on all and sundry subjects. Even though the council is not a government body, it is an institution in the public domain, its chairman is in some senses a public official. While citizen Katju has the full right to speak his mind on any subject under the sun, clearly he ought to impose some discipline on himself with respect to the range, volume and content of his views so long as he holds office. Since he speaks on so many public issues, sooner or later some of these will come up for consideration in the Press Council; as an ex-judge, would he recuse himself in that event? In any case such free expression of views is akin to the loose talk indulged in by Amartya Sen on fields well beyond his expertise. Charles Lindberg, the famous aviator, who did the first solo flight across the Atlantic, and who was a great national hero in the US was silenced in the public when he spoke on issues related to the second world war. Amartya Sen will perhaps carry greater weight in what he says if he sticks to the areas of his recognized expertise.

***

A recent *Washington Post* international survey has found India the 'second-most racist' country in the world after Jordan. Whatever the credibility of the survey, surely it will be foolhardy to reject it out of hand as 'biased'. Caste, communal, untouchability and other societal differences, indeed tensions and intolerance, are well known to be widely prevalent in the country. Caste and community are the two main factors influencing elections in our 'democracy'. The media could play a quiet role in improving the ground conditions. In nearly every television show or movie in the US, one can see, apart from the usual white, an Afro-American, generally a Hispanic, an Asian (mostly of Chinese origin), and these days the occasional sub-continental. In movies, or television comedies or other shows and also in advertisements you see this pattern, which has evolved and become a part of the organization of these shows in the US in a natural manner. Generally the non-white, unless the circumstances so warrant is shown in a neutral or positive light, in a natural manner, without apparent contrivance—be it a comedy or tragedy, or even in the ubiquitous advertisements. Surprisingly, most characters in our television shows, especially advertisements, have to be fair-skinned, 'handsome' men and women, carefully selected and conveying a subtle arrogant message of 'racial' superiority on the one hand and implied contempt for 'lesser humans' on the other. Without being artificial about it, I am sure that our media should now learn to be 'inclusive' in the best possible sense and learn to project people from all walks, backgrounds and segments in a naturally positive manner. That will be conducive to greater social cohesion. The US as a multi-racial society understood this long back that the media is a powerful vehicle for fostering social coherence, tolerance and mutual understanding in a harmonious society. Without appearing to be artificial, it needs to show different types of people in a positive light. This is clearly not a subject for a public debate, or for directions to be issued by the I&B ministry. This is a thought, if spontaneously acceptable and implemented in good faith by decision-makers in the media, will go a long way in naturally bringing more harmony in our complex multi-dimensional society.

***

I am frequently in demand as an 'expert' for many television talk shows, particularly where the issues relate to governance, administration or controversial issues relating to the 'common man'. I guess that I am seen as a 'neutral', but a strong critic of the establishment. When 'establishment-bashing' is on the agenda, I would normally be a good bet! Many of my friends ask me as to why I appear on television so regularly and accept nearly every invitation. I have a semi-facetious answer—'in my own house, or my golf or other private circles, nobody wants to listen to my views, even if I wish to thrust them on them. When somebody sends me a car, and politely asks me to comment on this or that, and gives me an audience, why shouldn't I do that!'

In addition, participation in television programmes and writing for the press gives me the feeling of being continually involved in public affairs and having the opportunity to contribute to the evolution of social thinking on matters of governance and public interest, however miniscule and inconsequential. Apart from these, these give me an opportunity to meet a wide range of people with diverse interests, thus broadening the range and scope of my involvement in matters of public interest. A number of my friends, well meaning, have asked me as to why I 'cheapen' myself by such frequent public exposure on television and elsewhere, particularly when I have no ambitions of any public position. The answer is that I believe that I have some experience in my service life of over 30 years and experience of public matters over a 15 year post-retirement period. For whatever it is worth, it is my duty to express my views on matters of public interest. In any case, apart from anything else, I enjoy it—that is good enough for me.

I live in NOIDA, less than a kilometre from Film City, where most of the television studios are located. 'Accessibility' is a key virtue that I possess—much like Michaela in Catch-22, her virtue was that she was 'available' whenever and wherever wanted, 'even keeping her broom held aloft as a banner'! So I guess the channels think of me first whenever they want to fill up a guest slot. I am only five minutes away, and can be counted on to give a 'first opinion' on 'Breaking News'!

Thanks to my regular television appearances and newspaper columns, I am now a fairly well recognized 'celebrity', in airports and in clubs. The predictable reaction of those who see me for the first time is to give the unspoken impression 'we thought you were a great person—we are thoroughly disappointed'; or the 'reality' is much worse than the television 'appearances'! With regularity, strangers walk up to me to ask 'have I seen you somewhere before?'. I have no ready answer except 'it is not my fault'. Others, even more frequently say, in effect, 'so, you are the *honest* Cabinet Secretary'. This is not said in a sarcastic or offensive vein but what is disturbing is the implication that practically every government servant—the senior one is, the higher the applicability—is dishonest. This poor opinion, implying (rightly or wrongly!) that I am the exception, is a highly worrisome thought, a scathing comment on the credibility of the system.

Finally, I need to mention a comment from my young grandson who visits me every year from the US. Now and then, when he is at home, the OB Van of a television studio gets established in my living room as a guest in some show. As it is broadcast, it is seen live on television by my grandson in another room. He believes that his grandfather is a 'TV star', that he is very 'rich', since all television stars are stinking rich!

5

WHAT IS MODERNITY—IS IT REJECTION OF TRADITION?

The problem in life is not that one does not get what he desires, it is that he does—anon.

In my younger days, I was inducted as an honorary member of 'PREM Sangh', founded by my uncle, a medical doctor at Palghat. This was something like a secret society, with initiation ceremonies, strong bondage of loyalty and togetherness among the members and an unwavering adherence to the principles of the Sangh, as well as total unquestioning loyalty to the leader—my uncle. The PREM Sangh stood for: P—Purity of Thought, R—Righteous in Action, E—Egoless Existence and M—Mukti is our Goal; the first three of these noble ideas relating to actions in life, and the last one relating to the Hindu concept of jeevan mukti or 'liberation' or 'nirvana'—the concept of the jeevatma merging with the paramatma. The 30 or 40 sworn members of the Sangh, from different parts of India, in different vocations, would meet for a ten-day camp every year in summer in some venue related to nature or religion etc. I recall attending meetings at Bhawani (near the Kaveri source), Sringeri (the seat of the Shankaracharya, with an unbroken holy tradition), Dakshineshwar and Belur near Calcutta (Ramakrishna and Vivekananda's ashram) and other places. As a young non-official, not-yet-formally initiated member of this secret society, I attended these camps, which included physical exercises, bhajans, meditation, and public service. One day was devoted to total *maun vrat* or a day of total silence, meditation and looking inwards. These were days soon after Indian independence and there was a strong feeling all over India that we needed to rediscover our traditional greatness by identifying and pursuing ancient paths laid out for us by our culture, through our scriptures and experience of life over five millennia. One surmises that the origins of the Rashtriya Swayamsevak Sangha (RSS) had similar roots and captured the imagination of young Indians in the days soon after our independence. There was a strong moral message in such ideology, an injunction that the traditional dharma, as interpreted needs to be followed rigorously, a moral dimension was intimately linked to our way of life. I lost touch with PREM Sangh in 1959, I don't know if it still exists.

Alas, as we see six decades after independence no school, formal or informal, teaches values, ethical lifestyles and subscribes in principle to PREM Sangh's injunctions—purity of thought and righteousness in action. In the name of secularism, which one suspects has been subverted to sub-serve the ignoble purpose of pandering to vote banks, we have given up the concept of 'moral studies', or a study of the teachings of great men in our schools and colleges. Our children are unable to imbibe values from their parents who are already too busy to eke out their daily harassed existence. Young growing minds get their role models and obtain guidance for lifestyles from television and other means of entertainment. Herein can be traced the tragedy of our times: generations growing up without anything moral or idealistic to look up to or to guide their lives.

***

It is the lessons, the pointers that reach your psyche early in life, that stay with you and guide your personality. One learns as one goes along, but to some extent this learning is circumscribed by the principles imbibed early in an impressionable period of one's life.

Among the first ideas that struck me from the *Bhagwat Gita*, and which stayed with me all through was the sloka in Chapter 6—उद्धरेत् आत्मनात्मानम् Uddharet Atamanatmanam ... (para-phrased by the injunction 'lift yourself up by your own boot straps; it is up to you to be your own friend or your own enemy, the choice is yours'). In older years, as one periodically goes back to the *Bhagwat Gita* for reference or just for a piece of '*shanti*' (peace of mind) one is struck each time with a new interpretation of the brilliance of a stanza. Chapter 9 talks of *yogakshema*—'I am present with you'—a commonsense interpretation of the concept that you have to work hard (yoga) to achieve something, and then you have to work to preserve and maintain the achievement (*kshema*). This elementary concept of creation and maintenance can be applied to any area of life, as to every aspect of administration and governance.

I wonder how many readers have had the unpleasant necessity of going through a full-body scanner, when one is buckled and strapped to the bed, going through the MRI tunnel. For anyone who is even mildly claustrophobic it can be a traumatic experience, a difficult 20 or 30 minutes to endure. In much the same manner, when one has to be on partial anesthetic for some physical operation the question always arises as to what one thinks of during these trying periods, when your instinct is to flay your hands and attempt to break out of the shackles. I wonder if people who have gone through such experiences would reflect on how they suffered through these critical times. Clearly the best path is through control of the mind. Through meditation the mind focuses hard on some object or thought or concept, that it is impervious to everything that happens around that person. It was said that Valmiki meditated for many years, oblivious of everything surrounding him, that over that long period ant-hills developed and enveloped him but he was unaware of everything, such was the level of his focus or concentration.

Having grown up in a pious ashram in my school days, having been exposed to the philosophy of Ramana Maharishi, with his truly original call to investigate 'WHO AM I' as the royal path for 'self-realization', having had the benefit of the grace of the Sringeri Mutt with its unbroken tradition of nine centuries of piety, wisdom, divinity and holiness, having been an associate member of PREM Sangh and familiar with the concepts and teachings of the *Bhagwat Gita*, I was an ideal candidate to withdraw into deep meditation at such times of physical and mental stress, like going through the MRI tunnel, or during a part-anesthetic operation. Alas, to my utter shame and sense of great failure, all these noble associations could not be invoked by me, to provide me solace, comfort and diversion during such critical times. I need to confess that on the three or four such occasions, I would relive, step by step, shot by shot, move by move, from the first tee-off, through the fairway and along the course—resort to a simulated dream-round of golf to give me comfort. I make this confession with a heavy heart. Such great blessings that one has been gifted with have not enabled me to lift myself up to higher levels of spirituality and philosophy, the clearest indication of a spiritually failed life, unable to grasp easy opportunities for self-advancement. Being born a human is the rarest of rare gifts. Worms, reptiles, fishes, bacteria and other animals spend their life-times on mundane affairs. Is it not unpardonable for a human being to profligately waste his good fortune and not use his precious gift of life to lift himself in the spiritual plane, to reach a higher level of consciousness, reach closer to the Maker?

There is the story of a young devotee of Ramakrishna Paramhansa, the great sage of the 19th century from Bengal, who 'worked' very hard to attain 'self-realization', and in course of time complained to his guru that despite his efforts, he was not reaching the nirvana stage. Ramakrishna counseled patience, and asked the young aspirant to persist with his yoga and meditation. After a few days the devotee repeated his complaint to the guru. The next morning, as they were taking the morning bath in the adjacent Hoogly river, suddenly Ramakrishna caught hold of the young man's head, pressed it under the water, and held it there for a half-minute. The young boy was struggling hard, trying to free himself with force; anon the guru released his grip. As the devotee came up for air, regained his breath, he glared at the master and asked him why he was being drowned. Ramakrishna gently told the young man that if he aspired for 'enlightenment' with the same urgency, passion and need for air that he displayed earlier, he would attain nirvana in no time! Nothing can be obtained without the grace of the Lord, even reaching the Lord has to be ordained by the Lord himself.

Things come around a full circle during one's lifetime

In Lucknow, playing golf in the 1990s, one of my partners in the group used to get his caddy to fix his tee before the tee shot. He could not bend enough, and would meticulously chide the caddy about the depth of insertion of the tee into the ground. Twenty years later, when I was suffering from sciatica I discovered that I needed a caddy to insert the tee for me as it was too painful for me to bend to fix it.

Going back even earlier, to my college days in Calcutta in the 1950s, we had a washerwoman coming to the house every day. She had a husky broken voice, attractive in a rustic kind of way. I made fun of her as a 'permanent *jalatoshi*'—one with a permanent cold. Sixty years later, I find that thanks to 30 years of heavy smoking, I carry a permanent cold, have weak lungs, have to use inhalers and get through three or four handkerchiefs a day, to handle a 'permanent cold'—this time for real—that I carry with me.

When my sciatica started troubling me seriously, I had to go through many doctors, much physiotherapy and receive much advice and sympathy from all and sundry. The breakthrough came when a friend gave me Robin Mckenzie's *7 Steps to a Pain-Free Life*. I followed the prescribed procedure and lo and behold, the back pain and sciatica vanished within a week. Mckenzie's prescriptions were simple; he merely advocated a thinned down version of our *suryanamaskar*—*s*un worship—which is very much part of our tradition and culture. My father used to practice it every day. One procedure involved prostrating full length, and lifting oneself slowly with both hands, as well as on both elbows, strikingly resembling the recipe prescribed by Mckenzie. Our *shastras* and *puranas* indicate the meditation—*tapas*—pose, squatting cross-legged with the back held up straight; imagine the standard pose of a Buddha, or Valmiki as depicted in our school books. The straight back ensures that the 'lordosis'—inward curvature of a portion of the lumbar and cervical vertebral column—is properly formed, as designed by human evolution. Again Mckenzie had brilliantly understood what our forefathers knew enough of to make it a part of their daily life. The US Marine Corps have incorporated a variation directly derived from the surya namaskar in their physical fitness programme, which they have labeled 'Hindu push-ups'. In our village, as in most parts of India, whenever a person met someone older than him, he would prostrate full length on the floor—doing this 20 times a day would correspond to the very practical and effective exercise to maintain one's back, as prescribed by Mckenzie. The older one gets, the fewer he meets people older to him so there is a natural arbitrage in the level of exercise prescribed for each age group!

During my childhood days, I used to go to Palghat for a month during the summer holidays, to stay with my uncle, a medical doctor practicing in those parts. The daily regimen included half-an-hour of yoga every morning before breakfast. At least 10 or 15 asanas would be performed in each session. It all came so easily at that age. I wondered, why bother with this kind of exercise? It did not tire me out at all. Indeed, wearing the *langoti* or the strip of loin cloth, I would not know the correct positioning of the male part it covered—in repose, whether it should be held vertically up or down! With the vigorous exercise and the excitement involved, and its consequent 'expansionary' influence, I would often invite a comment from my uncle that the natural position is 'down' and not 'up'! I would have to make a physical intervention by readjusting the langoti to make the necessary correction.

In later years, I just forgot how valuable yoga and asanas can be. In my older age, the doctor prescribes for me pranayam for breathing exercises and yoga postures for diabetes and blood pressure. If only one had followed a minimum level of practice over the years of a few asanas, one's health would have been much better preserved. I am sure there is a lesson here for our schools and colleges, and also for our society to revisit the healthy practices of yore, which we can re-imbibe with great benefit. As one goes to the US and Europe, one is astonished to see the number of yoga classes, schools and advertisements as well as health clubs which provide so much facility for maintaining health. One read recently that the 'उठक बैठक'— the exercise of sit-ups, which is standard prescribed 'punishment' in India for youngsters, has been discovered to be beneficial for 'brain development'. Many schools in the US now prescribe this as standard daily routine. We seem to have forgotten all our great traditions, without replacing them with anything substantial in return. On the one hand we have forgotten the healthy ways of living, as prescribed by our traditional systems and on the other, we have not supplemented these with meaningful substitutes.

***

India, of nearly continental proportions, has had great unity over the millennia. Pashupatinath in Nepal worships the same Shiva as in Suchindram in the deep south or Somnath in the west; the Jyotirlingas can be seen in every part of Bharat. Marriage customs, ceremonies and procedures are astonishingly essentially the same in every part of India. Valmiki's description of Rama and Sita's marriage, including all the religious and other ceremonies attendant thereon, have now been patented as standard procedure for marriages all over India. Thus, a marriage in the deep south of India will have *saptapadhi* or *agnipradakshan* as its common features, as anywhere else in India, East, North or South. Kamban's *Ramayana* in Tamil reproduces the same essential features of a marriage ceremony, as described by Valmiki; the other *Ramayanas*, in so many other Indian languages presumably also describe the critical features of marriage ceremonies in much the same manner. Clearly this is unity in diversity. The Indian mind, despite different languages, food habits and living conditions has a common denominator of thought processes, distinctly different from other regions in the world. For those who consider that the story of Rama was a work of fiction, recent research which plotted the stellar configuration at the time of Rama's marriage with Sita, as detailed by Valmiki (who was also an amateur astronomer) found it to be totally authentic, as calculated by a major computer study in the US. The event was genuine, nearly 3,000 years ago. We seem to have forgotten more than what others have learnt!

***

There are many childhood memories, many poignant, many happy, only a very few bitter. In the ashram in the suburbs of Tanjore, where I grew up for six years during school, some events are retained from those impressionable days. I recall a new litter of dogs in our compound, out of which only two survived—one black and the other white—called by us Blacky (*Karupan*) and Whitey (*Vellayan*). They were always inseparable and were always seen together within a couple of feet each other. I still remember that dusky evening, when a jeep distributing free advertisement tobacco packets, drove past slowly on the road in front of the ashram followed by 20 or 30 small kids, aged between 4 and 15 years. Every 20 yards or so, the attendant in the jeep would throw seven or eight tiny tobacco packets in the air, the kids would scramble to get hold of a packet. Many took home to their parents the product advertised. Some opened the packet out of curiosity and consumed the tiny bit of tobacco. Imagine the cruelty of the advertiser, the lasting impact on a child who ate that bit of scented tobacco. It is not only now that businessmen are heartless.

Anyway, in front of our house, this jeep ran over *Karupan*, right in front of our eyes. *Karupan* was in agony for a couple of hours, refused food and water and died in front of us children of the ashram. We buried him in a corner of the compound. Next morning, we found *Vellayan* close to the burial spot, lying down, whimpering in a low moan. For the next three days, he would not leave that spot, or his posture—refused all food and drink—and alas, fell down dead right next to *Karupan's* burial spot. Perhaps the atmosphere of piety in the ashram had a pervasive influence even on the dogs living there.

***

India is one of mankind's oldest civilizations. All human experience, of every sort, has occurred in this blessed land. For two-thirds of man's history on this planet, India has been a leading nation in the world. Its civilization has spread far and wide. At least three of the greatest religions have their origins in our soil. Christianity came to our shores even before it reached West Europe. The concept of ahimsa or non-violence is at the core of two great religions—Buddhism and Jainism. Hinduism is in many senses not a religion, but a way of life, and the path for evolution of man; it is all-encompassing. Islam came to India fairly early and has had a significant influence on the lives of a large number of Indians—Deoband and other schools of Indian Islam have followings even outside the country.

The great Indian religions and philosophies address issues of the mind as well as of the body, outlining elaborate prescriptions for their health. Every truth known to mankind is enshrined in our literature of the past. Notwithstanding great advances in the sciences, particularly in the west, no tenet or assumption in our scriptures has been invalidated, proven to be incorrect. On the contrary, ancient India has pioneered mankind's advances in the fields of mathematics, astronomy, natural sciences, ecology and economics: the range encompassing all sciences and arts.

In recent decades, especially after independence, one notices 'westernization' trends not only in superficial things like dress, hairstyle etc. (note that the चोटी—choti—the tuft of hair protecting the solar plexus from the hot sun is a local need) but also in values relating to interpersonal relationships, 'respect' for elders, concern for the family as opposed to an individual, and reverence for the environment. A host of value-related issues evolved to suit Bharat's conditions through the experience of millennia. The western/American 'way of life' has evolved through the western experience, including climate, food habits and other related circumstances. Replacement of the Indian 'way of life' and values by western concepts, has to be seen with some caution. We need to ensure that the solid inherited values in our system are not replaced purely by superficial ones; the baby should not be thrown away with the bath water.

Col. Sleeman, in the second half of the 19th century had noted in his memoirs that in his 40-year career covering large parts of India, he had not come across a single case of molestation of women. The prevailing culture respected the role of women in society. Can we say that of Delhi, say today? Can a single woman traverse areas of Delhi and feel safe? On the one hand there are no 'gurukuls' to teach, hands-on, the traditional values. In the name of 'secularism', our primary and secondary schools do not convey the concept of values, of 'goodness', the meaning of the ancient Hindu injunction 'सत्यम वद, धर्मम चर' (*satyam vadha, dharmam chara*)—speak the truth, do your duty; the results are there for all to see. There is a serious fall in interpersonal values.

Psychologists and experts from other fields may explore the detailed reasons for this. However, one set of values cannot be replaced casually. Values have to evolve with experience. India needs to introspect and review the treasures embodied in our hoary literature and experience. These are now being seen with great respect in foreign countries. Can we see them again through new eyes, to assist us in nation building in the changed circumstances?

In another book I have written about the lament of a near-illiterate man from East Uttar Pradesh, mourning the death of his wife, that she could not even take her tiny nose-ring with her when she went away, with this philosophical comment—'Even a trinket she couldn't take upstairs with her, but you see people hankering after buying land and houses and jewellery; do they think they can carry even a tiny bit with them when they die?' Our Indian scriptures give us the ideal recipe— 'अनायासेन मरणं, विना धैन्येन जीवनम्— (*anayasena maranam, vina dainyena jeevanam*)—a painless death after a full life, owing nothing to anyone.

Whenever one goes to the Golf Club in Delhi or NOIDA, there are always regulars who adorn or infest the place. There are morning regulars and evening regulars. One has now reached the age, sadly, that information keeps coming every now and then that x or y, your acquaintance or friend, is no more with us. In the Delhi Golf Club, if a person who is a regular is not seen for a month, nobody bothers to ask any questions. If he is around with us, he will turn up one of these days, otherwise 'may his soul rest in peace'. People assume that one is gone, suddenly someone refers to a permanent departure—all 'gentle' reminders that we are not immortal. Towards the end of the *Mahabharata* when the Pandavas were in their final journey, the Yaksha or divine creature asks Dharmaputra to recount four astonishing things that he has come across. One of them from Dharmaputra: 'one sees funeral processions, going towards the grave or cremation ground every day, but one considers himself immortal—nothing would happen to him!'

6

PUBLIC HEALTH—THE HUGE COST OF NEGLECT?

Mens sana in corpore sano—Juvenal

In the mid-1970s, I happened to spend a year at Harvard University in the US working at the Kennedy School of Public Administration, from where I took a course on 'The Economic Bases for Population Growth' at the School of Population Studies. The substance of a full semester course could be summarized as: 'There is direct correlation between economic development and reduction in rate of population growth'; the relationship is not in terms of GDP or per capita growth—it relates to the rate of growth of the poorest segments of the population. In particular, the key factors that directly correlate with population control relate to female literacy, mother and child health, nutrition levels as well as public hygiene—these have the direct maximum impact on reduction in population growth. All the reader needs to do to empirically test the validity of this thesis is to refer to the population growth of different states in India in the first decade of this century—Kerala's population grew by 4.9 per cent, while that of Bihar by 25 per cent; the Bimaru states (Bihar, Madhya Pradesh and Uttar Pradesh) showed the maximum 'buoyancy'!

The policy implications for India are obvious. Mahatma Gandhi, without studying at Harvard or Princeton understood this fully. He postulated that every policy decision taken at the highest level should answer only one question—'will it benefit the poorest person?' Alas, our great economists and post-independence leaders have not grasped this single fundamental. The mantra has been growth, with no concern for lifting the poor. No doubt, we are enjoying the benefits of the 'population dividend' today but without giving them education and health, this asset can turn out to be a major liability—indeed a catastrophic disaster. Their unemployability in an increasingly knowledge-based society can be highly counter-productive for national interest. Besides, 20 years from now the population will age, the average national age will sharply increase with massive attendant large-scale problems. Sometimes one is astonished at the vacuum in national policymaking. To put it simply, India and China started their development path about the same time. In the first two decades China focused sharply on education and public health and rural roads/electricity, then embarked on a massive urban development programme. We started in the other direction, and can now see the results 50 years later.

In any democracy, the most fundamental issues relate to the education and health of a citizen. On the specious ground that these are state subjects, national attention to these basic aspects of a citizen's welfare has been tardy—it is neither on the radar of the Centre nor of the states; citizens are the sufferers. India's current rank is a lowly 110 in the International Human Development Index; education and health make a huge contribution to this index.

***

The Directive Principles of State Policy enshrined in our Constitution envision good standards of life for the citizen. Good health is an integral part of good living. The Constitution also enjoins assurance of good quality nutrition. Let us see our progress in this basic aspect relating to a citizen's welfare, nearly six-and-half decades after independence.

According to the Nutrition Barometer report released by the International NGO Save the Children, India ranks with Congo and Yemen at the bottom of the 36 developing countries studied, which have 90 per cent of the world's 'stunted' children. The other South Asian countries, Bangladesh, Pakistan and Nepal fare much better in this regard.

Every third woman in India is undernourished; every second woman anaemic (55.3 per cent); three out of four children are anaemic. The child nutrition status has declined in many north Indian states; 53 out of 1,000 infants die within a year of birth. At least 44 per cent of the kids sleep hungry. Immunization levels which ought to be close to 100 per cent, at least upwards of 99 per cent, stand at around 52 per cent in India. These are appalling statistics which are unacceptable. Forty per cent of the world's undernourished children live in India; 48 per cent of Indian children below 5 years are stunted and 42 per cent are under-weight. All this is the result of poor nutrition.

The latest 'Lancet' report indicates that 45 per cent of deaths of under-5 children in India are caused by malnutrition. According to a WHO estimate, 26 per cent of maternal deaths globally occur in India. The Indian 'mother and child' care situation is rated to be at the bottom of the international pile.

Sixty-two per cent of the children under 5 years of age are vitamin A deficient; 31 per cent of school age children are iodine deficient. These deficiencies cause death and disability and retard brain development, IQ, cognitive skills, energy levels and productivity. India's performance on these crucial outcomes is among the worst in the world. Our nutrition indicators are far worse than those of even our neighbours Bangladesh, Pakistan, Sri Lanka and Nepal.

There is no awareness of the essential requirement of micro-nutrients for healthy growth of a body and mind, even among concerned national and state officials, not to speak of the population at large. Folic acid, vitamin A, iron, iodine, zinc (for diarrhoea), at minimum requirement levels are critical for health. According to a World Bank estimate, India ranks along with sub-Saharan Africa in this regard; it will take at least 25 years more to catch up with average African standards at present rates of growth!

Seventy-five per cent of an average Indian's healthcare expenditure is spent in the last 15 days of his life, based on a research paper discussed in a CII-Indus Entrepreneurs Healthcare Seminar recently. This cruel statistic illustrates the near-total absence of basic healthcare, insurance, availability of medicines and basic treatment in large parts of India. In most district and tehsil hospitals expensive equipment rusts and lies unused for want of spare parts or lack of minor repairs. The absence of medicines at the right time is chronic. A Union minister recently declared that 'India's public health system has collapsed'; can there be a more damning indictment of the present state of affairs?

In all civilized countries, healthcare for the public is placed at the highest priority in public policy. For instance, in the UK, the National Health Service provides free quality medical advice and treatment to all citizens. The public healthcare systems in the Scandinavian countries, fully free of charge, are of the highest quality, comparable to the best available. The situation is similar in most European Union countries. In many developing countries, public policy accords high priority to citizens' health and has many programmes to support these, nearly all free of cost. In South Korea, for instance, nearly every community (equivalent of our Gram Sabha) has a two-bed mini nursing home, with a trained nurse in attendance, and electronic/video connectivity with a major hospital. The first Obama elections in the US four years back saw, as one of the main issues, better healthcare coverage and affordable health insurance for all. During the election campaign in Brazil, President Lula promised delivery of measurable improvement in nutrition levels and micro-nutrient indices in the population; in the event, during his term in office, he gave personal attention to this element as a high priority and was able to achieve 90 per cent of the promised targets. President Rajpaksha in Sri Lanka made micro-nutrients a major policy issue in his governance. Over time, due to his personal commitment, the quality of life in Sri Lanka has significantly improved in this regard. It is an index of the contempt that our successive governments have had for citizens that Indian facilities in this regard are abysmally poor. Indian expenditure of 1.87 per cent of GDP for healthcare would rank among the lowest in the world. The Indian medicare system has been designed to benefit the top 10 per cent of the population (as are so many other 'public interest' arrangements), to meet the need of rapacious hospital interests—devil take the hindmost 90 per cent.

***

Nearly 80 per cent of the population lives in rural areas with poor access to healthcare and medical facilities; reinforced and perpetuated by the lack of skilled service providers and the virtual absence of accountability in the public health system. As a result, there is a huge unmet need for health services, with children and women being the major sufferers. According to the latest National Family Health Survey (NFHS) and District-Level Household Survey (DLHS) data an average of 15 per cent of the population that seeks healthcare services accesses government health facilities, while 85 percent opt for private providers—a sad commentary on the quality of our field governmental machinery.

A study has found that perceived quality of services was an important determinant of the pattern of utilization. Private practitioners were perceived to be providing better services because they included injections as part of every treatment and were willing to make home visits which were convenient, especially where transportation was inadequate. Government health services were not popular because of the longer waiting period involved, the attitude and behaviour of the staff and lack of medicines. Several other deterrents, such as bad roads, the unreliability of finding a health provider and costs for transport and wages foregone, make it cheaper for a villager to get some treatment from the local practitioner or 'quack', who may have limited knowledge and skills in either modern or traditional medicine. Taking good quality healthcare to the doorsteps to reach many of these under-served areas is thus very important. Initiating innovative public-private partnership models to capitalize on the preference for private sector services has not even been considered.

Elementary preventive medical advice and primary treatment facilities ought to be available to all, even in the remotest areas, of minimal acceptable quality and free of charge. Secondary and tertiary (specialist) hospitals could be left to private sector enterprise. The basic care of acceptable quality is the responsibility of the state. There are many healthcare programmes (mother and child, family planning, immunization, etc.) sponsored and funded by the state and central governments. However, these are department-centric, riddled with turf wars between various state government departments. At the field level, this 'specialization' is startlingly evident, when a worker popularizing the use of condoms cannot reach the women of the household; and with different departmental workers, crowding each other out, confusing the citizen, and being thoroughly ineffective. Departmental tussles at the secretariat, directorate and field levels are paramount—the citizen is nobody's concern. Trained multi-purpose para-medic workers, with capability of providing basic consultancy and facilities over the normal range of issues affecting a household has not been thought of seriously.

In recent years, I had the opportunity to become familiar with the progress in implementing public health programmes in different parts of the country. Nearly in every state, most senior officials, Chief Secretary downwards have scant concern for public health and nutrition/micro-nutrient issues. Even in the medical or public health or rural health departments, the focus is on hospitals, supplies and equipments, as well as on postings and transfers of doctors—all 'lucrative' in their own right. However there is little interest or care in issues like anaemia, mother and child condition, and immunization levels relating to preventive or primary healthcare issues. In one state, for example, in a meeting called on my initiative by the Chief Secretary, the four secretaries concerned and their directors argued that the immunization levels in their state was 99 per cent and anaemia less than 10 per cent. When I remonstrated, quoting NSS data for the state, I was pooh-poohed—the state produced 'its own authenticated data' showing nearly 100 per cent success! They openly said that the published figures of the Government of India were incorrect. There was nothing further to discuss or argue. Nobody in the state was interested in any innovation, improvement or enhancement of their programmes, they just wanted the money from the Government of India.

Nutrition and micro-nutrients

Fifty years ago Tamil Nadu started the mid-day meal programme in government primary and secondary schools. One is told that thanks to a persistent Education Secretary in the state government this far-reaching idea was introduced and implemented successfully, despite strong opposition mainly because the chief minister of the day, M.G. Ramachandran supported the idea. One is not surprised as my grandmother, with Kerala origins, in the early 1950s would talk of *narishmandu*, referring to 'nourishment'; such was the awareness those days. Clearly we have regressed in many areas in the past decades. Indeed our own Constitution, in its Directive Principles commands the state to raise the 'level of nutrition and the standard of living of its people and the improvement of public health as among its primary duties'—injunctions, as so many others, that have been so conveniently ignored by our political executive. One may surmise that the current pre-eminent position of Tamil Nadu in the Information Technology field could possibly be related to the foresight of one official in the state government decades back.

Thank goodness, the mid-day meal scheme in our schools is now a national programme. The overwhelmingly poor children, especially in our rural areas, do need the nutrition through this route as a minimum investment in the country's future. Besides, this is also an excellent vehicle for providing the children with essential vitamins and micro-nutrients through supplements in the mid-day meal. The technology is available; it is only that casualness and tendency for resistance to change at the Centre and in the states, which has not allowed a full focus on this vital programme to make it a significant engine for the nation's growth.

There have occasionally been mishaps, some very serious, in the mid-day meal scheme. In summer 2013, in one village in Bihar about 30 children died due to food poisoning. Other such events of lesser magnitude are quite the norm in India, sadly given the scant regard and care to field implementation issues. Indeed many 'arm chair' nutrition experts in India have advocated that food supplementation is not required; what is required, is providing a balanced diet—a strong motherhood statement akin to saying, 'if they can't afford bread, let them eat cake'. Surely if one can provide milk, eggs and green vegetables to every citizen the national nutrition levels will shoot up. If every poor person becomes rich, he would get good food! Till the population can afford natural nutritive food, supplementation is the second best alternative; the mid-day meal is an ideal vehicle. Asking for the scheme to be terminated because of implementation difficulties is like arguing for 'throwing the baby with the bath-water'. There are so many fatal railway accidents—do we close down our railways? Shall we ban trucks due to road accidents? The mid-day meal scheme needs to be improved, made efficient, implemented much better, with provisions for proteins and nutrients and supplements. This is the best investment that is possible in our country at this stage.

Till recently, I was the chairman, currently Chairman Emeritus, of the Micronutrients International Trust India, a subsidiary of the Micronutrients International (MI) based in Ottawa. MI in Ottawa, mostly funded by the Overseas Aid Programme of the Canadian government, is headed by Dr Venkatesh Mannar, of Indian origin—he has been conferred with the highest honour of the Canadian government for his services in improving nutrition in developing countries. MI's largest programme is in India. I have a clear picture of the attention to these matters in our states. Despite tardiness at the Centre, many states on their own have taken major steps to provide nutrient supplements to their populations. Particularly noteworthy is Gujarat's initiative of introducing vitamins supplements blended into the atta (wheat flour) supplied to the public, as well as promoting iodized or double-fortified salt (iodine plus iron) to combat anaemia. Many other states have similar programmes, on their own initiative. In many western countries 'fortification' of bread and milk with supplements has been standard practice for decades. In India, the Modern Bread brand used to be fortified with vitamins, so long as it was a Government of India company—they probably followed the British specifications; after it was denationalized and purchased by a private company, this practice, which adds a miniscule amount to the cost has been discontinued—clear proof of great corporate concern for the public weal!

Need for change in policy

The discussion earlier presents a depressing scenario. However, policymakers, politicians and bureaucrats do not realize the gravity of the issue, they are generally unaware of the broad contours of the problems in this vital segment, and the need to take effective measures to dramatically improve the situation in short order.

There is no question that major, far-reaching reforms are urgently required. There is no reason why available electronic technology (V-SAT, 3-G, etc.) cannot be used for well-equipped mobile vans, with real-time connectivity with a bank of doctors, say at the divisional or state headquarters to facilitate onsite basic tests (blood, ECG, eye-testing, etc.), and provide instant advice, with periodical (say, every three months) visits, starting with primary schools and reaching village mandis and in due course covering the entire population. These are entirely doable, and the cost implications are not likely to be mind-boggling; it is just that the system is too lethargic to innovate and come up with new solutions to old problems—there is just no political will.

One wonders why healthcare has not been made a major public election issue. Every party's election manifesto blandly talks of poverty reduction, welfare of the kisan or the jawan, good education and healthcare, etc.etc. It is time now to demand that before every national election, every major national party should commit itself to a detailed healthcare agenda, promising what it will do over the 5-year period, and specifying the objectives and targets against which they will be measured at the end of five years. Civil society organizations and other public workers should now demand these from major parties, and ask for implementation of major innovations and reforms in this sector.

Apart from the proposals in the earlier section, specifically the following action programme is suggested to address the persisting crisis of malnutrition:

- Decide on a firm vision to put India on track to eliminate hunger and malnutrition by 2025. Towards that goal commit to reducing the number of children with severe acute malnutrition by 90 per cent and chronically malnourished children in India by 50 per cent within the next five years.
- By simultaneously addressing the underlying factors that contribute to malnutrition, including poverty, the poor status of girls and women, food insecurity (especially in vital

nutrient-rich foods), poor health services and sanitary conditions, save the lives of at least 1 million children (under 5 years of age) every year.
- From 2014 start delivering on targets for several key nutrition indicators:

    - Over five years, address and reduce by 90 per cent stunting, wasting, anaemia and micro-nutrient deficiencies among young children through aggressive, universal growth monitoring and quality assured therapeutic services.
    - Over five years, reduce anaemia by 90 per cent among adolescent girls and women through a focused, collaborative programme between the departments of health, education and women and children for measuring and addressing undernutrition among adolescent girls and women.

- Regularly measure the extent of hunger and malnutrition in India using a credible, transparent and verifiable methodology to track and report progress:

    - Every birth, and birth weight, will be recorded, to provide a long-term nutrition and health indicator at the state, district and panchayat levels.
    - Universal growth monitoring using electronic data systems will be put in place to provide real time, community level assessments to address acute malnutrition and to prevent chronic malnutrition among young children.

- Each year, communicate widely to the public through the prime minister's Independence Day address, the nation's performance against the key nutrition benchmarks of reduction in cases of acute and chronic malnutrition among children under the age of five years and anaemia among adolescent girls and women.
- Ensure availability of quarterly tabulated information (tehsil-wise) on district administration websites on births, birth weights, growth monitoring statistics and the status of anaemia among adolescent girls and women in the district.

7

EDUCATION—IMPERATIVE NEED FOR A REVAMP?

Give a man a fish, you feed him for a day; teach a man to fish, you feed him for life ... Anne Isabella Thackeray Ritchie

Primary Education

The abysmal quality of India's primary education scene has been documented repeatedly. Right to Education was recognized by the United Nations as fundamental to man. In the immediate post-war years, as the UN was being established, India had argued vehemently in favour of education as a fundamental right. Nearly seven decades later, it is clear that India does not mean what it says, either domestically or abroad. Recently we enacted the Right to Education Act, an empty declaration without specifying how this right can be claimed or enforced, without provisioning for the funds required, and without taking collateral administrative steps—typical of the way, slogans like 'Remove Poverty', 'Jai Jawan Jai Kisan' are created, and then left in limbo.

Decades back it was recognized that neighbourhood availability of schooling, both in urban and rural areas was a key gap. By and large, this has been remedied as in most plains areas a primary school is available within one kilometre of each habitation; in the hills, generally, within two kilometres. However, the critical problem relates to the *quality* of primary education.

Recent ASER reports have given further cause for great concern. The latest report refers to many states, where a typical Class V student is unable to deal with the Class II syllabus. Alarmingly, there has been a 10 percentile point *decline* in reading ability in the past two years (as of 2012), indicative of the intensifying crisis in our primary education sector. This finding alone is a clear indication that our primary education scene is in serious trouble. The states and the Centre routinely trot out figures to prove 'improved' literacy figures, including female literacy, year after year. The fact is that the quality of primary education has deteriorated in absolute terms over the decades. Even of more concern, there is severe disparity in literacy rates and educational opportunities between urban and rural areas, males and females and among different social groups. This is a well-researched subject.

While access to primary education has now increased to 99 per cent, the drop-out rates have also alarmingly increased, as children progress to higher classes. Thus, the average enrolment rate at the junior school level is around only 84 per cent, declining to 63 per cent at the middle school level, and sharply falling to 36 per cent in senior secondary (school final) levels. This means that about 65 per cent of the students do not complete school. In the absence of development of alternate skills, they are let loose in society to fend for themselves, perhaps as unskilled labour or to join the ranks of the unemployed—a potential source of social unrest.

The reasons for this alarming picture can be summarized as:

(a) Heavy moonlighting by teachers—in many states, teacher absenteeism is endemic, many teachers hold other jobs and the existing teacher pool takes turns to be present, based on their own 'roster';
(b) Most of the election booths are manned by school teachers. No political party is willing to bring discipline into this group, for fear of adverse reactions in the teacher community, for obvious though invalid reasons;

(c) The classrooms are ill-equipped and crowded—the conditions are not conducive for teaching and learning. In many schools, buildings are not available; classes are not held in inclement weather—sanitation/toilet facilities are an exception;
(d) Coaching in fundamentals, particularly language and arithmetic skills in Classes I and II is weak, there is no systematic 'augmentation' to bring laggards up to the average level. By Classes III and IV, the gap between the class mean and the weaker students sharply increases, leading to progressively increasing drop-outs;
(e) Micro-nutrient nourishment available to our children is among the worst in the world, affecting relevant issues like concentration, brain-development, growth etc., all impacting the ability to learn and leading to drop-outs;
(f) There is no sound pedagogy, teachers are poorly trained and the quality of teaching and learning are highly sub-optimal; and
(g) Use of technology to bring higher quality educational material into the classroom has not been attempted seriously.

Each one of these reasons, along with their variants and combinations has contributed significantly to the current state of affairs. Sadly, all these are not seen as problems, or red-signals either at the Centre or in the states. There is placid inaction and indifference to ground conditions.

Clearly the solutions lie in recognizing the problems and issues listed here—and addressing them systematically. Unfortunately, there is no vote bank attached to this theme, the quality of primary education is not an election issue and our system gives no rewards for tackling this most fundamental of matters; conversely there is no punishment for neglect.

With the advent of technology, it is possible to bridge the gap in fairly quick time and rapid order. It is really a question of: (i) preparing high quality standard material, well designed with proper pedagogy to maximize the impact on a student; (ii) using 'delivery' methods, including mobile phones (3-G and 4-G), V-SAT, IPads, linked with local screening systems and other advances, optimally and imaginatively; (iii) training the existing teacher force to use these technologies and converting the sessions to greater efficacy; (iv) building a strong 'augmentation' method, where laggards are systematically identified, given supplementary coaching so that they can come up to the average class standards; and (v) introducing the concept of **90-90,** that is, in every class, 90 per cent of the students will learn fully 90 per cent of the material taught. Suitable measurement and augmentation systems need to be developed to ensure these objectives.

A technology-driven *virtual* teaching environment will also address the challenges of teacher-absenteeism and effective education outreach in rural India. Appropriate hardware and software infrastructure will help create a robust back-end technological infrastructural backbone with the potential to transform our archaic and conventional instruction delivery mechanisms. However, it is to be noted that a teacher is a vital component in the schooling process; the approach has to be to equip the teacher with the material and train him or her to use it effectively. A teacher-technology combination is the ideal way to proceed.

These are highly doable. Much of this is being done in small experiments in different parts of the country through private initiatives, as also in high quality urban schools. There is no reason why these cannot be built into a massive programme, well thought out and well designed, which will dramatically improve the quality of our primary and secondary education. Clearly nobody sees this as an issue, and no officially backed solutions are even tried.

The VidyaGyan Experiment

One significant experiment deserves to be mentioned. The VidyaGyan School system, established by the Shiv Nadar Foundation, has pioneered a new method of discovering talent in rural areas and providing opportunities for it to blossom. The programme is currently underway only in Uttar Pradesh. Ten students are selected from each district every year, to be taught in two residential schools from Class VI to Class XII. The boys and girls are given free boarding, lodging and quality education. The strict selection criteria includes:

(i) the children must come from purely rural schools—not from the town area, notified area or municipality or corporation, (ii) they must come from 'below poverty line' (BPL) families, and (iii) they must be talented and are selected through a computer-based test from among the toppers in Class V in their school.

With these criteria, clearly the children come from the most backward, rural parts of India, and from the most economically backward segments of the population. All of them, when they join VidyaGyan, are only familiar with Hindi language with no knowledge of English. However, three years after this kind of schooling, with high quality teaching inputs, the children are able to assimilate enough to be able to compete with their counterparts in the best schools in India. It is abundantly clear that India's children merely lack the opportunity and exposure. The quality of our children is uniformly of high quality, it is the failure of our system and our governance that seven decades after independence we have not given the children of India the opportunity to develop. An indictment of our governance model cannot be more severe.

One other element needs to be highlighted. At the time of selection there are no 'reservations'—caste or community based. However, the results have shown that by and large all communities and castes get well represented, without any need for reservations. Roughly 40 per cent of those who qualify are girls—it is abundantly clear that ability, talent and potential is spread equally across the state, with no considerations of caste, community or sex. All the posturing by political parties in these matters is purely vote bank-related. All the protestations of support to this or that community or caste is purely for electoral gains—no public spirit is involved. Experience has also proved that providing a good balanced diet improves the mental and physical ability of the children sharply. It also aids them in growth—much as theory would expect.

The programme is run by the Shiv Nadar Foundation in collaboration with the Government of Uttar Pradesh. The funding for all aspects of VidyaGyan is done by the Shiv Nadar Foundation; the UP government's role is to provide invaluable assistance in identifying boys and girls in a transparent merit-based manner from the 75 districts in the state. The 3-tier selection process consists of obtaining the names of one boy and one girl, topper from each rural school; running them through a computerized objective type test at each district headquarters, organized by a committee under the chairmanship of the District Magistrate; get a short list of candidates for a final computerized test organized by an independent agency, at two schools located in the state to finalize a list of 10 entrants per district per year; to take them on board to teach them for seven years from Class VI to Class XII. The model is to reach out to the top of the bottom of the pyramid, create leaders for tomorrow, and bridge the urban-rural divide.

As Chairman of the Managing Board of the VidyaGyan programme, I along with the team members have had many experiences in establishing the school system, and in running it for the past few years. The first year, in 2009, when I along with Shiv Nadar, the Chairman of the Foundation, went to the school to inaugurate the first classes, we saw the bedraggled, unkempt and 'God-help-me' looking children, along with their parents, who if anything looked worse. I had a twinge of regret, a presentiment of failure, indeed great frustration, about why I had got myself into dealing with these hopeless children. Today, four years later, as I go to one of the schools, I see bright, young shining faces, with sharp intelligent eyes—boys and girls who are not inferior to any children of their age, from anywhere in India. Remember most of these children come from the poorest segments of the population, from some of the most backward districts in India. Their innate abilities are not inferior to any child's from the best schools in the metros or the most famous public schools—Doon or Alwar or Rishi Valley. This is not a casual statement; it is borne out of actual experience in the past three years. Under the able direction of Roshni Nadar, and extremely dedicated principals and teaching staff, our school children have won national and international prizes in disparate areas like elocution, painting, as well as in academic fields, competing with the best schools in India and from abroad. There is clear proof that high quality talent exists in every corner of the country. It is merely the lack of opportunities that has kept all these children out of the race. India now holds a high position in the International academic arena exploiting the talents of just

5 per cent of the population; imagine India's potential if the resources available in the country are fully harnessed—again a testimony to the colossal failure of our primary education policy.

In the first year we had difficulties in recruiting the children. No one in the rural areas believed that their children could get high quality education free for seven years. The fact that the programme had the backing of the state government, and that I had been the Chief Secretary in the state, brought some credibility to the process. From the second year onwards, we did not have to worry. Our main problem was to ensure that imposters, frauds and those who did not meet our specifications were kept out. Training academies, like IAS coaching schools, have sprung up to coach people to do well in the computerized tests – what greater tribute is possible for this endeavour?

We have had to contend with our share of local level mischief—false certification regarding income or domicile; urban children obtaining token admission in village schools in order to become eligible, even children from other states, Bihar or Madhya Pradesh enrolling themselves in UP schools to gain admission—we have seen a lot of this. A clear policy is followed: anybody who enters through falsity or deliberate wrong certification is thrown out summarily.

Contrary to what we feared, we find that when the children go back to their villages for summer/winter holidays, there is no antagonism towards them—instead, they are treated as role models. They hold 'seminars' to inspire other children to study hard. One can see clearly the impact that they have on the school in the village that they come from; clearly they are part of a virtuous cycle, which benefits the system.

One comment about intervention by politicians and influential people needs to be mentioned. As the image of the school spread, we have seen the phenomenon of MPs, MLAs and Union and state ministers exerting influence on the Project Director or the District Magistrates to ensure that the child they recommend be given 'favourable consideration'. One District Magistrate did not follow the prescribed system, and came up with his own list—presumably due to pressures; we had to countermand that selection, and refuse to admit those children. When senior politicians approach me or

Shiv Nadar, we have a standard line—'even our own nephew or niece will not get admission, except through the merit list.'

Shiv Nadar summarizes the three things of greatest value that students need to get out of their education at the Vidya Gyan School—leadership skills, confidence to excel and compete with the best in the world, and value to give back to society and create spirals of inspiration for the larger community.

A full assessment of the impact of this experiment can only be known four years from now when those who pass out from Class XII, hopefully embark on higher education to become doctors, engineers, or lawyers or scientists, indeed leaders of society. We await the day when a new type of leadership will emerge in our rural areas.

***

In 2009, on the day that first Vidya Gyan classes started, one correspondent asked me at a press conference: 'You only cater to a miniscule insignificant number of the crores of children in UP who are in need of good education—how justified is that?' That triggered a new line of thinking, the need to tailor an innovative new programme to meet the needs of the average primary/secondary student, using technology, bringing quality education to the remotest rural areas. This is the genesis of the Shiksha programme of the Shiv Nadar Foundation, now in its experimentation stage, which could possibly be rolled out as an operational programme in the future.

In essence Shiksha will seek to usher in the 90–90 concept—90 per cent student in each class will learn 90 per cent of the material taught. If this concept is successful, this should be one answer to the issue of poor standards and high drop-out rates, the two banes of our primary education scene. Shiksha seeks to prepare high quality video/electronic teaching material, attractive and easy to follow by children, package it for delivery to near and remote government schools, train the teachers in optimal use of the material to have the best impact on students; use the latest technology for reaching the material electronically to classrooms in small towns, villages and the remotest areas. The roll out is in an experimental stage; if successful, it has the potential to impact the quality of our primary education, across the board. The next couple of years should be interesting, to see if Shiksha will succeed, or will hit a road block. Incidentally, it is imperative that other initiatives, sponsored by governments and concerned individuals/institutions experiment with differing models to dramatically impact the quality of our education system.

The conclusion that the country, through poor policies, has not allowed our children to grow and have opportunities to contribute significantly is inevitable. They have been suppressed, and kept in darkness. This is a severe indictment of our governance model. The solutions are obvious.

Secondary schooling

The same issues that we saw in the primary sector get carried into secondary schooling also. By and large, in government institutions, the situation is much the same as has been outlined earlier. However, many private schools, especially in urban areas have done a good job in this sector. Admissions are not easy as the 'capitation fees' (charged illegally) are high. One significant issue is the policy that no child shall be detained in any class for poor performance. In the absence of a meaningful 'augmentation' programme, the average level of teaching and learning will be pegged very low. Most classes address the level of the lowest student with consequent overall reduction in standards. Besides the system of learning is heavily rote-based, without providing the opportunity or incentivizing a student to seriously apply his mind and learn the concepts.

Many urban schools maintain high standards, but are not frequently accessible to poorer children. The best schools are as good as any in the world. Unfortunately, even in urban areas, apart from a few top-quality schools, for which the competition to enter is fierce, and quite often the capitation fee atrociously high, there is a sharp fall in standards of the average.

Skills training

The other issue relates to skill development. Not every high school student can, or ought to be allowed to, move on to college or higher education. No country in the world encourages this. Higher education ought to be reachable only to more talented students who will benefit from it. A dimension of training in skills needs to be inducted into our secondary school system. This is not capable of an easy or ready solution; however, no thought has been applied to this critical area. There is a huge 'skills' gap in the country but no steps to address this have seriously been undertaken.

With a burgeoning population and the growing impression among the populace that higher education is the only path to good jobs, we now find a situation where colleges and universities are overcrowded, they cannot cater to the demand and have become virtually education-shops with abysmal academic standards. The yawning gap in the system is that there is no escape route in the form of 'skills training' for those who have passed the secondary level. When the skilled workforce is heavily augmented, colleges will cater only to those who are seriously academically inclined and who will benefit from formal higher education. Thus, in most countries, at the middle school level, parallel opportunities in training in different skills are opened up. This contributes to the creation of new jobs as also to meet the large unmet demand for skilled services in urban and rural areas. Thus, the polytechnics, say in Germany and in other countries, play a vital role in the economy and in the education sector.

I recall that in the early 1990s, when I was the Secretary in the Ministry of Textiles, the National Institute of Fashion Technology (NIFT) was established initially in Delhi, and its schools branched out to three more centres in India. This was a pioneering experiment. As one of the earliest chairmen of this institution, I had the opportunity to help establish the curriculum in the various courses in this institute. Great care was taken to bring in the textile industry in preparing the curriculum and training material. The courses were designed, indeed tailor-made (no pun intended) to meet the requirements of the garment industry. Bright young boys and girls from high schools were recruited for a 3-year course in fashion technology, exclusively on merit. The courses were in great demand. It was found that the industry, both in India and abroad, welcomed diploma holders from NIFT with open arms, many getting enviable opening offers. Twenty years down the road, I can see with satisfaction, the role played by

NIFT in bringing new styling, colours, designs and patterns in the clothing of Indians. The impact can be seen even in the remotest areas. The quality of clothing used by even the poorest has changed dramatically. Additionally, the dramatic growth in Indian garment exports surely has some relationship with the establishment of NIFT.

I also recall introducing a skills training programme to expand the manufacturing base in weaving carpets in the Bhadohi-Mirzapur belt in UP in the 1970s. We experimented with a new formula that became successful. This was to create training programmes in collaboration with existing manufacturers and exporters. The scheme was drawn up in a manner that would attract the interest of all concerned groups—businessmen, locals and the government; perhaps it was this balancing of interests that helped make the project succeed. The cost of training was shared equally by Government (stipends to the trainees) with the private factory providing the premises and supply of raw material, mainly wool. We ensured that primary schooling was provided to the trainees for a minimum of three hours a day. This became a popular programme; all the elements fell into place. The trainees found gainful employment after the 3-months training period and the associated businessmen found the proposition profitable. I am sure this scheme contributed, over time, to the growth of the carpet industry in the Bhadohi and Agra carpet belt. The point is that innovative programmes can be started in hundreds of industries and vocations, which are meaningful and which contribute to the development of skills. The key is that this should be done in close collaboration with industry, which is the ultimate end user.

Our Industrial Training Institutes (ITIs) and other government sponsored training institutions have failed utterly in maintaining quality or in turning out qualified persons to meet the demands of the market. A new approach to this whole issue is now required for creating new avenues for job creation and for generating skilled labour. This is the crying need of the day—imaginative programmes need to be mounted. It is of the essence that such institutions should be established in close collaboration with diverse industrial and service entities to ensure relevant curriculum and absorption of the output in the market.

Higher education

In the 1950s and 1960s, the nation made significant moves in the higher education sector, with the establishment of Indian Institutes of Technology (IITs), Indian Institutes of Management (IIMs) and other institutional devices. However, in recent decades little has been done in this space. Other Asian nations have surged ahead. Even as recently as two decades back, at least 20 Indian higher education institutions were listed among the top 500 in the world. Not one Indian institute or institution now figures in this list. Even in Asia, we have been overtaken by a big margin, and our position has fallen precipitously. Amartya Sen, the Nobel Laureate has characterized our education scene as 'in a crisis'.

As in the primary education field, even in higher education this is a well-researched area, and the problems are well known, some of which are summarized as:

(a) Our colleges are now 'education shops', which are really essentially business ventures, providing degrees for money;
(b) There are a few good colleges, the others are purely for selling degrees;
(c) Standards of coaching are very poor, pedagogy is of a low level; and
(d) An average Indian graduate is of poor quality, not even capable of simple correct sentences to express thoughts.

Many 'advance' to college due to lack of job opportunities. There has been mushroom growth of poor quality engineering and other professional colleges, without corresponding growth in employment opportunities, thus debasing the quality of education. Commercialization of the education scene is now rampant and capitation fees is the key element in university education. One can find nearly every education institution linked to a politician for obvious reasons. Academics is no more a concern—commercialization is the only fact. It is quite well known that in nearly every medical college in south India, 'capitation fee', which is an illegal, under-the-table payment, is of the order of ₹40 lakh per seat for an undergraduate course; for a postgraduate course in a key area like orthopaedics, the 'entry fee' can go up to a whopping to ₹1 crore. It was reported in *Mail Today* (13 September 2013) that in some colleges, postgraduate seats are literally auctioned, which are conducted much like art auctions!—in one of the courses the highest bid was ₹4 crore—can anything be more absurd in our education sphere? In most private engineering colleges, the situation is not much different; the position nearly everywhere in India is much the same. All concerned—university/college authorities—anyone connected with education, each parent who has the need to pay, are all fully familiar with the 'facts of life' in this regard. In other words, openly and in full knowledge, a black-market higher education business is thriving in India. If you examine further, you will find that nearly every one of these academic institutions is connected with a politician or a business house. There can be no objection to market costs and profits legitimately becoming a part of education costs. However, the nation has, with full knowledge permitted an illegal business regime masquerading as higher education. The Vice chancellor of a major university mentioned recently on a public platform that 'the going rate for appointment of a Vice Chancellor in a reputable university is ₹40 crores'; an earth shaking statement, but one which sadly evoked no public response.

I also happen to be the Chancellor of the Shiv Nadar University, located in a 300-acre campus adjacent to Greater NOIDA. The admission is entirely on merit, with zero capitation fee; and the university aspires to be the national leader in higher education over the next decade. The first school is in the field of engineering. We already have a collaboration with the Carnegie Mellon University. The university, only in its third year, aspires to establish a number of schools on the US university pattern starting with a business school, a school of education and a school of entrepreneurship, each with high quality foreign collaboration. The ultimate aim is to be ranked as a world class research-oriented university in a relatively short time. As the only non-family member in the Shiv Nadar Foundation, I need to add that these large purely charitable investments in primary, secondary and higher education are all from the personal assets of Shiv Nadar, who aspires to set apart 20 per cent of his total income to charity. In India, alas, the practice of people who have made their fortunes in business, partaking of a substantial part of it to charity is highly unusual, indeed rare. We need to create a paradigm where rich people plough back into charity a significant part of what they have earned from society. Mahatma Gandhi had said that every businessman has to function as a trustee, and not as the owner!

I need also to make a brief reference to the SSN School of Engineering, sponsored and fully supported by the Shiv Nadar Foundation, spread over a 250-acre campus in Chennai. Now nearly a decade old, this is a landmark institution in Tamil Nadu, having climbed to the top-most position among the engineering colleges in that state. Many meritorious students prefer to join SSN even after admission to prestigious institutions like the Guindy Engineering College, occasionally even IIT. With its affairs ably guided by my good friend Srinivasan, who is the Chairman of the Board, this is one of the very few institutions where entry is entirely on merit, with no capitation fee. The college now enjoys many years of fruitful collaboration with the Carnegie Mellon Institute of USA, the foremost institution of its kind in the world. It is interesting to see that the alumni of the institute, now holding middle-senior executive positions in India and abroad, generously repay their debt by creating new fellowships for poorer students. Their need to give back to society, acknowledging the benefits that they have received, is worthy of note.

***

Even our quality institutes like IIMs and IITs have fallen sharply in standards. They now do not compare with their counterparts in the west or even in other Asian countries. The concept of 'research' is nearly non-existent in most institutions of higher learning in India. Where research is done, it is usually of a low level and of poor quality. Universities are the fountain-heads of research and new thinking in most countries; in India they are business entities with academics, research being of little concern. It has for long been well known that national regulatory agencies and other approving bodies in the field of education generally demand a large under-the-table 'consideration' for recognition or similar approval. This is quite well known to all in the field of education, including the minister downwards in the government. In short, like government posts, academic posts are also now auctioned. Can there be a stronger indictment of our higher education scene?

The situation is crying for reforms but no political party or government is interested in listening.

8

THE NEGLECT OF PHYSICAL INFRASTRUCTURE—THE HEAVY PRICE?

For rapid and orderly development, creation of infrastructure will have to be ahead of demand, not behind—anon

During Easter time in 1961, I spent three weeks hitch-hiking in four countries in Europe. One morning I found a lift in a Mercedes car, from the outskirts of Bonn to Frankfurt; I picked up a conversation with the owner of the car who was driving himself. (In post-war Germany, English is compulsory, I believe, in schools—everyone speaks English well, with odd exceptions). He mentioned to me that he preferred to live in Bonn, but drive everyday to Frankfurt for work, and return in the evening (about 100 miles or about 160 kilometres each way). I recall that the run from Bonn to Frankfurt took about 75 minutes; clearly my benefactor of that day used to spend less time commuting to work each day than most urban office-workers in India. The German resurgence under Hitler could be partially attributed to the massive 'autobahn' programme which Germany embarked on. The post-war Marshall Plan had its major stress on creation of infrastructure; the highway programmes in mid-20th century in the US opened up the country. Thus, the road to 'nowhere' created new growth opportunities—Zzyzx in California and Hohokus in New Jersey are examples of road building which led to America's prosperity. The Yamuna Expressway from NOIDA to Agra, if well managed in the next 20 years, will create high quality townships, employment and activity in the entire belt. The significance of creating infrastructure first to stimulate development has not been grasped in India.

There is little recognition in governance circles that the primary prerequisite for development is infrastructure. Thus, our agriculture is still languishing with poor growth rates due to terrible neglect of infrastructure—lack of electricity, as well as rural roads. These relate to physical infrastructure but equally failures in social infrastructure like education and public health are responsible for lack of development in rural areas; this is dealt with elsewhere. One sees the clear pattern that development is haphazard, uneven, patchy and frequently self-negating mainly due to non-creation of advance infrastructure to pave the way for planned development. This chapter addresses issues relating to the power sector, water supply as well as the roads sector, these only in a partial manner. So much really needs to be done for sanitation, management of urban populations, rural roads, airlines and port development—the list can go on. As a country we have failed to focus on the basics; lack of attention to infrastructure is a case in point.

The single most important reason why our agriculture has not developed is lack of a steady, reliable power supply in our rural areas. India sadly has not, even 70 years after independence, recognized the critical importance of reliable 24-hour power supply for development. We are unable to get the basics in position, but aspire to reach the moon.

**

For a regular traveller, it is necessary to know what the voltage is in the country he is visiting. In the US it is usually 110 volts ± 2%; in Singapore it is 220 ± 2% and in Switzerland it is 220 ± 1%. Visitors to India from abroad, need to prepare with special instructions. In India the prevailing voltage is 220 ± 100 per cent, that is, when it is available! My grandson who visits me every year from the US, whenever he sees the daily, frequent, irregular blackouts in NOIDA, calls it a 'power-surge'. Apparently, due to a surge, electricity went off in New York area for a couple of hours a couple of decades back; he heard about it, and has labelled all blackouts as power-surges.

My friend from Geneva travelled on work regularly in Africa, including to the poorest countries. He mentioned to me that nowhere has he seen power cuts or blackouts. As a pure vegetarian, he would carry a small bag of rice and some pickles, along with a cup-sized rice-cooker. He was always equipped with a complicated plug-in contraption, with about 10 different types of points, to meet the socket specifications in each country. However, he mentioned to me that he had never had the problem of not being able to get electricity even in the remotest parts of Africa. Cooking in his room was his second option. His first was looking up the local phone directory on arrival, start with the 100 or more 'Patels' listed and telephone them one after the other, referring to an earlier imaginary visit to Geneva where they had 'met'. By the time he got to the third Patel, they had built up enough conversation for my friend to cadge a dinner invitation; his multi-plug was rarely put to use!

The most fundamental infrastructure, ever since the time of Edison, is availability of electricity. F.D. Roosevelt, nearly a century back, had recognized this. At the time of laying the foundation for the Tennessee Valley Authority, he had declared that electricity is the 'truest servant' of man. In nearly every country in the world, including perhaps Zambia, Haiti, Somalia and Iceland, electric power is available in every habitation, generally always without 'cuts' or 'surges'. Even in medium-and-large-size towns in India, which aspires to be a super-power, routine daily power cuts of eight hours or more is not unusual. What makes the situation worse is that the cuts are random and frequent—there is no regularity or predictability. Many rural areas in a number of states including Uttar Pradesh, Bihar, Madhya Pradesh and Odisha often get power only for two to three hours a day. We have not been able to provide our farmers with this basic input and we complain that our agriculture has not been modernized. We expect some knight in shining armour to come from abroad with FDI and transform our agriculture and our rural areas. If this is not the height of illusion, one wonders what is.

This need not necessarily be so; we have large reserves of coal, among the largest in the world, sufficient at currently projected rates of demand for at least three or four more centuries. Contrast this with projected world petroleum/gas supply petering out in the next few decades and with gas prices going through the roof; as the prospect of petroleum shortages seeps into the market-psyche, the situation is bound to worsen dramatically. No doubt, Indian coal is not of high quality; however, beneficiation techniques are readily available, and the technology well known in India. Our failure on the power front essentially stems from not being able to manage basic optimal linkages between coal mining, railway-siding and transportation, finance requirements including guarantees etc. and coordination with State Electricity Boards. There is total failure of national policy in this vital field. Each player is asked to work out his own equations with a number of entities, each one of which considers itself 'sovereign'. The ostensible reason for the recent humongous Coalgate scam was due to issue of licenses freely so that coal is abundantly available for generation of electricity; in the event, as is to be expected in a totally venal system, policy instruments were subverted to fatten individuals in the public and private space. The people of India have been heavily short-changed; coal supply has stagnated, while the demand-supply gap has sharply escalated in the past decade leading to increasing imports of coal at prices four or five times that of domestic coal. It is not possible to muck-up our coal/power policy anymore than now, however hard we may have tried.

One further word about our energy policies may not be out of place. India is blessed with more sunshine than nearly any other country in the world. No doubt solar technology is not developed yet to the stage where it can compete on cost with petroleum or coal energy. However, there is increasingly extensive use of solar power in many parts of the world; solar powered farms are now the new norm, say in California. New commercial models of solar powered cars are now entering markets. The day is not far when use of solar energy will become common for many or most purposes. One would have expected massive experimentation, with large government subsidies, for entrepreneurs to invest in this field in India and pioneer a new power source, an alternative to natural gas. Apparently we wish all the experimentation to be done in Germany and Japan on the solar front. There is already large-scale use of solar power in China while we appear to be passive onlookers.

Our preoccupation with nuclear energy, particularly of the third generation variety supplied by the west, is astonishingly naïve. Clearly India has learnt nothing from the Fukushima nuclear disaster in Japan where two years after the tragedy, the core has still not been neutralized and the potential for serious nuclear pollution spread not yet been assessed; in short, the situation is far from contained. When much of the world is turning its back on nuclear power as the technology stands today, India is embracing this with open arms. This is recipe for potential disaster. Even our liability laws are tailored to meet the demands of suppliers not taking into account our national interest. There is a strong suspicion that our power policy is being influenced by a strategy mounted from far-off countries with the tacit, nay full, complicity of our decision-makers.

As of now, nuclear power accounts for only 2 per cent of India's current production and consumption. The extraordinary attention given to this segment, by encouraging new nuclear plants against international trends and arguably at great risk to the populace is inexplicable. The main attention given to thermal power based on Indian coal, accounting for 70 per cent of production in recent years has been the manifestation of Coalgate! Clearly the nuclear 'tail' is wagging the energy 'dog'. The Parliament has been arm-twisted to pass an absurd Nuclear Liability Law, limiting the manufacturer's liability to Rs1,500 crore and for a period only of five years—a sure invitation to build obsolescence after a 5-year life. Astonishingly, even this weak law is sought to be circumvented by seeking to allow the foreign manufacturer to go totally free of risk. Clearly our policymakers have greater sympathy for the commercial worries of foreign manufacturers, than the concerns of the poor Indian citizen.

If one were to look at nuclear power, we need to seriously consider or at least investigate 'fourth-generation' nuclear technology. A number of countries have already started experimentation in this regard; prototypes and model plants are already in the process of establishment. Clearly our policymakers are totally oblivious to these developments. Note that the 'fourth-generation' technology has the potential to be much less expensive, completely safe and not weaponizable. It meets nearly every possible objection to third-generation technology. Is it merely ignorance or deliberate sell-out that we have not even allowed a public debate on this subject, as if this potential technology is unknown to the world?

India has vast thorium reserves, probably the largest in the world. We have accepted unquestioningly the western research opinion that thorium cannot be the feed-stock for nuclear energy. Recent developments in fourth-generation nuclear technology suggest that thorium can become the source for energy in this field and a breakthrough may not be far away. In this context, it is baffling that the government has not embarked on sponsoring large-scale research on use of thorium for this purpose. It is even more astonishing that thorium is allowed to be smuggled out of the country, allegedly in very large quantities, right under the nose of our authorities, who do not know what is happening in their mining sectors. Recent reports (summer 2013) from Tamil Nadu indicate large-scale mining of thorium-rich sand and its exports. Clearly somebody outside the country has understood the potential while we do not even realize that it is being smuggled out.

In short, our energy policy, as our approach to nearly every other major issue confronting the nation, is vapid, vacuous, irrational, illogical, non-existent and heavily influenced by outside interests. A country which cannot produce enough power to meet its needs has no business flaunting itself as a potential leader or performer in the comity of nations. Among many things we need to be ashamed of, this would lead the list!

***

Indian highways are among the deadliest in the world, with the highest mile-accident ratio. Truck driving is a hazardous occupation. It is prudent for every passenger, before entering the highway, to pray to Lord Ganesha. As in every other aspect impinging on a citizen's life, urban road conditions in India are in a terrible shape.

Registered motor vehicles have grown in the past decade at a compound annual growth rate (CAGR) of 13 per cent while surfaced roads in metropolitan areas have grown at an annual rate of less than 1 per cent. This mismatch, and its potential consequences over a 10-year period, will be obvious to a high school math student. Apparently, however, the implications are beyond the comprehension of our management systems. In many urban arterial roads, 'peak hour' is round the clock while in others, during morning and evening hours, passage is tortuous and prolonged. One surmises that urban commuters reached their destination faster four decades back; at the differential rates of growth between road availability and increase in vehicular traffic, the days of logjam are not far away.

The roads in residential colonies appear to be primarily meant for parking vehicles. Pedestrians take their lives in their hands when they take their morning constitutional walk. High-powered cars drive at breakneck speed, causing terror and damage. In many upper-middle class colonies, it is not unusual to see three or four cars, often Mercs and BMWs, parked in front of a house. The value on wheels per household can be as high as a crore of rupees or more. The owner prefers to use the public road as a garage. Why should a parking fee of say ₹10,000 per month not be charged by the municipality or the RWA for each vehicle? Why should cars parked for long periods on the main roads in bazaar areas not pay a heavy charge? Why should public passageway be used for private parking? In cities like New York, parking rates for just eight hours can go up to $200. In many countries in Europe one needs to purchase a 'local shelter', bought through the manufacturer when you purchase the vehicle, or pay each time of parking. Why should this facility be free in India? Parking wars and road-rage are inevitably on the increase.

In cities like Singapore, London and many others, a heavy 'per entry' tax is levied in designated areas. In many cities, purely residential colonies have been converted to highways, in the sense that traffic enters the smallest bye-lane to take 'short-cuts' adding to the misery of harassed pedestrians and ordinary residents.

Expansion in urban infrastructure is the key element in the planning of most cities in the world. Even towns likes Barcelona, Taegu (Taegu?—where is it?) had metros 60 years back. South Mumbai's sea connectivity with the mainland ought to have been completed 50 years back—one hears with dismay that 'technical objections' have surfaced against a new plan in this regard.

The Kolkata metro took 40 years to build; the Delhi Metro, early last decade, did the job in five years. Delhi should have had its metro three decades earlier. It is heartening to hear that 25 cities in India are in the process of creating their metro rail systems. In each case the construction period is inordinately long with much harassment to the citizenry. By the time the new systems are ready, traffic growth will have outstripped supply, as in the case of Delhi. The key to planned growth is having infrastructure created ahead of demand. Why are we permanently playing 'catch-up'? It is the same story in power supply. Primacy ought to be given to multi-modal public transport, as opposed to private transport.

Why is there no bold aggressive plan to have elevated urban highways, vaulting over colonies to ease congestion in the arteries and to provide a quick transportation mode for vehicular traffic? This has been successfully tried in Delhi with the Barapullah flyover—a wonderful experiment, marred only by lack of imagination in not providing direct connectivity to the main destination of NOIDA, prompting a wag to comment: 'We always knew they were corrupt, but clearly they are also stupid!' We need hundreds of Barapullahs in our cities over the next five years, though more imaginatively planned and designed.

Many readers will not like the suggestion that cars are heavily under-priced and under-taxed in India. For example, a Honda Civic in Singapore costs about ₹1 one crore. Indian roads are not built for Ferraris, BMWs and SUVs so why are they not taxed at, say, 500 per cent? The less said about the standards of policing, and optimal management of urban roads the better. The only training that the traffic police get apparently is in quietly pocketing the regular bakshish or hafta, or fleecing the rule violator; they have no concern for the smooth movement of traffic. Senior police officers in-charge of traffic in most urban areas appear to be chosen carefully from among the most unimaginative and non-serious among those available. The quality of supervision of our traffic is abysmal. Apparently there is no 'vote bank' in organizing smooth traffic; but there is much profit to be made in creating bottlenecks! The disdain for our rural areas is only matched by the neglect of our urban areas.

Again for regular international travellers, it is an important issue as to whether you drive on the left side or the right side of the road. Those who take their cars from London to Paris through the 'Chunnel' have to switch from the left-side of the road to the right side once they reach France. In the US and Europe, it is right hand drive. In Japan, Emirates and in many other countries of the old British Empire, it is left hand drive. Foreign visitors to India need to know that in India, it is 'officially' left hand drive, but right-hand drive is not unusual, certainly not forbidden. Thus, whenever there is a level crossing without a divider, traffic builds up on either side to cover the entire road. On a two-lane each way highway, about ten lanes get created on either side. Motorcycles and smaller vehicles fill up all available space in all directions. On the NOIDA-Greater NOIDA Highway, where vehicles often drive at more than 120 km per hour, it is not unusual to see vehicles coming on the wrong lane, at considerable speed, ostensibly taking the democratic position that the road belongs as much to them as it does to anyone else. No wonder the vehicle-mile accident ratio in India is among the highest in the world by a big margin.

It is not just a question of availability of roads, urban or rural; it is equally important as to whether the existing road infrastructure is optimally utilized. When one drives in small and medium size towns anywhere in India, the main streets are nearly always jam-packed. There is continuous one-upmanship, with everyone trying to cut through in whichever direction. The person who manages to get away feels that he has climbed Mt. Everest, never mind the chaos and log-jam left behind him, indeed probably caused by him. One car, or one cart or truck 'strategically' placed, can hold up traffic for hours. The police in that area watch nonchalantly, the jam is not their problem so they are not concerned. While on the main roads in cities, you should not allow even an inch of space between your car and the vehicle in front of you as someone cuts in promptly and feel he has achieved a victory. Besides, leaving space in front will be seen as 'weakness'—your macho will not permit it. Never mind if there is a bumper scrape; this provides an opportunity for exchange of abuses, even the occasional fisticuffs and entertainment for the large crowds that gather in a jiffy. Never mind polite exchange of telephone numbers or insurance policy details; if a mild person gets away without physical damage post the accident, he can thank his stars. At any rate, traffic has to be bumper-to-bumper. Shopkeepers and onlookers have a good chance for regular entertainment, following 'a verbal duel' or a 'pugilistic drama', where they can have a ring-side seat.

As an aside, when one is entering into or waiting to alight from a plane, or standing in any queue, one feels cramped, with bodies pressing into you particularly from behind. Perhaps this may be enjoyable if it is of the right sex, with the right perfume but almost always the person has a tendency to perspire and probably has never heard of deodorants, and to make it worse usually also has bad breath! One can imagine the plight of those who were in the 'Black Hole of Kolkata', or in one of those 'slave-ships' from the West African coast to the Caribbean. Again leaving the airport pushing the baggage trolley, one strongly has to watch out for a bump into one's Achilles heels by the trolley behind—a frequent occurrence, even if one takes great care—it can be a very painful experience. When you glare at the culprit, he may or may not look contrite, but will almost always say, generously, 'never mind', essentially telling the victim not to get too excited. Clearly he has more concern for your blood pressure, if not your ankle!

Once in Switzerland, driving through to the Austrian border, I got caught in a traffic jam, on the two-lane auto-route due to an accident inside a tunnel. Even though the emergency lane was completely free on our right, not one car overtook me. Lane discipline was maintained for the full three-hours of the jam. I once saw an aerial picture of a 60-mile long, 11-day traffic jam somewhere in China over six-lanes on the highway, due to collapse of a bridge. The aerial picture showed, on the third day, not a single car out of line, no attempt to lane-jump, remarkable discipline. If we can see this in one 'developing' country (China), it is a mystery why similar discipline cannot be displayed or enforced in India. Again, many years back, at Victoria Railway Station in London, on a heavy rainy day, I saw a long queue just outside the station on the portico, waiting for taxis. Due to the inclement weather taxis were in heavy demand but no one tried to queue-jump. Even the old people did not ask for preference; nobody ran out of the station to intercept arriving empty taxis; everyone bore the situation with fortitude and patience, waiting for his turn. I wonder why our psychologists have not tried to analyse this issue in the Indian context to identify the underlying tendency for indiscipline in India and suggest measures to be adopted to enforce better discipline.

Perhaps one answer lies in enforcing traffic rules and regulations. I recall that in Switzerland in the 1980s, the bus fare was SF 1, per trip. In general, one purchases a ticket at the automatic ticket booth in front of bus stop or buys the monthly concession ticket pass, say for 50 trips and has the ticket punched for each trip. There is no one to verify if a passenger in the bus has purchased a ticket or has freshly punched his pass prior to entry; in the normal course it appears to be left to one's 'honour' not to travel free—but is that really so? In reality, every now and then suddenly the two doors of the bus, one in the front and one in the back, are closed; two inspectors quickly check each ticket or pass. A defaulter is fined 120 francs on the spot. If he does not have the money, at the next stop the Marshall is called and the defaulter is taken to jail to spend the night there and stay there till somebody pays the fine on his behalf. In effect, the verification of validity of the ticket has a 1:30 chance; the penalty is 1:120. Only a very foolish person will take a chance. The principle involved is simple—trust the citizen, however, verify him in a thorough manner periodically. In case he is found to be a defaulter, punish him in a disproportionately high manner; there will be no escape clause or excuses under any circumstances. These are the principles that will ensure that rules are obeyed. It should not be difficult to bring these into practice in Indian conditions—there is just no desire to do so.

In the US, for example, anybody caught and convicted for drunken driving has to forfeit his driving license. This caution is clearly inscribed in the license itself. The systems are managed in such a manner that effective random checks are effected periodically, the 'drink-test' is administered in a thorough manner that will stand scrutiny in court and special courts take up cases within weeks. These kinds of measures have practically eliminated drunk-driving in the US. In Singapore, drivers who have caused death through drunk-driving, are liable for execution. Such severe measures are required in our system to counter the present general impression that one can violate the law with impunity. For example, Salman Khan the actor is under trial for 'drunk-driving'. It is a joke of sorts that the trial, with legal shenanigans has been going on for nearly a decade now.

***

I was asked by one of the local engineering colleges near Karur, a tehsil town in my childhood, now a district headquarter, to be the guest of honour and address the students. This was in April 2013. Despite the inconvenience of the travel just for one lecture, I readily accepted the invite, mainly because my home village is located very close to the town, across River Amaravati, which forms the boundary of the town. The road from Tiruchy, where my plane landed winds alongside River Kaveri, all the way to Karur, about 80 km away. Amaravati, a tributary, merges into the Kaveri, a few miles short of Karur on the route.

During my childhood, I spent nearly every summer holiday in our ancestral home in the village, basically a one-street Brahmin village those days, but now with its character much different. My grandfather who settled down in the village after a career as a revenue official, rising to the level of tehsildar by the time he retired, was perhaps the most prominent and respected citizen in the village. As I mentioned, the village was next to River Amaravati, and between the village and the river, there was a small irrigation canal. My grandfather's memoirs, written early in the 20th century in English, are likely to be published soon, giving a graphic picture of life in a typical village in early last century, also with references to government service during the British period, as seen by a junior official. He refers to going to town—Karur—nearly every day, crossing the canal which we used to call in Tamil *Vaikkal* which almost always had water flowing at some speed, at least waist high and then crossing Amaravati, usually swimming across the river—there was no proper bridge across the river during his times.

During my summer holidays, the canal always had waist high water, and generally clean, even though the village did its washing in the canal. We waded across the canal, went on to the river, played a ball game in the sand bank and returned to our homes. I never saw the canal having less than waist high water. Amaravati was always a perennial river, though during summer time water flowed only in about a quarter of its width.

On the drive from Tiruchy airport to Karur that afternoon in 2013, I was quite surprised to see that Kaveri river, which always had plenty of water, one of the perennial rivers mentioned in our scriptures, appeared to be completely dry. I had not driven on that route for many years, and asked the driver of my taxi as to why there was no water in the Kaveri. He had come to that area only about five years earlier; he mentioned that he had never seen water in the river except briefly after the rainy season every year. As I reached Karur, drove close to Amaravati, I noted that there was not a single drop of water in the river. On the day I reached Karur, I went to my village to pray at the Ganesha Temple, established by my grandfather, paid a visit to my old home, very familiar to me through at least 15 annual visits where in an outhouse in the mid-1950s, down with chicken-pox and in 'quarantine', I had read the 'complete Shakespeare' in those seven days when I was out of commission. I had many intimate memories of that house. As I walked to the temple alongside the canal, I was astonished to see not a drop of water in it. In fact it had been converted into a sewer canal, where all the waste water and sewerage was diverted. Uncovered as it was, the canal—surely it has to be called a sewerage ditch now—raised a stink as I approached it. In the course of one day, I had discovered that three water channels, the Kaveri river, the Amaravati river and the village canal, all of which had a 24x7x365 water flow had become totally and probably irrevocably dry. The canal had become an effluent and sewer discharge passage.

In the tehsildar's house, by a pure coincidence the new owner was also a retired tehsildar, a gentleman by the name Subramanya Bharathi (presumably named after the great freedom poet). He had grown up in a neighbouring house, joined the government service and had risen to retire respectably as tehsildar. He received me warmly, and called his mother who was in the adjoining pooja room to join us. Lost as she was in prayer and meditation amidst the hundred or so pictures of Hindu gods and goddesses, she reluctantly came over to us. When the tehsildar introduced me as a retired Cabinet Secretary, and even mentioned that I had earlier been a Chief Secretary in some state, there was no reaction, this did not register. But when he mentioned that I had been 'Collector', there was a visible change in her demeanour—she became highly respectful, looked at me with great admiration, regard, animation and warmth and went out of her way to offer coffee, sweets etc., mentioning how honoured she was that such a great person, that is, a Collector, should take the trouble to visit her. After all everyone will have his own heroes; greatness is in the eyes of the beholder!

On finishing my lecture the next day, I drove straight to the airport at Tiruchy, flew to Chennai, took a connection to Delhi, landing there late the same evening. It was quite dark as I crossed the Yamuna by the DND flyover on my way home. Suddenly a stench hit my nostrils and I asked the driver what it was. He looked surprised, and said to me that it was the foul smell emanating from the Yamuna. Yes, even the Yamuna has now become an effluent discharge canal. So much for our perennial rivers, mentioned in daily prayers: गंगे च यमुने चैव गोदावरी सरस्वती, नर्मदे सिन्धु कावेरी ... ... referring to the perennial rivers of India—Ganga, Yamuna, Godavari, Saraswati, Narmada, Sindhu and Kaveri; Saraswati has long since disappeared underground, alas literally and figuratively; Sindhu (Indus) has been ceded to Pakistan; in one single day I discovered that Kaveri had become totally dry, and the Yamuna is now a sewage canal. The count is on and it is a question of time before the others also go the same way. Within a month or so thereafter, one learnt that the Mandakini, a tributary of the Ganga got flooded for a brief period, caused untold destruction and desolation and swiftly ran on to the Bay of Bengal, to return to its normal thin stream. I wonder if there is any policy recognition of the criticality of the situation, the impending catastrophe in terms of what the future has to portend in terms of water supply in India. A few years back one heard of a grandiose scheme to connect the major rivers of India—I do not know what the feasibility is. However, the way things are moving now, it may actually amount to creating a national sewage grid—I cannot comment on its desirability.

About a decade back, I had the opportunity to drive across Continental USA, from the Pacific Ocean to the Atlantic Ocean in a leisurely ten-day trip, in semi-holiday mode. After passing through the vast Colorado river mountainous areas, after Nevada, Utah and Colorado states, we drove through the vast plains of Kansas in the night, to reach St. Louis in Mississippi, where we crossed the Missouri river, of Mark Twain Riverboat memory—'Ole Man River'! Between St. Louis and Washington DC, one crossed at least 15 large rivers, each carrying more water than Ganga, Yamuna, Narmada and Godavari put together. Every 50 miles or so, one crossed a major waterway. Lake Mead and Hoover dam have irrigated California, a naturally barren area converted to a highly fertile fruit belt through imaginative use of the waters of the Colorado river. One sees the Ganga or the Godavari reach the sea with abundant mile-wide water. But by contrast the Colorado river irrigates the desert areas of Utah, Las Vegas and Arizona, apart from California; it becomes a trickle, round the year, as it reaches Mexico—water management is the key. A country's wealth is measured by the amount of water it has, and by the quality of education of its children. We have seen elsewhere how in India, the world's best human material is prepared for life on the planet, through abysmal lack of educational opportunity. On the other hand, rivers are all drying up, slowly getting converted to carry the national refuse. This is a matter of great concern. I recall great ancient literature in Tamil referring to 'wealth of water', as a sign of prosperity. We need to introspect on what we are slowly getting into.

The water table in NOIDA is visibly going down; Gurgaon has nearly reached panic stages with regard to water; in Bangalore, a cruel water-mafia is emerging, supplying potable water to colonies at robbery rates; the recent drought in Maharashtra has an entire state reeling. Is the looming crisis seen by anybody? Are medium and long term measures under contemplation, under implementation? What about water-harvesting techniques? Are they being optimally employed? Many years back there was the check-dam programme for ground water retention in many areas—has anyone heard of these in recent years? The unchecked digging of bore wells, in urban and rural areas, many coupled with powerful submersible pumps are playing further havoc to the rapidly depleting public water supply. Is any kind of regulation in place, or being contemplated? I have written elsewhere about the havoc caused by reckless construction of irrigation canals, which destroyed natural aquifers, as I saw them 20 years back, when I was the Agriculture Production Commissioner in Uttar Pradesh. Does anyone realize that a major water catastrophe is around the corner? Does the PM or the Planning Commission have any views on the subject? Does Montek realize that if the nation does not start serious thinking now, we could jeopardize our future agriculture potential, as well as even availability of drinking water. Is there a problem? Apart from sterile official notes on files, and indulging in inter-departmental turf wars, is anything else going on that is worthwhile in the Planning Commission? As a citizen I would like to be assured in this regard; and if there is a likely problem, I would like to be assured that preparatory steps are being thought of and being taken.

9
STRATEGIC ISSUES—ARE WE A SOFT STATE?

O Lord forgive them, they do not know what they say or do—but surely they are not innocent

To a casual observer, it may appear that the response to major situations and policy issues is based on immediate political considerations and generally without deep thought and without the basis of a medium-long term strategy. The observer may not be wrong. In many major policy issues relating to external and internal security, a strategy for removing poverty or say reducing corruption and in nearly every other major issue, one does not see a well thought-out plan in action. Naturally no long-term plan can be rigid, it needs to be supple, and to respond to evolving circumstances. This does not mean that all action is based on knee-jerk responses, with no structural framework for placing a major issue in perspective. Short-term electoral considerations and parliamentary tactics, as well as the predilections, preferences and personal interests frequently influence large policy issues in a decisive manner. I try and give below three or four instances of lack of a well considered long-term policy framework; these examples can be multiplied to cover many other themes and subjects.

***

In December 2001, our Parliament was attacked by armed men in a brazen project obviously sponsored from across our borders. The security in our 'temple of democracy' was woefully inadequate even after many warnings had been received from international security agencies of potential attacks on parliaments, including specifically the one in Delhi. Be that as it may, it was only providential that the attack finally did not succeed in the manner it was meant to. Actually, the assailants had penetrated the first two barriers and were thwarted only by the extreme bravery and devotion to duty of two police jawans in the final ring. This literally saved the 60-odd parliamentarians, who were then in the main hall, from a horrible massacre. Surely if that had happened, the consequences for India as a nation would have been unimaginable.

If this was not an act of war, what can be termed as one? If an armed assault a few years later on the Arabian sea route, by a well trained, well armed and fully equipped team, coming to Mumbai from Pakistan is not war, what then constitutes war? What was our reaction to both these major events? Let us ponder for a moment.

India is supposed to follow 'rule of law'. We allowed our legal processes more than a decade to pursue both events, for showing to the world that we are 'law abiding' and forever follow 'due process' and 'due procedure'. So far so good, nobody can object, except that the 'process' has to be swifter. What substantive pre-emptive and preventive military and administrative action did we mount? Did we have a strategy to meet such situations? Did we see the need to generate a strategy for future situations of this sort? Do we want to be seen as 'soft targets', on whom pot shots can be taken at will by any neighbour, small or large? Even now, is there a strategy in place to identify real or imaginary incursions or attacks, grade them, evaluate them and have a graduated response based on our analytical conclusions? In both these events, is there an iota of doubt that these were both 'state-sponsored' or state-supported? What direct or indirect action did India take to pursue its long-term interests? The feeling is inescapable that our foreign policy relating to our neighbours is prisoner to our domestic vote bank considerations. The ruling party is conscious of the criticality of the minority vote and is unwilling to risk it, even if it costs the nation massively. Sadly our own policymakers implicitly permit Indians to have dual loyalty, to the 'secular' Indian state, as well as to society/creed/nation outside our borders. This is clearly indifference to national interests and cannot be attributed merely to a namby-pamby, effete foreign policy.

What did we do in these two instances? In December 2001, after the Parliament attack, the army was sent on full alert, across our entire western border with Pakistan. This was peak winter, when 'every square-inch' in Kashmir including the highest ranges were patrolled by our forces in harsh conditions. Four months later, during the following summer, the 'full alert' phase continued—at temperatures of 110 degree Fahrenheit our forces in full uniform guarded the Rajasthan borders in extreme cruelty conditions. Nobody in Delhi had a thought on what would happen to the morale of our armed forces. Surely they can't be on full alert for months on end, in harsh conditions? In early spring in Kashmir or late summer in Rajasthan, the forces would have been so exhausted that they would have been 'sitting ducks'. From Delhi's perspective, prompt 'strong' action had been taken—ordering 'full alert'—and nothing further needed to be done, not even quietly withdrawing the order for alert at the appropriate time! Apparently no decision-maker in Delhi could find a 'legitimate reason' to rescind the order for alert, which continued by default. We may think that we are ready for war; perhaps we even are from a technical and military point of view. But Pakistan knows clearly that we are not ready for any disturbance to our cosy and comfortable and venal political and commercial life.

After the Mumbai attack, what did we do? There was a charade of weak-kneed exchange of documents, 'evidence' and shadow discussions on the legal and evidentiary aspects with Pakistan. We wanted to convince the 'criminal' that he had committed a crime by asking him to agree with the documents that we produced. We converted a major political/military response situation to one of an anaemic diplomatic exchange, with high courtesy and low content when millions of Indian viewers had seen live on television the war being waged on our soil by foreign invaders. The final insult was that many years after the event, the lone invader caught, Kasab, was executed, with great reluctance and in stealth as if the nation was abashed and ashamed to put to death an enemy who had attacked us openly. In summer 2013, when our prime minister accompanied by the chairperson of the Congress Party (or, was it vice-versa?), visited Kashmir, it was touted as the 'first' visit by the PM after the execution of Afzal Guru, one of the plotters of the Parliament attack. He was a convicted criminal—was his execution a 'landmark' national event to be celebrated or commemorated or mourned? How much cowardice can a nation show? Can anyone deny that the 'soft' treatment given to Kasab had everything to do with our own vote bank politics, and the need to ensure that a significant segment of our population should not get alienated? This is the greatest failure of our secular democracy—we are not sure of the loyalty of our own citizens. The people of India need to reflect on this.

***

The Naxal or Maoist problem is not new to India. Even in the early 1990s it was in a simmering stage. I recall that sometime in the mid-1990s, the then Home Secretary (who himself originated from Bihar but had worked in another state) had done a study in then undivided Bihar, and reported that in 13 districts, there was no administration to speak of; the block and thana officials stayed in the district headquarters and went to their respective places of work under heavy armed guard only once a month to draw their monthly salaries. The situation has continuously become worse since then. While local 'insurgency' can stem from different local factors, the common thread is that the agents of disruption were able to capture the imagination of the Adivasis and local tribes in the affected areas; these poorest of the poor in India, hardly with any kind of education facilities and with little physical infrastructure (roads, schools, hospitals, electricity), in areas where the local state administration hardly had any presence, were ready fodder for insurgent leaders (who were, without doubt, funded from outside sources).

The handful of districts in two or three states affected in the 1990s has now blossomed into at least about 200 districts, some slightly and others severely disturbed. At least in 50 districts today in about seven states, there is hardly any administration. Local revenue, police and development authorities are generally not present in their positions; the poor Adivasis are left to the mercy of armed insurgents, or the armed police—the latter only marginally less brutal. Sadly this slowly growing cancer has not received adequate national attention and no national strategy has been adopted.

The issue has traditionally been evaluated as a purely law and order matter. In the late 1990s, the first national meeting on the subject was called by the home ministry in Delhi—only of the home secretaries and Directors General of Police in the then seven state governments were involved. It was soon thereafter realized that the issue had to be addressed on many levels—law and order, social justice, land reform, development etc. Hardly any worthwhile initiative has been taken by the Centre to tackle this national menace on a campaign basis, in a meaningful and coordinated manner.

In first decade of this century, the prime minister made a thundering announcement that this is a national menace, and will be given highest priority; hardly any follow up action resulted. The subject continued to be dealt with as a law and order matter, conveniently seen to be in the purview of the state government with the role of the central government being to respond, often with great miserliness, to demands for central armed police forces. The central intelligence agencies have failed to develop reliable information channels. Their role has so far been to issue periodical 'advisories', predicting potential insurgency acts in most general terms and demanding that the state may be on 'alert'. Not surprisingly every few months or so a major ambush by the insurgents is reported, resulting in massive carnage, usually of police and para-military personnel. While such incidents, on a smaller scale happen nearly every day, and generally go unreported, periodically a large event catches national attention. Something like the Gadchiroli or Dantewada or the recent Sukma massacre raises large anxiety levels in the country but after a few days of media focus, the issue dies out, to be played out again in another place after a few months. It is astonishing how little strategic sense is displayed by our national policymakers. One gets the impression that the authorities have become fully desensitized to major insurgency events. The routine response consists of high level political visits to families of the victims, a highly publicized visit by the home minister to the state capital to 'review arrangements' and a helicopter/airplane survey of the affected part of the forest. With these formalities, concluded in the first four or five days of the tragedy, the issue can be consigned, forgotten. As and when another 'strike' takes place in another part of the country, the formula can be repeated!

About 50 districts are very severely affected where there is no local administration to speak of. The local residents, the Adivasis, already leading the most miserable existence, are caught between a rock and a hard place—between the insurgents and the armed police. Politicians jump-in periodically with their bit of trying to fish in troubled waters, and to generate some local partisan advantage. Leaders of the state recklessly hand over the land and mines to big business—crony capitalism plays a large role in adding to the misery of the locals. In all this mess, there is no well thought-out strategic plan to tackle the menace over a period of time. Many observers glibly recommend 'sending the army in', even to send 'helicopter gunships' to tackle the menace—it is little realized that the cannon fodder can only be the local residents, Indian (not foreign) citizens. Perhaps some economists and social strategists, educated abroad, genuinely believe that one credible way to develop India is by quietly 'doing away' with our poorest citizens, much like the conquering Europeans in North America 'did away' with the Red Indians and buffaloes some centuries back. Economic theory will profoundly propound that fewer the poor, higher the per capita income!

Delhi needs to see this as a national issue. Where insurgency is at a very incipient initial level, it can be tackled by determined use of force—as was done in Chandauli in UP and Erode in Tamil Nadu in the 1990s. But once the menace has taken roots, a multi-pronged approach is essential. In a democracy the public has to be wooed, no solution will result through threats or subjugation of the Adivasis—their hearts and minds have to be captured by carefully thought-out measures. Special problems require unique solutions. Perhaps we need to identify the 50 most-affected districts, bring them under direct central administrative control, cut out local politics and politicians totally for about 10 years, bring a generous dose of development, along with strong use of force as required. Some such dispensation is likely to succeed. In riot-hit areas all over India, the local District Magistrate generally bans visits (or visitations) of all 'politicians'. Note that the Naxal areas are actually chronically disturbed. If one goes back a few decades, the British brought in special management arrangements in specified areas for a period of time. Perhaps we need to think of such out-of-the-box directions. If the present Constitution does not permit it, there needs to be political will to amend it suitably to meet special requirements.

This recommendation for a 'special dispensation' is not to be construed as 'softness', or an approach where force is abandoned in favour of 'development'. Instead, a focused development orientation, delivered with a mailed fist without the distractions, complications and irrelevancies brought in by the normal democratic administration (as applicable in 'settled' conditions) are special measures which are advisable to bring back highly disturbed areas to normalcy. Such a dispensation will be able to target, very specifically and in a precise manner, terrorists and mischievous elements, simultaneously allowing the local people to see administration—without any political colour—as their friend and well wisher.

***

The failure of forming a strategic approach, coupled with sustained implementation can be seen best in the context of our dealings with neighbouring countries. Can India point to one single country among our neighbours, that we can count on as our 'friend'? Is it credible for India to stake a claim as a 'world leader', when it cannot rely on the support of a single neighbour? In these days of the internet and easy communications, when business interests in different countries can interact easily without the intervention of their respective embassies, foreign policy requirements with respect to, say, the western world have not been of great complexity—they rarely have been in the past. We need not unduly worry about the UN and its agencies; these are not significantly relevant any more in international affairs. We need not also stick to a childish demand to become a Permanent Member of the Security Council—we are likely to gain nothing substantive out of it. In fact, in 'negotiating' for it, we may needlessly pay a heavy price, to get little in return. The key foreign affairs issues relate to our neighbours, where the nature of the problem, or the opportunity, is very specific and needs to be studied and tackled purposefully.

There is a border problem with China; the longer the settlement takes, the more difficult it will be in the interim period. We cannot wish it away. India has strategic interests, so has China. With increasing asymmetry in our respective economic and military capabilities, a solution to the border issue will get harder and the terms will worsen from our point of view, as the decades go by. Once upon a time, when Rajiv Gandhi was the prime minister and commanded a three-fourth majority in our parliament, it may have been possible for him to 'negotiate' a compromise formula with 'give' and 'take'. In such matters, in any such compromise, both parties will have to give but both will gain if there is a compromise; the certainty is that both will lose if a settlement is not done. India progressively will be worse-placed in this regard, as we have seen in the past decades. The potential for Indo-China cooperation in the international fora is very high if we can find ways to trust each other. The trans-Atlantic alliance ruled the world for over a century, despite the individual interests of the US and individual European countries. If such an arrangement, not to the detriment of India's long-term interests, can be worked out, the next 100 years could see a Sino-Indian world domination.

Unfortunately, we have no credible policy with regard to Pakistan. There has been no sustained strategic approach through the decades and no one in our administration is clear as to what and how our response should be to every event and provocation. Solving the 'Kashmir problem' is not going to get easier with time. There was a time in the 1940s when we could have found a military solution; we lost at least two opportunities in later decades to hammer through an agreement based on resounding military victories. Clearly Pakistan is highly unpredictable with a deadly mixture of Islam and anti-India sentiments which hold it together. We need to be quite clear as to how far we will go—how much we will accept. Are there clearly drawn lines, which if crossed will elicit a strong reaction? Do we have a Pakistan policy?

At the time of independence, we took a conscious decision to become a secular democracy and to give an option to the Muslim community to live in India or to migrate to Pakistan. With this major step, whose implications our founding fathers perhaps did not sufficiently comprehend, there is no option except for the majority and the other minority communities to live in harmony with mutual accommodation in religious and social matters. However, we forgot that while Indians follow different religions, creed, practices, languages etc. there has to be a basic Indianness in all citizens and no discrimination can be done. This is the premise, promise and guarantee of our Constitution. Sadly successive generations of politicians saw a vote bank opportunity in 'wooing' certain communities and religions. If you sow the wind you will reap the whirl-wind. Today it cannot be said that all Indians see our country as Indians first and community later. The US is also a multi-racial society, and has gone through many transformations over the decades and centuries but every citizen has pride in being an American. Vote bank politics should not erode this element. Every Indian should place India first, our polity needs to guide this wisely, but forcefully. Dissenters will have to be dealt with firmly till everyone falls in line. It will be fatal to induct vote bank politics into the scene.

The policy mess with respect to Sri Lanka does not need elaboration. The Government of India, astonishingly never took into account that Tamil Nadu has strong ethnic ties in Sri Lanka; this should have been kept in mind while interfering in Sri Lankan affairs by sending our forces three decades back. If the move was deliberate, and well thought out, we should have seen it through and not beaten a retreat. We have consistently given the impression to Sri Lanka and to the world that the Government of India's approach and that of Tamil Nadu/Kerala is quite different; no effort has been made to reconcile the two. The failure is palpable.

Our relations with other neighbours have their own specific features. One common thread is that we have no sustained and credible strategic approach to each one of them, as well as to bringing that in unison with our overall approach to neighbours and to world issues. Ultimately strategy has to be devised on our perceived long-term interests, not to be improvised on a month-to-month basis by whoever may be the foreign or finance minister, or prime minister of the day. We seem to have forgotten that effective diplomacy is a combination of a mailed fist, playing footsy under the table, a kick in the groin when none is looking, a quiet passing of the envelop suitably filled up and a number of other things performed in public and private. Diplomacy is not just wining and dining, and regular trips abroad. We need to grow up, if we have to make a mark as a world leader.

***

The same approach to paper-over disasters, shy away from strategic decisions and failure to mount sustained campaigns have been the hallmark of our approach in many key sectors. For example, our railway system is crying for modernization and reforms. While the management of our railways, one of the largest systems in the world, is by and large free from political interference at all levels and is relatively professional (only relatively and that too with low quality), there is hardly any major new innovative advance in the overall system. The average speeds have remained the same over six decades, creating new lines has hardly kept pace with demand, segregation of freight and passenger traffic corridors has not even been seriously attempted; linkage of railways with coal, iron ore and other mining areas has not been approached in a cooperative optimal manner; and the signalling systems are outdated—the glaring failures can be recounted endlessly. On top of this, one sees the sleaze in the higher management levels—the recent ministerial-board level expose clearly is the tip of the iceberg.

How often have we seen after a major accident, the minister and board members descending on the scene nearly instantly to 'organize relief'? Surely they can do this job better sitting in the headquarters, leaving the local operations in the hands of the lower railway hierarchy and local district officials. Invariably an inquiry will be ordered. While constructive responsibility always vests on the highest levels, this is never admitted. The only person usually punished is the local linesman or the station master at most. Our railways need to grow up. One merely has to take a look at the wonders achieved in China in the past two decades in the railway sector. The mind-boggling progress and modernization, even if only partially emulated in India, will take us quite far.

***

The recent Uttarakhand tragedy, in the Kedar Nath Valley in summer 2013 has brought to the fore the issue of vulnerability of the system and lack of preparedness in the face of natural disasters. While the proximate cause was the breach of a water-body north of Kedar Nath due to very heavy rains, the extensive damage caused was from reckless lack of preparedness, apart from wanton permission to degrade the environment in the area, resulting in probably ten times the loss that should have been there. Indiscriminate felling of trees, unfettered pilgrim traffic facilitated by heavy road-building without consideration for the capacity of the land to bear it, free permission to construct shops, hotels and residences right on the river bank; in other words reckless disregard for the fragility of the environment clearly is to blame for the severity of the loss.

In 1993, as Chief Secretary in Uttar Pradesh, I had got a rapid study done on the stability of Mussoorie, as well as of the impact of quarrying and mining on the Dehradun-Mussoorie road. Based on the alarming picture that was presented to me, I got the approval of the then Chief Minister Mulayam Singh to totally ban all construction in Mussoorie, as well as quarrying and mining activities on the entire hill side. Half-complete buildings were not allowed to be completed, and I gave very strict instructions for full, complete and detailed compliance. The political backlash and furore could be expected. Many lobbies got together to attack the ban. To the credit of Mulayam Singh, he stood firm and did not amend or dilute the ban. Today one can see the result—Mussoorie is alive, it has greened and its survival today can be attributed almost certainly to the advance steps taken earlier. Very similar is the story of Nainital.

In the early 1990s, the Apex Court had intervened to declare a five-mile patch alongside the Arabian sea as an ecologically sensitive 'coastal zone', and had banned all construction in that area, except in some specific circumstances. I recall that as Cabinet Secretary in the late 1990s one faced enormous pressure to dilute these provisions—this was successfully resisted. I do not know what the present situation is. It is imperative that we realize the ecological sensitivity of certain special areas and tailor development consistent with ecological requirements. Development is essential, but it has to be sustainable otherwise the entire process will get violently disrupted—nature cannot be trifled with.

Already one hears the chief minister of Uttarakhand promising 'development' in that area, and return to 'normal' tourism at an early date. While this is desirable, indeed essential, this has to be done very carefully within the constraints of the fragility of the local ecology and keeping relevant factors in mind. Remember that in countries like Switzerland or Austria, great care is taken to ensure that all development in the mountain areas is 'sustainable'. Sustainability is the key-word, not reckless construction, allowing the forest, tourism, building, road and other mafia to dictate the pace and nature of development.

The damage caused by the Planning Commission—of omission and commission

Many of the issues listed earlier, along with so many others not touched upon, need sustained effort over a long time, based on a strategic framework. One wonders what machinery is available to do the strategic-thinking part. The PMO and the Cabinet Secretariat are immersed in day-to-day management. They have no time for thinking through the issues; the line-ministries are equally on a fire-fighting mode. Many of these issues cut through different departments and ministries, requiring an over-arching all-encompassing approach, bringing high level intellect and experience to be brought to bear, without the distraction of having to respond in a knee-jerk manner to immediate stimuli, or to react to the political developments of the day. One would have expected the Planning Commission to perform this role as the 'super-think-tank' of India. Alas that has not happened.

In fact the Planning Commission was originally conceived as an agency for preparing the working plan in each sector and working closely with line-ministries in implementation. Traditionally not so much stress had been given to long-term policy formulation.

Thus, the Planning Commission is in near-daily touch with different ministries on implementation matters. It will be a fair assessment that the Planning Commission is de-facto a stumbling block—one more hurdle to be crossed—in the process of implementation, and is seen almost on each occasion, probably rightly, as a 'pain-in-the-neck' by the implementing ministries. It has enormous powers with no responsibility. If one agency is to be blamed for non-abolition of poverty, poor education standards, abysmal infrastructure and a host of appalling failures, I would vote for the Planning Commission as the main culprit—its role has been one of a 'dog-in-the-manger'.

This has been the experience over decades. With the advent of a 'free-economy' advocate like Montek Ahluwalia, one would have expected him to bring a large broom and clean up the Planning Commission, conceived from the period of an era aping the erstwhile USSR pattern. One would have bet in 2004 that Montek would have perceived his first task as dismemberment of the Planning Commission, making it disappear and creating a major think-tank for 'strategic planning'. Alas this has not happened; 'Circe' was able to suck in and embrace the newcomer and give him the illusion of power, pelf and authority; bureaucracy has again succeeded in perpetuating itself.

Whether or not the Planning Commission is dismantled is not the real issue. It is merely a nuisance, and a hurdle to be suffered. What is of consequence is that we need a high level, slim, thinking body, manned by people of great experience, vision and wisdom (not a dumping ground for people who need to be conferred with political favours for services rendered). Such a high level intellectual body, attached directly to the PMO or the Cabinet Secretariat, is a crying need in the country. This is required to prepare medium and long-term strategic thinking on a host of large policy issues.

10

DOES PARLIAMENT REPRESENT THE PEOPLE ANYMORE?—REFORMING POLITICS AND POLITICIANS

> *This tree gives no fruit, this cow no milk... ... anon*
>
> *The Indian politician—'Others abide the Question, thou art free'*

There is a growing feeling that our Members of Parliament (MPs) (and legislators in the states), once elected from a constituency, do not need it any more, till the next elections come around five years or so later. Rather than acting as a bridge between the constituency and the government, a MP in India perceives his role as one of following his party's directions, apart from looking after his own personal interests. A MP gets a mandate from the constituency, treats it as an irrevocable power of attorney, and thereafter the people have no say in how they are administered on issue after issue.

Let us consider a few examples. When Anna Hazare's Lok Pal was discussed in Parliament, one intuitively felt a very large degree of public support—a growing revulsion against corruption, and the need to take strong action to combat this menace. One did not find this general mood of the people reflected in the goings-on in Parliament. This was treated as another political matter, to be settled at convenience, and in a manner suitable to the various political parties in Delhi. Is Parliament concerned only with political manoeuvering and jockeying for party positions? Has it nothing to do with tackling issues? If a poll had been taken at any time whether the CBI should be under government control or not, there would have been a loud voice from the people to make the CBI free. The Parliament surely was out of tune with the people.

Let us take the instance of the policy on 'reservations in promotion'. Accepting that the various deprived classes need special attention, and affirmative action, there could be two views on the subject. Many polls on television channels, while supporting reservation at 'entry', indicated a 90 per cent or thereabout opposition to reservations in 'promotion'. Astonishingly nearly every party in Parliament supported the move (except one, but for reasons not on merit); can there be a greater mismatch between the Parliament's views and that of the people in general?

India may want Electoral Reforms—Our politicians certainly do not!

In the Gujarat and Himachal Assembly elections in 2012, 74 per cent and 65 per cent respectively of the winning candidates were crorepatis (31 per cent and 21 per cent respectively had criminal cases against them). In theory, a legislator does not hold an 'office of profit'. However, nearly each one multiplies his wealth while in office. A Congress spokesman, now a Union minister, in November 2012 let the public know in a media discussion that one candidate for the seat of MLA spent ₹20 crore in his assembly segment election campaign. Assuming a 'modest' ₹10 crore expenditure as the norm for each assembly segment, the 'speculative investment' is of the order of ₹40 crore, assuming a 1:4 success ratio. A person willing to invest that much will not be satisfied without a 500 per cent return in one term. This translates to a ₹200 crore project for each MLA's post; perhaps double that for an MP. These are turnovers bigger than many universities, hospitals, indeed large industrial projects.

In June 2013, a senior BJP party leader, Gopinath Munde, let it be known in a public speech that he had actually spent about ₹8 crore for his election as a MP, as against the formally approved limit of ₹40 lakh. This generated a major furore with the ruling party demanding immediate 'action' against the MP, as he had openly confessed to 'breaking the law'. The Election Commission apparently is issuing him a show cause notice in this regard. What is remarkable is that every single MP and MLA, practically every politician knows that the prescribed limit is broken by 20 or 30 times or more—this is the most open secret in our politics. If Election Commission members are not aware of this fact, clearly they are nincompoops and undeserving of the high positions that they occupy. If they actually know the 'facts of life', it is a moot question why they have not taken strong action against rampant violation of the rules, nearly by every candidate. The EC should use this 'confession' to start a major campaign, to ensure the elimination of money power in elections. The black money requirements for election purposes is the prime mover for the massive parallel economy in the country. Action just against Gopinath Munde would be pure tokenism, the EC needs to make a significant move to bring the fear of god in defaulting politicians, to ensure that the limits are by and large stuck to. Munde has provided the EC with an opportunity which needs to be fully utilized.

The largest and least regulated 'industry' in India is politics. The players make their own rules, break them at will, change their own goal-posts and do not want any umpire (Lok Pal?—perish the thought!). The Parliament and the assembly are 'of the politician, by the politician and for the politician'. Why is the EC an idle spectator, when the Constitution and the law demand of it that it does its job?

The Election Commission regularly brings out a report after each series of elections on compliance with the existing regulations on expenditure limit by each candidate in each constituency—in general this is of the order of ₹50 lakh or so. Past practice has indicated that in about 10 per cent of the cases, the candidates have declared their expenditure as going up to 90 per cent of the approved limit; in 90 per cent of the cases, only up to 50 per cent of the limit is reached! These figures are unbelievable—it is surprising how the Election Commission accepts these patently false figures. As mentioned earlier, the limits are exceeded by 20 or 30 times or more in each case. Everyone knows that the official figures are absurdly off-beam. Clearly a change in approach is called for.

After T.N. Seshan, while we have had a number of high quality Election Commissioners and Chief Election Commissioners, none has so far attempted to begin the clean-up of the electoral process, in terms of cleansing it of 'money power'. Seshan himself had shown how a major issue can be addressed. In later times, Vinod Rai showed how a strong ethical adversarial approach can bring skeletons out of the government's financial cupboard, and contribute to bringing greater financial discipline. We have had high class commissioners in the past in our Election Commission—men of the of the calibre of T.S. Krishnamurthy have headed the Commission. However, the Election Commissioners in recent years have not fully discharged their functions; they have not used the full authority vested in them by the people through the Constitution to take effective measures to address money power distorting our elections. Nobody stops our Election Commission from hiring chartered accountants, their own financial secret agents to act as their eyes and ears and when false certification is made, to come down heavily and hand down punitive decisions, to act as deterrent. The Election Commission needs to look at itself in the mirror—it is not sufficient if it 'conducts' elections 'peacefully'—it needs to conduct it 'fairly'. That will happen only when money power is substantially eliminated; till then, no kudos whatever to our Election Commission.

The early 1990s saw the termination of muscle power in our elections (exceptions such as Kunda, only prove the rule); pre-Seshan, two gun-toting goondas, at the village entry point, would ensure that the 'wrong' people did not leave the village on voting day. It is the height of irony that two-third of the population is in deep distress and politicians are emerging as the crorepatis in India. The menace of money power is grossly distorting our electoral process. There seems no move from any quarter to reverse the trends. It is a safe bet that any new emerging Seshan will be nipped in the bud, the same way Anna Hazare was.

The so called 'model code of conduct' in practice has little teeth. One does not recall any person or party disqualified in any election till now. None is frightened of it; it is flouted with impunity, using ingenious devices. Much like cumulative football offences, should not the violations be allowed to pile up through successive elections, so that at some time they reach a point where a party or person is disqualified from the contest?

Why is the Election Commission so placidly supine? Why can't it arouse itself and enforce the 'model code of conduct' with greater pungency and efficacy? It is a constitutional authority, it need not behave like a namby-pamby poodle to be coddled by government. It represents the interests of the people to ensure free elections—this trust is not being fully discharged now. Clearly the Election Commission is too soft, wants to please all political parties, does not want to be seen as unpleasant; its allegiance is to the Constitution and the people of India, who require the Election Commission to be bold, aggressive and do all that is necessary to weed out 'money power' in elections. The Election Commission after the days of Seshan has reverted to its standard mode of a pleasant comfortable friend of the government and political parties in the process betraying their trust. This is a call for the Election Commission to wake up, stand and be counted and ensure that money power is wiped out in our electoral system. The Constitution gives it unlimited powers to devise its own methods.

It is also important that the selection procedure for membership of the Election Commission be amended, to be bipartisan, neutral and seen to be completely impartial.

***

Other distortions are bedeviling our electoral process. Designs borrowed from the UK, US and France, where predominantly two major parties are in contention, have been imported into the Indian system. With multiple parties competing for each seat, the winner can have a mandate supported by as little as 20 per cent of the popular vote. Should a 'transferable-vote' system or 'run-off' not be envisaged to ensure that the winner or winning party gets at least 50 per cent of popular support? Will that not ensure greater stability and higher acceptability and credibility in dealing with contentious issues?

In theory, we have a parliamentary form of government, of the British model, as compared to the US presidential model. In nearly every state, the chief minister rules like a despot, supported by a kitchen cabinet of staff officers and a personal secretariat. To some extent, the same is also true at the Centre. Is this what our Constitution makers envisaged six decades back? Are there effective checks and balances on the Executive? Have we drifted into a presidential mode in substance, while retaining a Parliamentary façade? If this is so, this should be a conscious, well thought out and debated decision, not a matter of convenience for those in power to slip it in on the sly.

In a country where two-third of the population is struggling for two-square-meals a day, what is the extent of political involvement of the citizenry in policymaking and its implementation? The so-called middle class, the social sector and the educated classes can debate issues till the cows come home—the real voting power is elsewhere. Policies and practices need not be based on rationality or logic; they are merely to be fine-tuned to look good for electoral results at the right time.

RTI—Transparency of parties

Sometime in May 2013, the Central Information Commission, taking up the petition of an activist, gave its orders that the Right to Information (RTI) Act was applicable to national political parties, giving technical and legal arguments to buttress its decision. Clearly this will be challenged in the apex court, and it remains to be seen as to what is the final legal view that will prevail. However, immediately after the finding, nearly every national political party roundly condemned the decision, referred to it as impracticable and wooly-headed and said that it was un-implementable. I recall that in 1997, when I got the first draft of the RTI prepared and took it to the Cabinet, nearly every government servant from the Joint Secretary to Secretary level that I spoke to, referred to it as impracticable, un-implementable and utopian and that it would seriously hamper the internal processes of the government. The objections now from political parties heard were nearly on identical lines! It should be remembered that in 10 years of implementation, RTI has brought out more 'facts' in the realm of the public, than 60 years of 'Question

Hour' in Parliament. It has done a good deal to clean up the internal processes and to give spine to officers who want to stand up within the system. In an era where our electoral processes urgently need to be cleaned up, a new Seshan is required to emerge to purge our elections from the hold of black money. Clearly this new order of the Information Commission will contribute to the commencement of the process. For decades, practical recommendations for electoral reforms have remained unimplemented, indeed have gathered dust with no attention whatever from Authority. When there is no desire to reform the system by those concerned, the reforms have to be rammed through—this is what the RTI is seeking to do. Ironically, parties which generally oppose each other on nearly every issue, have gotten together to stand shoulder-to-shoulder to oppose this move!; much like they all worked together, overtly or covertly, to kill the proposal to create a Lok Pal a couple of years back. If one were to have a referendum in the country on whether political parties should become more transparent, whether their income and expenditure details should be widely available, one imagines that there will an overwhelming response in the affirmative. It is ironical that in this 'democracy', political parties which control our governance, appoint the prime minister, the cabinet and other executives take a position totally contrary to what the public wants or demands. It is only in the democracy-model of this country that one can see a total dichotomy between what the public wants and what their 'representatives' decide.

Detailed information regarding source of every income and where and in what manner the money is spent is essential to be available in the public domain for every party. After all, it is the parties which determine the chiefs of the executive branch, and have a major role to play in governance at the Centre and in the states. He who pays the piper calls the tune. People have the inalienable right to know who has money power over the parties. So much black money enters the electoral process, more information on party funding and expenditure will definitely inhibit the role of black money in our elections. Besides, the details of expenditure on helicopters/planes being hired and other related issues are of major public interest. Do businessmen pay for the political travel by party men is a relevant question. When a party person lands somewhere by private helicopter or plane, it is a very relevant question for the public whether the 'leader' paid for the ride from his own pocket, or was the expense covered officially by the party, or whether a private businessman funded the trip. Accordingly the finances of a party ought to be in the public domain. Whether this is done through the RTI Act, or by an administrative fiat by the Election Commission, or through voluntary agreement between the parties, the modality is irrelevant. The substance is that the detailed finances of parties should be in the public domain.

Not surprisingly nearly all political parties oppose exposure of their finances to RTI. They have all ganged up to legislate the exclusion of political parties from RTI. Legal 'luminary' Kapil Sibal, who propounded the 'zero loss' theory in the 2-G context, had announced that the Chief Information Commissioner's verdict bringing political parties in the ambit of RTI was 'flawed'. Clearly the flaw, under the concept of rule of law, ought to have been 'rectified' through an appeal in the apex court. However, the government chose to bring a hammer to the table—to ram through a legislation excluding parties from RTI in the process telling the citizens of this largest democracy that they do not count, that the hammer will smash the concept of 'transparency' if it impinges on the privacy of the political executive and the politician—in other words, utter contempt for democratic principles. Can a greater example of Parliament not bothering about what the citizens wants be given? Will this attract Article 14 of the Constitution of India?

Need for a Referendum procedure

Many countries have a 'referendum' procedure while considering policies or projects touching a cross-section of the population, either locally or nation-wide. Thus, for example in Switzerland, one of the best run democracies, each Canton has a referendum system; similarly so too in each US county. The only channel available in India is the Member of Parliament; he does not 'represent' his constituency—he 'commands' it—he is accountable to no one except his party boss.

Let us take the issue of FDI in multi-brand retail, where there is large-scale opposition. Without taking a position, we note that there are strong interests to support the policy and a vocal group opposing it. Chief ministers representing 70 per cent of the national population have expressed strong reservations. Is it prudent to plunge hastily into a policy decision, irrespective of what the people think? Is it a pure economic decision, not involving our people? Is it a mere matter of 'proving' a parliamentary majority? Should this not be subject to ascertaining the people's opinion in a national election which is due in a year or so? For something that has not been done for nearly 65 years, is there a tearing hurry to do it today, in the teeth of major apprehensions? Are we a true democracy? Are the people important, or have we outsourced all our authority, power and interests to our politicians and Members of Parliament?

In the course of the FDI in retail debate in the Rajya Sabha, 18 parties spoke; of these, 14 spoke against introducing FDI in retail, while only four members of the ruling coalition spoke in favour. Of the parties who opposed the move, at least four belonged to the ruling coalition; all spoke vehemently against the move, mentioning that the medium and long term effects would be disastrous for small retailers and farmers, who constitute the bulk of the population; that the measure will eliminate jobs in the country, rather than create new employment. At the time of voting, however, one of these major parties abstained, and the other three voted for the proposal, having earlier stridently opposed the move. If all the parties had voted on the lines they took in the House, the executive decision on FDI in retail would have been defeated.

What is the morality of a party taking a strong position in the House, and voting against its own position when the matter is brought up for counting of numbers especially when it was made clear that the ruling coalition will not collapse if the vote went against it. What is the message sent by these Janus-faced parties to their own constituencies, as well as to the country at large? Is there a feeling in the country that it does not matter what position, principled or otherwise, that a party or a politician takes—the public can be hoodwinked and the prevaricators will not be punished? Is all our politics about vote banks, caste and community issues, all of which having nothing to do with major matters relating to our economy or culture or security? It is a terrible thought that the electorate in all likelihood will not punish those who say one thing, and vote the other way within the hallowed precincts of the Parliament—our temple of democracy. Indeed is this temple being treated by our pandas and pujaris with contempt? How can one expect the citizen to take Parliament seriously?

Given the mismatch between the way our Parliament performs and the thinking of the people, is it now time to consider introducing a 'referendum' procedure in our constitutional practice? A regime needs to be considered for adoption where major policy matters would be tested from time to time, to ascertain what the nation as a whole thinks about it, rather than depending exclusively on the interests of our parliamentarians to decide the nation's direction. This will mean curtailing the powers of the Parliament, which has to some extent forfeited its right to represent the people, through a poor performance record over decades. The owner now desires to amend the power of attorney he signed and gave, to make it conditional on his consent on major issues!

Great Britain had a 1,000-year history of struggle between the Parliament and the monarch, before it could reach the current stage of democracy, where genuinely the citizen is supreme. Perhaps India got its independence too easily; strangely the struggle in India now appears to be between the citizen and his Parliament—the citizen may not be able to trust his own Parliament fully anymore to represent him! With the growing mismatch between the needs of our politicians and the interests of the people, and given the large levels of venality, vote bank politics and callousness exhibited by the political class, has the time come now to examine the need for a 'referendum' procedure in our constitutional practice?

In the past 60 years or so, a very large number of unresolved problems have continued to persist; many new serious difficulties have cropped up. No doubt issues like poverty, illiteracy, public health have all been victims of poor public policies, and worse implementation; but there are other kinds of issues which have lingered on for decades without a solution. No doubt time is a great healer, and many issues get resolved with efflux of time.

However, there are many other kinds of issues which keep festering, occasionally come to the boil and generally become slowly intractable. For instance, the issue of settling our border with China, or the contours of our relationship with Pakistan, or say how to deal with internal insurgencies—Naxalism or Maoism. These have been with us for decades, flare up to fairly serious proportions from time to time and generally become politicized whenever they surface as an immediate issue. Whereas these should be treated as national problems, with a long-term national strategy and approach, these lend themselves to the buffetings of the politics of the day. Take, for example, the issue of our border with China—there is no question that if we get a reasonable settlement, it is better to settle the border, than to leave it open. However, with our present approach to the issue, every time an incident takes place, it assumes inordinate proportions, becomes a political football, a lot of loose comments are made and we lose strategic momentum. This is a national issue to be tackled as such. However, given the contentious political scenario, with none holding a clear majority in Parliament, postures and positions are taken often for the sake of the politics of the day, with little relevance to its long-term implications.

We may refer to the decision of the Cabinet taken in summer 2013 for the creation of Telengana by bifurcating Andhra Pradesh. This is a major decision, not only affecting the 13 or so crores of Telegus, but also with potential implication for many other states. Note that demand for creating new states is in different stages of intensity in many parts of India. The general policy hitherto had been on creating new states on a 'linguistic' basis. On these grounds, there is no logic in creating the new Telengana state. Indian experience has shown that the quality of administration is 'size-neutral'—the quality of governance is a function of the people in-charge of affairs, rather than the size of the state. It can also be argued that given the increasing venality of our political class, the more distant decision-making is from direct political attention, the cleaner it is likely to be. Be that as it may, it is obvious that the Telengana decision was taken on grounds purely of expediency, from the strategic and tactical perspective of the party in power in Delhi, that is, the Congress Party. The timing of the decision also leads one to suspect that the creation of Telengana is related to the political fortunes of the Congress Party in the forthcoming elections. We may note that this decision, apart from anything else, is likely to intensify demands for new states in many locations in India.

We will have a piquant situation if the undivided Andhra legislature votes against a bifurcation! What will Delhi do? Will the Centre 'overrule' the state legislature? By now it is well known that politicians/members of legislatures do not represent the views of the constituencies; they act only in pure self-interest. Is not this an appropriate issue for a referendum in Andhra, whether a separate state should be created or not? Should this decision be taken only in Delhi by politicians who have no particular concern about the citizens of Andhra, and have an interest only in their own electoral fortunes? Given the current mismatch between the interest of the citizens and that of the legislature, which purports to represent him (citizen), the introduction of a 'referendum' procedure for certain types of important decisions seems to be highly desirable.

In 1984 Rajiv Gandhi came to power with a massive majority. At that time many of the long standing problems that the country faced like our international borders, many major domestic inter-state and state-Centre issues and others could have been sorted out, if there was some statesmanship available in the scenery. The fact is that Rajiv had no comprehension of the nature of the issues to be tackled, and how to go about it. This is the danger of having tyros in-charge of complex operations. However, that opportunity was lost, the goodwill and assets which Rajiv brought into his office were scattered away with careless abandon with both hands in a very short time, and we were back to square one. Now, sadly, we are in a position where no serious large national issue can be settled by consensus, and without a debilitating fracture in Parliament. This is where the device of a 'referendum' could come in handy. The most fractious issues, where consensus cannot be obtained due to political posturing, can be brought to the people from time to time to get the issue finally settled. After all, in a democracy, the citizens are the final arbiters—the Parliament is only a convenient way to represent their views and positions. While national sovereignty vests with Parliament, the citizen is supreme in a democracy—when he decides by majority vote, that should be final. There is a strong case for introducing a referendum procedure in our political process.

None need fear that the induction of a referendum process will lead the country into a constant 'election mode'. We could have a referendum on selected issues, say, at the time of every general election, and perhaps a mini-referendum on urgent matters once in-between the main elections, coinciding with state elections. It should not be difficult to work out the details, nor should it add significantly, if at all, to election expenses.

It can be nobody's case that our electoral processes and functioning of elected bodies are not in need of major reforms. Surely it is time to examine electoral reforms in a holistic way, through the appointment of a credible commission to consider in depth some of the issues mentioned here (and many other related ones). Many old recommendations have been gathering dust – none in authority seems interested in pursuing any reforms.

This is not likely, as our politicians are quite happy with the status quo, and the people are powerless—a strange democracy indeed!

***

The past history of performance of Joint Parliamentary Committees (JPCs) to investigate major events in the country and to recommend remedial measures has been sub-optimal, to say the least. One can recall the four or five previous JPCs, which were built as mountains but turned out to be mole-hills. The Bofors or Harshad Mehta JPCs produced nothing worthwhile, they were merely political exercises in making a grand show of major activity, with no serious action intended. The JPC on the 2-G scam is going the same way as the three key witnesses, who were closest to the final decision-making, have steadfastly been prevented from tendering their evidence—contrary to the first principles of any investigation. In this continuing saga, one sees further failure in our Parliament to do the obviously right thing—to hide behind narrow technicalities, using brute political majority, to thwart the uncovering of truth. Parliament's reputation has taken a further beating and the public is now seeing how openly it is being hoodwinked.

The JPC on the 2-G scam has concluded its inglorious existence. As expected, we have now an insipid, vacuous report (sharply divided), with little substance or punch, delivered without credibility, and consigning the real issues to limbo.

Two developments (summer 2013) need to be noted. The main accused in the 2-G case, previous telecom minister A. Raja had formally asked to depose before the JPC. The JPC, in its wisdom, denied his request and the Chairman of the JPC advised him to send a 'written deposition', if he so desired (it has been reported that Raja indeed has since sent a 15-page 'deposition' in writing to the JPC). The ostensible reason why Raja cannot depose was that he is an accused in a criminal case, and that it would be 'inappropriate' for him to be 'examined' by the JPC. At other times, the 'reason' trotted out was that calling him as a witness may entail asking all previous telecom ministers to depose before the JPC.

Both so-called 'reasons' appear to be hogwash. Firstly, a Member of Parliament can always make a statement in Parliament, whether being an under-trial or not. The Parliament and the judiciary are separate fora—there is no reason why an individual cannot engage or be engaged with both. Raja is not a convict, at present he is merely charge-sheeted. It is common practice that even convicts have interacted with Parliament and been allowed to be present on special occasions. Raja can be examined under Section 313 of the Cr.PC by the trial court, with no reference to the proceedings in JPC. Raja is squarely in the radar for the 2-G scam—if earlier telecom ministers need to be called to provide information, so be it; they should be called.

New information has recently emerged in the public domain that the details of all decisions, including those relating to policy and implementation, were known in the PMO, were analysed there thoroughly and that all concerned were in the loop. Similarly, a detailed internal government memo, mentioning the major developments relating to the scam (including the strong notings in the finance ministry arguing for market-related pricing), going to the extent that the then finance minister could have prevented the loss, has been in existence. In fact this paper purports to prepare a 'common' inter-departmental position on the 2-G matter. Can this not be interpreted as tampering with evidence and influencing witnesses, which possibly is another criminal act? A detailed analysis by a then senior officer in the finance ministry was quietly sidelined and that person shunted out, allegedly being deprived of a prestigious foreign posting.

It is astonishing that the three individuals who know most about the scam, two of whom have offered to give their versions of what happened, have not been asked to depose. The logic of Section 311 of the Cr.PC clearly applies—anyone who has information on the subject should be called to provide evidence. If the three are not called to provide information, there is the danger that the proceedings may be seen as a charade or farce.

Should not Parliament find out how such a humongous failure of governance took place? The JPC may not be a court of law, to award punishment to wrong doers and enforce the law; however it has a larger role to play—its duty is to find out the circumstances under which such massive failure took place, how the system was subverted—and make proposals on how to improve the system. How can this task even start, if there is refusal by the JPC to ascertain the basic facts from the people who know most about it? A refusal to look at the whole truth can be seen as a betrayal of the purpose for which it was set up.

***

It can be recalled that there was a petition against P. Chidambaram's election from Sivaganga constituency in Tamil Nadu on the issue of alleged electoral malpractices, in particular of tampering with electronic voting machines (EVMs), during the elections in 2009. This was nearly five years back; the new elections are due in months and there is still no verdict from the court whether the election was valid or not. As soon as the present Parliament is dissolved prior to the general elections, one presumes that the petition against Chidambaram will lapse. This is not fair either to him or to the public at large. In all possible likelihood, there was no serious malpractice. In that event, there ought to be a declaration by an appropriate authority that the election process was fully valid. On the other hand, it is possible that there were malpractices, unlikely but possible. It is unjust to the nation to allow a person to hold a high office in the country dealing with Home and Finance, and then to declare that he was there without legitimacy. Either way there clearly ought to be a better method to decide the legitimacy of membership to the House within months rather than letting the issue fall by default.

I recall that when I was posted in Geneva in the late 1980s, I heard about the fodder case, and inquiries against Lalu Yadav in Bihar. The other day, in summer 2013, one saw in the newspapers that proceedings are on, and very recently he has been convivted in one case (autumn 2013). This really is an issue that concerns our justice administration, rather than a legislator. However, it is unfortunately a fact that rich, famous and influential people can get away with dilatory tactics and avoid facing real charges for decades. For instance, actor Salman Khan has managed delays for at least one decade on two very specific charges, without the matter actually reaching the trial phase. A large number of MPs/legislators are able to manipulate the system to ensure that the cases against them rarely advance.

With politicians having so much influence through their offices on public welfare, clearly there is need to fast-track issues which could have a bearing on their continuation in office or as members of a legislative body. While this issue does not directly relate to the executive, rather more to the judiciary, perhaps some thinking is required to see how a satisfactory arrangement to determine legitimacy can be ensured.

How effective has Parliament been? Do we need one?

Many have raised the question as to what is the real contribution made by Parliament in the process of governance. As one of the three major pillars of the Constitution, does it carry its share of the burden of governance? Firstly, Parliament is a place where important facts relating to the nation are recounted, specific actions or activities of the executive are questioned and facts elicited to keep the executive on its toes. Towards this we have the Question Hour, where 'inconvenient' questions demand credible, truthful answers. I really do not recall any information newly available to the public through the medium of the Question Hour, over the past six decades. On the contrary, the ten-year old Right to Information Act has produced much more information and facts relating to the executive than decades of Question Hour.

The other important purpose of Parliament is for major national issues to be debated and the perspectives and points of view of the political parties to emerge facilitating a citizen to take an informed view on public issues. This role is now being effectively done on television. Every evening, on every channel, parties express their views on national issues ad nauseam. I have not recently known of anyone who turns to Parliament to find out what a political party thinks on a particular issue. Ironically, many parties take a position outside and inside Parliament on a particular issue, but vote on a contrary manner when the time comes—this tendency to hoodwink the public is mentioned elsewhere.

The third major function of Parliament is enacting laws. In this context, much lament has been heard in the past couple of years about the opposition 'obstructing' the work of Parliament by denying a debate. The government of the day has blamed the opposition for lack of progress on reforms, and non-enactment of important legislations, due to obstructionist tactics, not allowing the Houses to function. This is totally absurd. Firstly, during the past two years, the Parliament functioned about 66 per cent of its total work schedule. Surely, it would not have achieved much more by functioning for, say, 90 per cent of its capacity. Secondly, in 2010 or so, 12 Acts were passed in Parliament within the space of eight minutes. That is all it really takes for an Act to be passed, if the government of the day wishes to impose its rude majority.

In summer 2013, the UPA government brought in the Food Security Ordinance, about a month before the scheduled monsoon session, which as per the Constitution, has to be confirmed in the following session. This was clear contempt of the concept of debate in Parliament and the sanctity of its functioning. The government had been in power for nine years so there was no tearing urgency, or emergency need for an Ordinance on this subject. In the monsoon session, which was getting stalled due to many other issues, the question was raised as to what the government would do in case it was unable to pass the relevant legislation. Astonishingly, the spokesman of the Congress Party, on a television debate (NDTV 18 August 2013) openly stated that it was the prerogative of the ruling party that it could bring an Ordinance at any time. If the Ordinance was not confirmed in the monsoon session, it would wait for the session to be over, at which time the Ordinance would lapse as per the Constitution. He then aggressively added 'we will then re-promulgate the Ordinance the very next day after the session lapsed'. Can there be greater contempt for the concept of Parliament from the ruling party? Can there be greater proof to establish that debates and discussions are redundant in Parliament and that the ruling party will rule with or without Parliament.

Parliament is the repository of the sovereignty of the nation; it is the highest temple of democracy in the country. We have seen earlier how over the decades the priests have desecrated this hallowed institution. Of the major pillars of the Constitution, it is really the legislature (at the Centre and in the states) which is the weakest link – nearly non-functional in performance over time. Let us imagine a scenario where the Parliament (or state legislature) meets only once a year for two or three days, passes a vote of confidence on the executive (alternately dismisses the executive through a vote), passes a clutch of laws by vote and does nothing else. Would this scenario in any way reduce or impinge on the quality of governance as we have it today? Will the people notice any difference? Is the Parliament in effect irrelevant for India except for periodically renewing the mandate of the government in power? Sadly, this appears to be the case. Any country, where the Parliament and parliamentarians appear to be objects of ridicule or pity, or are seen to be brazen, is in trouble. The situation is surely in need of an effective remedy. It is for parliamentarians of different colours to ponder this issue, and see how they can bring credibility back to this highest institution. If this is not done seriously, one could question the future of democracy in the country with much anxiety.

11

THE CBI NEEDS FIXING (ALSO HOW IT TRIED TO 'FIX' ME)

Ou sont les scammes d'antan—with apologies to Joseph Heller

That the CBI (Central Bureau of Investigation) has been a handmaiden of the government in power is well known in all inside circles. Most outsiders also suspect that this is so, without having definite knowledge or information about it. The senior echelons of the central government, in particular the prime minister and his office, and the party in power treat the CBI as an instrument of governance—to suspend a 'Damocles Sword' over persons who could be potential allies or enemies, and dangle it with appropriate finesse at the right time to meet short-term and long-term needs; as also to critically alter the pace, substance and direction of investigations into alleged wrong-doings by those in authority or opposed to it. If in the early stages of investigation critical documents are allowed to be destroyed, 'disappeared' or handled strategically—also evidence 'planted' judiciously where appropriate—these can impact the progress of the investigation in a definitive way. This can be used to 'kill' a case or create a suspicion where none is possible or open a case and keep it hanging to ensure continuing support. All of these with infinite variations, are deadly games that are played all the time.

I can recount in broad detail, a CBI case that was registered against me, its circumstances, contours, motivations and its objectives, and its progress. Since, as far as I know, the case has not been formally closed, friends have advised me not to talk about it openly. I am not young any more, I have had the matter with me for more than a decade now. I think that the time has now come to bring out the facts as I know them, state them to a degree of detail, so that an example of how CBI functions can be illustrated. All elements central to CBI's character are illustrated in this episode, in microcosm.

In early January 1998, the finance ministry, in its internal notings had expressed apprehensions about shortfall in wheat production in the country. In a series of notes between 6.1.1998 and 9.1.1998, with contributions from the then head of the economic section, and the Chief Economic Advisor (who later became planning minister), it was said that it was 'inevitable' to go for the import of one million tonnes of wheat, in view of the potential shortfall in production, consequent reduction in food procurement quantum, and therefore potential impact on prices. This had the approval of the finance minister, who sent the file to the Cabinet Secretary (myself), for his views. I quickly consulted the Agriculture Secretary and Food Secretary, and replied that as of that date there was no need to panic, that we could wait for some more time before deciding on import; that since the Cabinet Committee on Prices (CCP) had not met for some time, should not an early meeting be called to discuss the issue. The finance minister asked for the meeting on 19.1.1998—on that date the latest estimates of wheat availability were seen to be even lower than what was predicted earlier. Immediately following the CCP, at the same venue, the finance minister asked the assembled ministers to stay, the Additional Secretary in the Cabinet Secretariat apart from me being the only officials present. In a short meeting, the finance minister indicated that there was no option in these circumstances but to immediately order the import of one million tonnes; this should be done very quietly, without a formal announcement so that there was no impact on world prices.

Accordingly, a note was prepared on the basis of this meeting of the Cabinet Committee on Prices, approved by the then food minister and the then finance minister, who chaired the meeting. This was sent for information/approval of the prime minister, which was given with his signatures. Based on this, the Cabinet Secretary constituted a committee consisting of the Food Secretary, Agriculture Secretary and Chairman STC to take further action to conclude the imports, without undue publicity, and on the best possible terms. A second meeting of CCP was held on 26.2.1998 on the initiative of the finance minister, where after a full review, the five ministers present ordered an additional import of one million tonnes (making a total of two million tonnes). The minutes were approved by the food minister and the finance minister (who indicated on the file in his own words that this should be approved 'today' itself in view of the urgency), and the proposal was approved in writing by the then prime minister. During this period, at least five operational meetings were held under the chairmanship of the prime minister, on issues relating to details. A number of meetings were held to handle operational issues by the Committee chaired by the Food Secretary, and including the Agriculture Secretary and the Chairman STC. I demitted office on 31 March 1998 and had no idea what happened thereafter. I recall that the file was also sent to the new Prime Minister, Vajpayee, for his perusal, soon after he assumed office—he was kept informed of the decision to import.

When questions arose later, prompted by vested interests, about the need and justification for the imports, the then food minister (of the new NDA government, which was not in power at the time the imports were approved) made a statement in June 1998 on the floor of the House, fully justifying the imports, mentioning that it was a considered 'government' decision, that the imports were necessitated due to reports of imbalance between production and demand, due to shortfall in procurement and consequent potential impact on prices. Taking into account the needs of reserves, he fully justified the decision inter-alia stating that the best prices were obtained, all aspects of quality and purity attended to and declaring that the government's decision was in the 'best interests' of the nation. Thereafter, at some time the CAG had gone extensively into the details of this case, and came to the categorical conclusion, rare for the CAG, that all procedures were followed fully in the government decision-making process and that the imports were justified.

This was the background; I had forgotten all about it, when much later, in 2001, while playing golf one day, I got a phone call from my sister about a newspaper report, headlining that the ex-Cabinet Secretary, naming me, is a CBI accused, in the 'wheat scam'! I had no clue about any of this and spent the next few days trying to understand what was happening. I could not get through to the CBI Director, nor any senior official in CBI. Nobody could furnish any information to me except that the CBI had flashed my name as an 'accused', registered an FIR against me, the then Food Secretary, the then Chairman STC, and 'others unknown'.

I have given the broad details of the background. Right or wrong, the decision to import was formally taken by the government. I believe that it was the correct decision. Even if it can be opined that it was incorrect, it was in the province of the central government to take this decision, and this was done lawfully, with proper procedure, well documented and with the repeated approval of the highest levels of government. It was preposterous to name me as an accused. If any wrong-doing was suspected, the FIR should have included the names of the then food minister, the then finance minister, two other ministers including the late Murosoli Maran, as well as the prime minister, who had seen and approved the matter not once but at least five times, and also Vajpayee who had approved the imports ex-post facto after the decision; also the then finance secretary (Montek Ahluwalia), who had opined that the import was inevitable; so also the food minister in Vajpayee's government who had made a 3-page statement in Parliament unambiguously and categorically supporting the decision. Since the matter had been reported to the Gujral Cabinet twice, perhaps every member in that Cabinet also should have been named in the FIR. The Cabinet Secretary, Cabinet Committees and the Cabinet routinely take hundreds of decisions every month on important issues—should we have an FIR, CBI inquiry, potential arrests, bail etc. against all these functionaries for taking everyday decisions, which one may agree with or not?

Why did the CBI pursue the matter, lodge the FIR, convert it into a charge-sheet, in the face of the facts I have mentioned here, in well-recorded documentation? Did some person, someone senior in authority, ask the CBI to 'fix' the ex-Cabinet Secretary? Because it was expedient to commence a fraudulent case against him, to ensure that he is placed on the defensive, for him to be seen by civil society as 'corrupt', as an 'accused', and cripple him so that he is not to be considered for any advisory or other role in government circles and to be made an 'untouchable' by government .

I have a shrewd, indeed definite, idea as to who wanted this to happen, and how it was orchestrated. Clearly 'directions' or 'suggestions' or 'advice' or 'gentle hints' were given to the top brass in the CBI to 'fix' Subramanian, and keep him out of 'circulation'. The then Director of CBI who had seen the papers thoroughly, had noted strongly in the CBI files that this matter should be closed forthwith. However, after his departure, at a subsequent informal meeting (I have strong reasons to believe that the meeting did take place, though without minutes), it was 'directed' to revive the matter—presumably a look at the notesheet of the CBI would bear this out—the 'resurrection' of the case would coincide, soon after the new Director's arrival, when another Joint Director was made in-charge of the investigation. The formal concurrence to ask the CBI to investigate was given by the Department of Food. A look at the internal noting (which I had a chance to do) will make it abundantly clear that the person in-charge asked for the inquiry, when none was warranted. Clearly high-level footwork, on an informal plane had resulted in the attempt to 'frame' me. I should add that these shenanigans are not at all unusual. Framing innocent people is as regularly practiced as deliberately allowing wrong-doers to escape, as is clever bye-passing of clear evidence—these are standard games being played from the top.

The point I stress now is how, with no evidence or even basis whatever, can one start treating someone as an accused, level a charge against him and let him find his own devices to defend himself? Meanwhile he is out of circulation from any public activity for a decade or two. The eminent lawyer that I consulted, who had worked in government in a very senior advisory capacity earlier, and who knew the CBI and its actions well, warned me that he would not put it past the CBI to 'plant' evidence, that I should be 'careful'— though I did not know how I should go about doing that—surely, I am now violating that well-meaning advice!

Two curious sidelights on this episode need to be mentioned, which cannot even now be deemed to be completely finished. Much later, when P. Chidambaram, the then finance minister wanted to see the papers, I met him at his residence in Chennai late one evening. The brilliant lawyer that he is, he quickly perused the papers and pronounced that no court in the world can take this matter against me beyond the first hearing, when on the first sight of the facts, the case will be thrown out, with strictures against the CBI. I quipped to him, only half-jokingly, 'If I go to jail for one year for this "offence", you will go to jail for 10 years, for your part in this crime!' The other curious element was that even though the then Agriculture Secretary, who I know to be an honest man, was not named in the FIR, even though he was very much part of the 'wheat import scam'. Could this be explained because he was the Cabinet Secretary when the CBI was 'directed' to go after me and therefore the CBI followed instructions, but dutifully left out the Cabinet Secretary of the time since there was no directive from the top to 'fix' him!

I lost track of the matter of the 'wheat import scam' after March 1998. The actual import orders were finalized by STC, sometime in the second half of 1998, well after I had retired. I believe the imports actually started in 1999. Even today, in summer 2013, I have no clear idea if the case is hanging somewhere or the other, or it is finally closed against me. As one has seen in so many other instances, a CBI case is a like a trap-door—a one-way valve—the case opens, but is shut only with the demise of the accused, a few decades thereafter!

***

This narrative also brings into focus the question of permitting inquiry agencies to mount investigations on senior government servants, with respect to decisions that they take in the course of their official duties. Very correctly, the principle of the 'single directive' or 'prior' approval before launching an investigation is a necessary safeguard to protect against reckless attacks by investigating agencies. This is not to suggest that all government servants are 'dyed in the wool', or are 'pure as the driven snow'. There are many black sheep, even at very senior levels, alas alarmingly on the increase. A reckless regime of launching investigations against senior civil servants will merely, in the current venal scenario, result in prosecutions launched against honest civil servants, with the crooks going scot-free. Clearly a balance has to be found without doing away with the 'prior approval' requirement, which is heavily abused and misused by the government by denying or never giving approval. The variant adopted should be that if within a specified period, say three months, the approval is not given, the investigating agency can proceed as if approval has been given; in other words, the default mode is one of approval, in case it is not denied within three months. However, it is to be noted that the root cause in my case was vendetta from a senior government functionary. The initiative was not taken by the investigating agency, its fault was that in its eagerness to please those in authority, it was quite willing to create an investigation where none was warranted. When the CBI Director of the period handed over charge on retirement, he called me on the phone to tell me that he had seen the papers carefully and that no case was made, hinting that the CBI move was under external pressure. To this day, 13 years later, I have not heard if the case has been finally closed, whether I am still an 'accused' or what my status is.

***

That the CBI has been a handmaiden of the central government for decades is well known. Without questioning the agency's competence, there are genuine, well founded apprehensions about its neutrality—propensity to accelerate or soft-pedal, be amenable for command performances and generally be an instrument for wielding power. Despite enormous pressure, the demand for giving independence to the CBI will not be conceded by the ruling party. It is their governance instrument of the last resort. This was also the sticking issue which broke the Lok Pal legislation—the government was willing to incur national wrath to protect its 'interests'.

With the 'caged parrot' comment of the Supreme Court, the stage is now set for wide ranging reforms of the CBI, to provide it 'autonomy' in investigations. A large proportion of the cases under the CBI's purview involves the interests of government and its functionaries directly. The caveat in the Vineet Narain pronouncement by the Supreme Court in 1997 specifically directed the state not to intervene in any manner in the course of investigation—a reiteration of the dictum that the 'suspect' should not be allowed to dictate the direction of investigation. Flagrant violations of this principle have now prompted the apex court to insist on the functional autonomy of CBI.

Happily, the nature of the debate has now changed from 'whether' to 'how' the CBI needs to be reformed. With this basic shift, the technical aspects of CBI reforms need not pose too many difficulties. A squirming government will now attempt to find a cosmetic, eyewash solution to 'free' the CBI while actually retaining effective operational control—this should not be allowed to happen.

Enactment of laws is not in the province of the apex court. However, pronouncing the principles to govern the functioning of CBI is well within its purview. No doubt the Parliament may or may not observe the court's directive to pass a 'CBI Law'; however, till this is done, the directives of the court will have the force of law as 'continuing mandamus'.

No agency can be allowed to have total independence or autonomy, without checks and balances—in Indian conditions, this will mean the creation of an uncontrollable monster. If an independent neutral Lok Pal were in position, it would have been ideal for him to oversee the functioning of CBI. Ironically, it was mainly on the question of the 'independence' of CBI that the Lok Pal could not be established. In the absence of Lok Pal, the second best alternative could be to link the CBI to be 'guided' and 'supervised' by a special committee chaired by the Chief Vigilance Commissioner, consisting of four or five members with experience of the judiciary/administration, selected on merit in a bi-partisan manner. This is one model—others could be examined—but a neutral mechanism to watch over the overall functioning of the CBI will be essential to be put in place. This will replace the umbilical cord relationship with the government that the CBI suffers from at present. This interim arrangement can be in place till an independent Lok Pal is created.

CBI's 'control' by the government basically is on four different platforms—finance, personnel, investigation and access to expertise.

It is obvious that full autonomy in investigations needs to be given to the agency. No functionary, however powerful, will have the right to interfere in the details of any investigation. There are many government agencies which perform autonomously while being financed by government like CAG, CVC and EC. This issue should pose no operational difficulty. The CBI's budget can be under the purview of the CVC Special Committee. This oversight committee can also deal with CBI's operational issues requiring additional expertise of different sorts on an ad-hoc basis, from time to time.

The issue of personnel for the CBI requires some thought. The selection for the Director and top three levels of the organization ought to be in the domain of the CVC supervisory committee, referred to earlier. A judicious mix consisting of a permanent CBI cadre, along with deputationists from the police cadres, as well as expertise from outside, can be designed to ensure optimal results. We need to remember that the CBI is an efficient agency—its malaise stems from government interests dictating the course of individual cases.

A view has been expressed that the agency can function under direct parliamentary oversight, on the analogy of the experience in other countries. This will not work in Indian conditions. Imagine a scenario where a possible list of members of such a parliamentary committee includes, say, A. Raja, P.K. Bansal, Bangaru Laxman, Raja Bhayya, P.C. Chacko—so many other names can be mentioned—Gresham's law will come into play! Like in other cases of statutory and constitutional bodies, an annual report on the functioning of the CBI could be placed for debate in Parliament—the control of the House ought not to extend beyond this. We have seen the havoc caused by executive 'oversight'; the higher judiciary cannot be burdened with monitoring every case or investigation. We need to find our own unique Indian model.

My memory goes back to 1997, when the Supreme Court was hearing the now famous Vineet Narain PIL, in which the apex court intervened under Article 32 of the Constitution to issue directions relating to the independence of the CBI in an investigation. I recall the furious discussion we used to have in the chamber of then Prime Minister I. K. Gujral, usually with only the Advocate General Ashok Desai, and Principal Secretary N.N. Vohra present.

In essence, Chief Justice Verma had understood the CBI extremely well, and was keen to 'uncage the parrot', even at that time. As Cabinet Secretary, I probably did not have enough understanding of the need for loosening government's control over the CBI. I argued strongly against the apex court's vision that ultimately public interest would be served better by affording freedom of investigation to the agency. Desai clearly was caught between the strong position of the court asking for reforms, and the government's position that we should not give up our 'grip' on the agency. While Gujral was fully neutral, I recall that N.N.Vohra—who had authored earlier the insightful 'Politician-Mafia' Report, was leaning towards a higher degree of reforms. In retrospect, I now realize how wrong I was. If I had strongly argued to support Ashok Desai, the freedom now sought to be given to the CBI would have been a reality in 1997. In the event, due to the intervention of Ashok Desai on behalf of the government (half-hearted as it was), the Verma judgment did not go the whole hog. It is still a major landmark judgment, emphasizing the role of the Supreme Court in interpreting the Constitution, and the first judgment of the apex court to stress the citizens' fundamental right when it comes into conflict with the role of the executive. This was the first judgment that recognized that the executive does not have full, complete and exclusive jurisdiction over all administrative matters where public interest is involved. Indeed Verma's judgment is a 'continuing mandamus', the current basis for defining CBI's role with respect to an investigation. I need to record that I was instrumental in delaying the process of administrative reforms, due to insufficient comprehension. I hope there will be an opportunity in this life to atone for it meaningfully.

I need to make a reference to the Bofors papers. In a breakthrough by the CBI, the Government of Switzerland had agreed to provide the full banking statements of certain key accounts related to the Bofors issue. Obviously this was explosive, deadly material. The papers in original were to be given in a sealed cover to our representatives in Bern, to be hand-carried to Delhi. The then CBI Director Joginder Singh was extremely worried that someone may tamper with the originals, or there could be physical loss of the same, deliberately or otherwise. Looking at the great significance of these papers he came to me for help. It was arranged that a Joint Secretary from the Government of India would accompany him and a senior representative of CBI, to go to Bern to collect the papers. I spoke to our Ambassador in Bern, directed that apart from the original, two extra copies be prepared, in the personal presence of the Ambassador himself and the CBI/government representative, to be sealed then and there, with a clear notation from these high officials certifying their authenticity. The arrangement was that one set would be retained in the safe personal custody of the Ambassador, one sealed set would be retained in the Cabinet Secretary's office in Delhi, with the original going to CBI headquarters. The intention was to pre-empt any over-writing, tampering or destruction of these vital documents. Joginder carried a large trunk for this purpose, but apprehending possible mischief, sent the CBI copy (ostensibly the only original) through a courier, and brought the empty trunk to India ostentatiously! In the event, the procedure went without a hitch. I presume a sealed copy is still in our Embassy. I am reasonably sure another sealed set is available somewhere in the bowels of the Cabinet Secretariat—at least one hopes so. I made it a point to ensure that none in Bern or in Delhi would be privy to the detailed accounts given to us, arising from this break-through. It is entirely another matter that the case was totally botched up thereafter. Evidence available on a platter was not used and a clear-cut case failed. It can only be in India that no one needs to take responsibility.

As noted, the CBI on its own is quite efficient. However, nearly in every state, the vigilance directorates and the 'crime branch' exemplify inefficiency, coupled with total political control. After the 'reform' of the CBI, the next major step needs to address the issue of revamp and autonomy of these state agencies.

Our Constitution makers did not account for the level of venality of our political class; they did not provide the necessary checks and balances. Bringing in a Lok Pal will meet this gap. Till this materializes, the way forward is to enact a CBI law and hand over the supervisory powers to an ad-hoc committee, chosen with care to ensure independence, quality and experience. While details of what has been suggested could vary, it is time to un-cage the parrot—this is what public interest demands.

12

HOW CAN GOVERNMENT ENSURE IMPROVED DELIVERY OF SERVICES?

Genius is 1% inspiration and 99% perspiration—Thomas Edison

Governance is 5% policy, 95% implementation—anon

In the mid-1960s I was the District Magistrate in Ghazipur, east of Varanasi. River Gomti shrunk in the summer months before the monsoons, leaving a large dry sloping area on its banks on either side. We wanted to conduct an experiment on whether the water from the perennial river could be lifted through diesel pumps for irrigation of the adjacent land. An elaborate experiment was mounted, and the District Magistrate was invited for the commencement of the innovation, about 20 miles away from the district headquarters. It was about 5 pm; I reached the site, the hose-pipes were set up, the motor primed, and the engines spurted to life. One could see the flat canvas pipes suddenly filling up with water and the wave of expansion carrying it on through the upward slope of the banks, as we clapped. Suddenly we saw an unexpected phenomenon—the hose-pipe suffered hundreds of punctures, water squirted out in a shower all along the hose-pipe line, and spread out about 10 feet on either side, as we suddenly saw a spectacle—hundreds of snakes, mostly small, wriggling out of the dry banks! Clearly they thought that monsoons had arrived and hibernation was over. Spectacular as the scene was, we also realized that all the water was being ejected out of the hose-pipe, due to a manufacturing defect in the canvas. It took me many years to realize that what I had seen that day was the standard norm in all our development projects; all the money gets leaked out in the delivery process—the intended ultimate beneficiary gets cheated.

Manifestation of the problem

Rajiv Gandhi had once remarked that only 16 per cent of the subsidies reached target persons. This may appear to be an exaggeration, but he may not be far off the mark. Sometime back, I asked a District Development Officer in Tamil Nadu, a relative of mine, her assessment of the quantum of leakages. Her answer, after some careful thought, was that about 30 per cent actually reached the intended beneficiary—and this in a relatively better administered state. I recently came across an instance of distribution of surplus village land during the 1990s to specified categories of villagers—480 persons had been allotted land; only 70 (15 per cent), on detailed inquiry were in the eligible category. That the problem is widespread, and that the quantum of leakage is of a very high order, is quite evident.

The problem is not new. When I was a District Magistrate in Uttar Pradesh in the 1960s, I was asked by the Directorate of Handlooms to distribute handloom marketing subsidies to 27 societies in the district. When I sent teams of senior officers to do a physical verification, I got the report that none of them actually existed in the address/village indicated—these were ghost societies! When I returned the money to the Director with my comments to have his societies verified better, I got a surly reply that thanks to my bull-headedness, the financial 'allocation' had lapsed!

A senior colleague of mine in the 1970s, who was then Regional Food Controller in Meerut, caught his deputy red-handed who was directly and personally involved in serious irregularities in purchase of wheat during procurement. He sent a detailed report to the government, with facts, statements of witnesses and other necessary particulars. For his pain, the Deputy RFC implicated his boss with false allegations, used his political clout to have an inquiry against him. Ultimately in disgust, my friend had to leave the service, seeking voluntary retirement. These kinds of lessons are administered early to All India Service officers, who are fairly quick to learn. If they persist in serious field inspections, they may put their careers at risk! The Durga Nagpal case in summer 2013 brings out clearly the jeopardy of officials who are serious in discharging their duties.

Governance consists of 95 per cent 'implementation'. This of course includes proper project conception, planning, appropriate technology, coordination among the implementing agencies, as well as sound project management—these are prerequisites for success. This chapter does not address those issues, instead it addresses the sad Indian reality of corruption and leakage of intended funds through intermediaries who are involved in implementation.

Analysis of the issue

The problem is well known, to any insider—politician or bureaucrat. Indeed it is a grand conspiracy that no one will interfere with the enormous leakages that take place. All that the managers directly concerned need is reasonably authentic looking records and documentation—none at any level then takes the trouble to verify their accuracy. There has been colossal failure of the system to identify the problem, and to take remedial measures. It is the continuing failure ultimately of the Planning Commission not to formally recognize this well known problem, build it into their programmes and to find remedies while planning for development. Its attitude is that 'implementation is in the hands of the states'. Any plan that does not take into account implementation aspects is hardly likely to succeed.

At the local block/thana/tehsil level, the reality in every state in India is generally as mentioned below, with honourable exceptions, and with only minor state-to-state variations. Some common features include: there is no ethic that corruption is bad, only 'do not get caught'; a strong local nexus between the various local functionaries to ensure that falsification of documents and records relating to beneficiaries will not be exposed; and a strong local political influence of the local politician in all aspects of distribution of subsidies etc.—he would be a major beneficiary in each case.

Any BDO/tehsildar/thanedar will be transferred instantly if he interferes in the process. If he persists, he will be harassed, false charges will be made against him till he becomes 'pliant' and 'realizes' that overall it is lucrative, less worrisome and more comfortable to play ball. The 'intelligent' thing to do is to collaborate.

The local MLA, notionally a policymaker, would have a direct hand in influencing and directing his own political assistants in his own beat. All local contractors, working on various projects need to be in the 'good books' of the local MLA or MP, doing all that is required. This underlines the importance of winning elections, since it is a lucrative business. All contenders invest heavily and the victor can take home manifold dividends. There is lack of real supervision by any higher official authority. Any person who indulges in serious verifications is likely to get summarily transferred, at the least.

At the district level, the district supervising officer (the District Magistrate and other departmental chiefs) would not generally take the trouble to do any detailed field verification. Many departmental district heads, especially in the engineering and some other departments, are directly in the chain of 'beneficiaries' and may not have the moral authority to take their subordinate to task. It is not infrequent that during his tehsil visits, the District Magistrate would ask the rhetorical question of his tehsildar 'Is everything alright?' He would be annoyed if any actual problems were brought to his attention!

The District Magistrate is always looking to the state headquarters. His focus is on handling VIP visits and responding to queries, comments and recommendations from the state's political and bureaucratic bosses, as also keeping the elected representatives in his district in good humour. The one or two special informal representatives of the chief minister in the district also deserve to be looked after.

Attention to ensuring correct implementation of field programmes is low in the DM's list of priorities. This is because of a variety of reasons, which include the time and energy required to deal with state headquarters and VIP movements, and possibility of immediate transfer if he 'meddles' in field implementation issues to the discomfort of this or that important person. For him, recognition by the people who count in the state headquarters is the key. The system does not reward him for better implementation, nor punish him for poor implementation in his district. The same applies more or less to all other district level functionaries like the Superintendent of Police, District Medical Officer, District Irrigation Engineer, etc. With this lack of accountability, is there any surprise that implementation is poor.

***

During the British days, one of the main functions of the District Magistrate or Collector was to tour extensively and intensively within the district and make surprise inspections to see the quality of field work. Increasingly this practice has nearly come to an end in post-independent India. Apart from the pressure of headquarters work, most DMs would not have the power to take punitive action against officials found errant during field visits. The political pressures he would have to face if he took action would be enormous—he could rapidly be turned from accuser to accused. The local politicians would jump to the support of the accused local official—in this scenario the state political/ bureaucratic leadership would not support him. In short, there is no atmosphere conducive to ensuring good delivery of services at the district level.

At the state headquarters level, quality implementation is the least of the worries of the political or bureaucratic chiefs. This is of nobody's concern—failure is not punishable—attention to quality is not rewarded. With rampant departmentalization, the ministries compete for funds and prominence. Quality is not the issue; there is no accountability of the department for poor implementation. So long as the paper work is complete its accuracy is of no major concern. The pipelines frequently reach up to the political head of each department (ministers, through independent informal channels), that there is no incentive for senior officials to take undue interest in quality, and in the process annoying their own political bosses. Recall that the chief minister of Andhra Pradesh, in early September 2013, while welcoming the latest batch of IAS probationers to the state, practically told them, nearly in these words, 'not to concern themselves with political corruption, as this money comes back to society; instead to focus on bureaucratic and business corruption'—as unbelievably absurd a statement as can be from a person in authority; astonishingly the media at large, (except Headlines Today) did not pick it up, and highlight the unsuitability of such a person to be the chief executive of a state.

At the Government of India level, the mantra is that implementation is an issue with the state governments—so certification of spending is the only document to be looked at. Quality of implementation has never been questioned by any ministry for fear of raising political hackles. The tendency is only to look at macro figures, not micro processes. Equally, departmentalization and turf issues are rampant at the Government of India level. Thus, for example, elements of micro-nutrition required by every growing child is looked after by a number of ministries—health, food, child and women welfare, education, industrial policy and promotion etc. There is generally no coordinated look at the needs of the beneficiary; the only concern is the point of view of the ministry or department concerned. The Government of India is satisfied with 'utilization certificates' furnished by state governments; they definitely do not want to get involved in the authenticity or correctness of these.

Audit and accountability

The accounts are maintained at the block/tehsil level and audited there by the state audit teams. Very little field verification takes place, for reasons mentioned earlier. These are verified/countersigned at district levels and certified at state levels, without much ado. This suits all concerned. The department head at the state level accepts the district level audit without question. There are no special teams to verify the quality of implementation and to touch base with the beneficiaries, for reasons mentioned earlier. The Government of India's departments accept the macro expenditure certificates of the state governments, without question. Any questions only relate to balancing the books—not quality.

The Comptroller and Auditor General (CAG) does not go into the quality of a local audit, particularly to verify on a regular or test basis the accuracy linking programme with beneficiaries (once I came across a batch of Indian Audit & Accounts Service (IA&AS) officers, who would man senior positions of the CAG in course of time, during their 'Bharat darshan' tour. I checked as to how much time they spent on familiarization with field implementation and delivery issues at the village or block level. The astonishing answer was that there is no provision for this; implementation is a state issue). CAG only audits the macro picture presented by the states. There is no provision for independent field verification at the state or central levels. There are no dedicated inspection teams to make surprise visits and identify wrong-doing. In some cases where the wrong doers are identified, the procedure for punitive action is so flabby and cumbersome that it is more often than not, not resorted to. It is not uncommon that 'inconvenient' persons are frequently deliberately targeted with departmental action.

Macro issues in quality of implementation

There is lack of accountability at all levels with no systematic means of re-verifying accuracy of field records and field documentation. Rampant political interference and direct linkages with implementation issues are the norm. The District Magistrate has no time for quality of implementation—he does not get credit in this regard, nor does he get punished for neglect.

In addition, there is rampant departmentalization. A plethora of field officials visiting each village, from different departments, without effective coordination is standard practice. Administration is not left alone to implement; there is active participation by the local political machinery, which is motivated and has strong interests in pursuing party interests, concurrently with sharing the financial benefits.

There is no credible availability of personal identification cards to facilitate test checking. Panchayats frequently function on political lines and their functionaries partake of the proceeds. All these are compounded with the fact that there is no work ethic or moral stigma attached to corruption—low level corruption has existed from the Moghul and British days and is taken as a way of life.

At the field/district level, the head of every department is well aware of where the weaknesses are, specifically the areas where corruption is strongly prevalent. He should be made directly responsible for corruption and non-performance within his specific areas. Likewise, the head of the department in the secretariat would have a very clear idea as to where the weak spots are. He should be made accountable for lapses in integrity within his agency. Unless constructive responsibility is enforced, the system is not likely to respond. If there is active involvement in improved implementation by the head of the department agency, the likelihood of quality, clean implementation is much higher.

Possible approach to solutions

There is complete satisfaction and strong vested interests within the machinery (at local, district, state and central levels) to maintain the status quo. While quality of implementation has been talked about in many fora for many decades, simply put 'there is no political will', for obvious reasons.

Use of available technology (smart cards, fingerprints, etc.) should be resorted to the maximum possible extent. A number of technical improvements can be introduced including creating special verification teams at all district/state/central levels, cutting across different departments, reporting to a central agency on the quality of implementation. Past experience has shown that there is little appetite for this approach, also probably because the testing machinery itself has a tendency to get immersed in the same practices. Thus, independent cross-verification teams at vertical levels will also have to be created.

Very carefully selected NGOs should be encouraged to do independent field verifications and report to a suitable independent authority. There are many issues in this regard, which need to be carefully sorted out. Private sector chartered accountants could be inducted into the process in a careful manner, to support CAG.

CAG itself should accept quality field implementation as its responsibility to ensure verification in a suitable manner.

There is correct and proper recognition that we need to bring 'technology' to address issues of reach and field level delivery problems. A variety of initiatives are on hand—the Aadhar card, BPL card, payment for MNREGA through bank accounts etc. All of these in principle are extremely welcome. However, ushered in as they are by 'experts' from Delhi, whose knowledge of rural India is very limited, it is necessary to inject a strong note of caution while embarking on such innovations on a massive scale in a diverse and vast country like India.

The fact is that ours is an essentially illiterate or at best semi-illiterate community, especially in rural areas. The women-folk are highly susceptible to frauds and other forms of exploitation. Giving numbers for operating bank accounts may be an excellent idea in the case of anonymous Swiss bank accounts, but needs to be approached with caution in rural areas. As is well known, there are strong mafias which have got established in the distribution of food grains, kerosene and other ration items through large-scale misrepresentation and fraud. Great care needs to be taken that in the process of bringing technology to rural areas, new mafias do not spring up, so well thought out safeguards are required.

I have discussed with many field authorities in different states the problems of providing a 'final' identity. The potential for large-scale collusion and fraud exists so these should be built into the equation. In the case of MNREGA, the richest beneficiaries have been Panchayat secretaries—the fastest growing new-millionaire category in India. For every 'enrolment', a hefty fee is required. With numbered accounts in rural areas in the names of elderly men and women, many illiterate, the possibility of benami transactions will increase manifold, so major safeguards are required.

It is a tragedy in India that a citizen requires a very large number of 'cards', now fashionably called 'smart cards'. As Chief Secretary in Uttar Pradesh in the early 1990s, I had seen the problem of illegal entry into India along the Nepal border; most border inhabitants on either side could not establish a clear identity if they were Indian or foreign. I recall that I had made a strong recommendation at that time that a single identity card, which will establish citizenship along with other entitlements, with a unique number, much like the US Social Security number, should be issued in a nation-wide programme, eliminating the need for multiple cards for different identity purposes. This was not accepted by the home ministry. Today's technology was not available then but the idea was not pursued. However, the real reason may have been administrative lethargy, a tendency not to embark on anything new. PAN, election and ration cards are among the plethora of cards required by a citizen. From what I have seen of the debate in Delhi, I have no confidence that anyone has a full and comprehensive understanding of the issues involved. The approach seems to be highly theoretical. This is the surest way to create new mafias operating in rural areas.

This should not be seen as inhibiting the reach of technology in rural areas to aid the quality of delivery. On the contrary, it is imperative to use relevant technology to improve the ground situation, taking into account the levels of high illiteracy, as well as poor power availability in rural areas, coupled with the genius of our field machinery to convert every situation into a personally lucrative one. This is an area where we should hasten, but slowly, deliberately and cautiously with enough safeguards. No deadlines relating to national or state elections should come in the way of a sound programme to be established in this regard. In sum, we need technology inducted into our delivery systems, desperately so. However, we should do this with careful deliberation and due speed.

Conclusion

Implementing projects, programmes and schemes at the field level is of primary importance in governance. High quality in conception and formulation of schemes, taking into account local conditions is of course of prime necessity. Proper project management, vertical and horizontal coordination for optimal performance, supported by suitable technology are no doubt keys to success. In addition, the following issues relating to leakages in project funds need to be addressed.

Leakages of a very high order are now recognized to be a serious matter. The high interest in a political office at the district level can be traced as one of the root causes, as well a major consequence. Leakages are now well entrenched in the system, and it will require enormous political will to improve delivery systems. Such will, despite protestations at all levels, does not seem to exist. The administrative machinery for implementation has to be totally segregated from political influences. This is easier said than done, but is a primary prerequisite for a clean delivery system.

Stable tenures in state government posts for District Magistrates and departmental officers is essential as a first step for improving the quality of implementation. Senior field officers and heads of field departments should be held directly responsible and accountable for clean and efficient functioning of the work of various departments.

A strong independent machinery to credibly test-check implementation, to rapidly process punitive action and provide a climate for impartial but swift action without political intervention is a *sine qua non*. The processes should be structured such that judicial intervention cannot be resorted to too readily and casually. An independent verification mechanism involving NGOs and private chartered accountants needs to be introduced.

Technology is now available to facilitate implementation issues. Widespread use of IT in all aspects of implementation, including at the field level would be essential. Smart cards and personal identification mechanisms will certainly help. This is the way of the future.

***

In my 40 years of directly working in public affairs, I am sad to relate that I have not seen even one senior politician or anyone in political authority, whose agenda included tackling corruption—this is the astonishing reality. I am not suggesting that all politicians are venal; there are a few, indeed a very few, sadly not too many, who are quite honest and straight-forward. However, they will not raise their voice too strongly against corruption, as it may adversely affect their political fortunes. Corruption everywhere, particularly at policy and headquarters levels, is very debilitating; it is not merely a side-transaction between the bribe-giver and bribe-taker, it affects the entire system adversely and is a prime contributor to poor governance. If the political will to tackle corruption is available, this is one malaise that can be addressed with a high degree of success in a relatively short time. We may have to wait for the top-most leader, whose primary agenda includes elimination or severe reduction of corruption levels, to give relief to the country.

13

DIRECTION OF CIVIL SERVICE REFORMS?

Something is rotten in the State of Denmark—Hamlet

Who will rid me of this meddlesome priest?—Henry II

In any democracy, a politician and a civil servant are seen as 'necessary evil'. A political executive reflects the mood, requirements and demands of the public, and is primarily responsible for forming policy and legislation. A civil servant implements the mandate given to him or her, within the ambit of the Constitution. Because of their training and experience, the higher civil services also have a key advisory role in forming policy though the final decision is that of the political executive. In most democracies, interference by the political executive on purely implementation issues is negligible, indeed non-existent, except in India and in some other developing countries. The political and permanent executives work together as partners in governance; the relationship is not one of master-and-man, it is rather one of elder and younger brothers.

Since independence, politicians and bureaucrats, whose close interaction is essential for good administration, have worked in an atmosphere of camaraderie and near equality, even though their official relationship is of a formal nature. However, progressively in recent decades, a 'durbar' atmosphere has sadly crept in, with the permanent executive forced to assume a subordinate, indeed a subservient role, with the political executive, untrammelled by checks and balances slowly assuming a 'master of all' posture. This surely is not conducive for sound governance in a democracy.

***

In April 2013 I had the privilege of being invited to the official reception given by the Cabinet Secretary on the occasion of Civil Services Day. This day is dedicated to issues relating to the administrative apparatus, and was brought into the national calendar about seven or eight years back with a seminar on issues relating to administration being the central item, followed by the reception. Hitherto the reception was held on the lawns of the Cabinet Secretary's official residence with invitations going out to all ministers, service chiefs, heads of all national departments, as well as secretaries to the government. The occasion also has hitherto been graced by the presence of the president, the vice-president and the prime minister. This was an occasion for the very high dignitaries, as well as the various ministers present to mingle and discuss matters in an informal manner with the officers present, including the various secretaries. It hitherto had a social reception atmosphere for informal exchange of pleasantries and the odd official matter.

The April 2013 reception was held in the Grand Ball Room of Ashoka Hotel. The format was astonishingly different—a veritable royal durbar atmosphere was created with the president, vice-president and the prime minister seated on 'thrones' on an elevated stage; with the ministers seated, presumably in a 'pecking order' arrangement below the stage, at a distance of 15-yards or so. The next row was taken up by senior heads of the bureaucracy, many outranking mere secretaries to the government, seated again in terms of assumed or adopted seniority, with the general audience or spectators this time constituted by the secretaries to the government—thronging the perimeters of the large hall. I had a sudden feeling that I was in the court of Sultan Mehmet in Ankara, or Emperor Babur at Diwan-e-Khas. It was a disgusting spectacle. Elsewhere I have written about a visit to Manila, to Marcos's 'Court' in his Palace, where the dictator was sitting on a high throne on an oblong table, one-and-half-feet higher than his cabinet ministers on one side, and us visitors on the other side of the table; his secretaries and ambassadors were kept standing throughout the one-hour meeting. The parallel could not have been more striking! The three dignitaries on the elevated podium, separated from the hoi polloi, appeared like three Alexander Selkirks, each one a monarch of all that he surveyed. One wonders if they were comfortable on the joint throne; perhaps in modern times, the only comparison could be with the durbar of the dictator of DPRK. One wonders how an Obama or a Merkel or Cameron, clearly from 'democracies' inferior to that practiced in India, would have conducted themselves on a similar occasion. It is even likely that they may have seen an opportunity to mingle with the 'minions' and the 'civil slaves' (note the elevation from the civil servant status).

***

In the decades after independence, the political and official executive were seen as two sides of the same coin, the political side being the 'head' and the bureaucracy being the 'tail'—inferior, but with close relations to the political leadership. Even till ten years back, in every large meeting or conference, one used to find the secretary sitting next to the minister, even when the event included chief ministers sitting in the hall. In public, and also largely in private official environs, the secretary was given a degree of courtesy, treated with some dignity and given the feeling that he was part of the team though it was quite clear as to who the boss was. Things started changing in the 1980s and 1990s, but even then the Chief Secretary/Secretary in the states, as well as secretaries at the Centre deserved and got near-human consideration from the minister. There is this story of Lalu Yadav as chief minister of Bihar talking to his Chief Secretary and secretaries with a mouthful of paan (betelnut); While addressing them at close quarters, particles of the red paan-paste would be spat out, frequently lodging on the face of the secretary concerned. Very soon, a Chief Secretary, when subjected to this punishment, told Lalu that he desired to be transferred immediately, as he was not used to being spat at. Many long-suffering, pusillanimous officers were too meek to take up the issue and had to resort to using a disinfectant to wash their faces every day! In recent television pictures of large conferences, conducted by the PM or the home minister, I have noted with much concern that senior-most officers are consigned to the second row, a clear announcement to the public that the politicians are in command and are the masters and the officials are merely vassals.

The painful durbar I witnessed on Civil Services Day is now clear confirmation as to how our highest level of administration treats the senior-most bureaucrats. The system now demands total, complete and abject compliance not only to written and spoken orders; it now also shows that the civil servants are treated as an inferior-breed, have to be 'shown their place' and have to function as 'hey-you' boys. Clearly Mughal days are back in Delhi; this happened in states a decade or two back. Sadly this uncivilized exhibition of power by the elected authority is now nakedly on display in Delhi. Sadly again, one may argue, probably with some justification, that civil servants have brought this situation on themselves!

***

One of the more difficult functions I had to perform during my term as Cabinet Secretary related to selection of panels for the post of Joint Secretary, Additional Secretary and Secretary to the Government of India. The selection was done by a small committee chaired by the Cabinet Secretary including two other senior-most secretaries. The thumb rule was that only 50 per cent would be promoted to the Joint Secretary (JS) level from those eligible; and again from the JS to Additional Secretary level only 50 per cent would be identified to be on the panel; likewise from the level of Additional Secretary to Secretary. Accordingly contrary to popular belief, usually only one in about 15 entrants to the IAS in a particular batch would find place on the 'secretaries panel'. The selection task was not usually easy, since in many states there is the practice of giving liberal and generous annual CR entries while in some others, senior officers were more parsimonious in this regard. It was not unusual that in a group of 30, nearly 25 would have 'outstanding' annual entries over the previous ten years. The task would be to identify the 15 among these who deserved to move to the next level; a thankless task indeed. The other side of the coin is that it is so easy to give/receive a 'lukewarm' annual remark; that is enough to destroy the career of an otherwise excellent officer permanently—such is the tragedy of the hierarchical system. Such power is used ruthlessly by the political executive. Contrary to what one hears these days, I never had a single intervention from any political level relating to empanelment, 'suggesting' that a particular person should be looked into 'sympathetically', barring one instance.

I had mentioned in an earlier book that Deve Gowda had asked me only for one favour—I had not elaborated on this at that time. He had called me to his residence, told me with great distress that he was being harassed by a particular senior politician, who would not leave him alone for a moment, insisting that a lady officer who had been overlooked for promotion, must be promoted. The prime minister told me plaintively that he was unable to concentrate on official matters, as the politician insisted on repeating this point from morning till night every day. Deve Gowda asked me whether I could look into this matter, in 'public interest'! I saw the file; though the earlier supersession was probably justified, she had already been overlooked for a year. At the next meeting, I took up her case, and 'in public interest' she was 'elevated' to the post of Additional Secretary. Within six months, she was at my throat, this time insisting that her batchmates were being made secretaries, while she was still only Additional Secretary. As a matter of fact, even if I wanted to help, I could not, since the rules clearly insisted on a minimum tenure of one year in the post she was holding before she could be considered. No explanation was acceptable or adequate; her anger had no bounds. A couple of months later at a lunch party in the Cabinet Secretary's lawns (probably the annual Diwali party), her husband who was in a small group with me, while passing by quietly and surreptitiously gave a karate-type elbow punch on my kidney; it was done so casually; more than 200 persons were present but nobody would believe that the Cabinet Secretary could be assaulted in his own house. I couldn't even speak to anybody about it but I had to go to a doctor to get his advice on the severe pain that persisted for a few days to ensure that there was no serious damage. The doctor surmised that I had been lucky; the blow was only a glancing one, but could have been more serious. Who said that the Cabinet Secretary's post is not a dangerous one!

In one instance, a person with whom I used to play golf on a daily basis, did not make it to the secretaries panel. The final call was with me, which I took with a heavy heart. One had to dissociate one's personal relationships while doing this onerous job. Another officer from my cadre (UP), whom I had known closely, practically since he joined the service, did not make it. Many who knew both of us were quite surprised. The officer who was personally very close to me earlier, would not even greet me and would look the other way, when we happened to meet—for me a heavy price to pay indeed.

I have one regret in the matter of selection to panels for higher posts and I have had much heart-ache in this regard. This related to an officer called PSA Sundaram, who was Additional Secretary in the Personnel Department. He was the key man in the Government of India who pioneered the concepts of Right to Information, Transparency, Citizens' Charter, etc. While so much credit was taken by so many NGOs and social organizations much later, perhaps not totally unjustified, the real credit for initiating these reforms should go to Sundaram. I gave him full support at my level, and as mentioned in another chapter, major pioneering significant work of great importance was done during 1996–97. To my eternal regret, when the final secretaries panel was drawn up that year, when the other two members of the committee were either negative or lukewarm about him, as chairman I did not put my foot down. I did not overrule them and ensure that Sundaram was on the panel. I do not know how this lapse occurred on my part. If there is one regret that I have regarding my posting as Cabinet Secretary, it is that I did not do the right thing in this regard. The gentleman to the core that Sundaram was, he did not come and meet me thereafter, and very soon sought repatriation to his state from where he resigned to join academia. I needed to come out with a clean breast to expiate my soul—I still relive this lapse with pain.

***

Let me illustrate the overall decline in the ability of the higher civil services to coordinate policy and implementation issues through a personal experience. During 2005–06, my good friend and colleague B.K. Chaturvedi was the Cabinet Secretary to the Government of India. He was a dedicated and committed civil servant, reputed to be a good officer. During that period, I happened to be the Chairman of the Micro-nutrient International India (MI) Trust with headquarters in Ottawa, with their largest country-programme in India. MI's vision was to generate awareness relating to micro-nutrient deficiencies and popularize solutions to improve nutrition levels in India; note that the nutrition levels in India are among the lowest in the world. Since these issues at the Government of India level relate to six or seven ministries—health, women and child welfare, labour, education, industry, rural development and the Planning Commission etc., many of the Government of India programmes lose efficacy due to poor coordination of intervention policies. Nearly every programme has an inter-departmental character; and with rampant turf wars, the quality of programme implementation is the casualty, as in so many other fields. With actual field implementation entrusted to state governments, where the problems are even worse, the situation is compounded, leading to very poor delivery. Chaturvedi, having held the position of Secretary, Women and Child Welfare Department at the Centre, had full understanding of nutrition and micro-nutrient issues and was fully committed to the need for enhancing the quality of intervention, and lay greater stress on coordinated programmes. Incidentally he was conferred with the high national honour of 'Padma Bhushan' after his retirement. I approached Chaturvedi to help out, bring the different agencies in the Government of India into 'mission mode' to provide coordinated direction, advice and guidance to the states. Chaturvedi was enthusiastic and understood the need for this.

On my prompting, he held at least four, or perhaps five 'coordination' meetings, all of which were attended by senior representatives of the departments concerned, attended by myself and the senior staff of MI. During these meetings, everything was very pleasant, every ministry nodded to every suggestion and all agreed that concerted action was required. The Planning Commission representative was also on board and generally agreed that it will be useful to ensure a coordinated mechanism for superior programme implementation. However, after a 6-month process, nothing moved. To put it crudely, the Cabinet Secretary was ineffective in ensuring an improved operational mechanism. I did my best to prod him and to push him. However, it became painfully obvious that he carried no clout with the various ministries, which all functioned as independent 'empires'. While part of this failure could be due to the personal inability of the chief, due to his mildness to push his way through, the larger point is that the system has tended to become loose and structurally uncoordinated with each element tending to take its own direction. Clearly the system has deteriorated enough only to respond effectively to a political command from the top, which normally is given only for a hefty quid-pro-quo.

There would have been absolutely no political opposition to improving coordination on this issue. The failure of the attempt is entirely to be laid at the door of the higher bureaucracy. We need to multiply this instance with failures in the power, steel, coal, highways, infrastructure sectors etc., referred to elsewhere. The system has now lost the ability to coordinate effectively. Higher level posts of Cabinet Secretary, Secretary, whose job has little technical content except coordination, have lost their 'teeth' and 'bite'; they only occupy chairs. Clearly there has been a sharp deterioration in the ability of the higher bureaucracy to coordinate policy formulation and programme implementation. The instance mentioned by me is not an isolated one. I see the same phenomenon now in state governments also. Civil servants, while correctly blaming the political executive for poor governance, need also to look in the mirror—they don't look, as a class, so beautiful.

This incident is not directed at Chaturvedi, who is as good and pleasant a person as is possible to know. It is a lament about the fall in the efficacy of the implementation machinery. Again, I hope I have not lost a friend.

***

Some time in the early 1990s, Vohra, the then Home Secretary prepared his famous report, referring to 'The Nexus between the Politician and the Mafia'. This was a seminal contribution to the analysis of administrative collapse in India, identifying for the first time that mafias of different shapes, sizes and character operate in every district, in every field of government work. Thus, in petroleum distribution, forest, land, mining—the list can go on and on, the government directly or indirectly encourages the formation of mafias for mutual benefit of the politician and the mafiosi. Most ministers encourage such arrangements; the malaise in the system stems from the top. Any number of district magistrates, SPs and other departmental field officials have been threatened, assaulted and in many instances even killed by one mafia or the other. This is an all-India phenomenon, known to every politician and administrator. The country saw this in the recent cases of Durga Nagpal and Khemka—however, these represent only two of thousands of such cases which are rampant in every district and in every secretariat in every state in India. Transfer, premature postings out, adverse annual performance entries and departmental proceedings are the instruments used to bring the 'errant' official, who merely does his duty, to heel. Sooner or later, a local mafia chieftain will go to the minister or chief minister, complaining against an official—'will you get rid of this meddlesome priest'? Presto, the transfer orders will issue the next day. This is the anatomy of the failure of governance.

***

It is widely acknowledged, including by the Government of India, that poor implementation and weak oversight have distorted and reduced the effectiveness of government policies and programmes. Thus, the Second Administrative Reforms Commission (ARC) acknowledged that 'governance is admittedly the weak link in our quest for prosperity and equity. Elimination of corruption is not only a moral imperative but an economic necessity for a nation aspiring to catch up with the rest of the world. Improved governance in the form of non-expropriation, contract enforcement, and decrease in bureaucratic delays and corruption can raise the GDP growth rate significantly' (Second ARC, Fourth Report on Ethics in Governance). The 10th Five Year Plan noted that 'People's welfare is largely determined by the efficiency of public delivery mechanisms. The best plan cannot compensate for poor implementation; accountability and efficiency in all our public institutions is the key to unlocking the potential of our country and to sustained social development.'

Since the implementation of government policies and programmes is the responsibility of the permanent civil service, the lacunae and fault lines in this regard can be traced back directly to a civil servant. While proximate causes can always be identified for under-performance in individual sectors, the consistent failure to achieve targets, across the board and over time, clearly indicates that the basic problem underpinning each failure lies in implementation arising out of poor governance. Any attempt to improve the administration must therefore necessarily focus on the micro-issue of civil service reform, which in turn affects all aspects of service delivery and implementation. Addressing this fundamental issue will directly and significantly improve the quality of delivery and implementation of government policies and programmes, and thus the quality of governance in general.

As a backdrop, to understand the nature of the issues it will be useful to recall comments made by two distinguished former civil servants. T.N. Seshan, who had in the 1990s made a major contribution to reforming the electoral process, commented in effect 'senior civil servants are like sophisticated call girls'. His distinguished successor J.M. Lyngdoh, in another context commented to the effect 'politicians are a growing cancer in society'. At first sight these comments appear crude and tasteless. However, in public affairs we need to go deeper into the substance of what has been said, rather than to base reactions on issues on the surface. Seshan's comments, surely while not being universally true, certainly have more than a grain of truth that senior civil servants have often been intellectually dishonest. This is something right from the ICS days that few will seriously dispute—perhaps many bent slightly to accommodate, some more than others. However, increasingly, in recent years senior officials tend to crawl, when they did not even have to bend; sadly today many senior civil servants are not averse to cash-corruption—a situation unheard of even a decade back. One makes this statement with some trepidation, with profuse apologies to a very large number of extremely able, ramrod straight, morally, financially, ethically and intellectually incorruptible officers.

Our system is blessed with a large number of such people; indeed our system still functions with reasonable efficiency, perhaps only thanks to such people at decision-making levels.

One need not be unduly apologetic about endorsing Lyngdoh's comments, however tasteless they may be. Politicians are never liked anywhere in the world. In India they give ample opportunity to be intensely disliked and deservedly so. I may have liked Lyngdoh to have phrased his comments a little more elegantly (thank goodness, he has always been true to himself); on balance I fully agree with him. We need to look at the issue of administrative reforms also in the background of Seshan and Lyngdoh's comments.

***

Public administration in the country is compromised by: (a) corruption within the administration, (b) a 'spoils system' that has meant an irresolute system of tenure, transfers and promotions, (c) political interference and pressure on civil servants, leading to wrongful decisions manifestly not in public interest and engendering both corruption and the 'spoils system'; and finally, (d) the non-implementation of consistently recommended reforms for institutional change. These interlocking phenomena have been repeatedly addressed by numerous government-appointed committees as being primarily responsible for the poor state of governance in India. There is an urgent need to make a civil servant accountable, sensitive and responsive. If this is achieved there will be across-the-spectrum benefits. Since civil servants at all levels, from the village to the block/thana to the tehsil, district and state secretariat are directly in touch with citizens, an improvement in the quality of their output will surely positively impact the overall quality of governance. It is imperative to address the micro-causes which have rendered a civil servant apathetic, callous, ineffective and corrupt. There is an urgent need to usher reforms.

The Union Government as well as the state governments have set up numerous committees which have studied and made recommendations with regard to administrative and civil service reforms. All these committees have concurred on the need to protect a civil servant from extraneous pressures and make him/her independent so that he/she can render his/her considered advice freely and frankly, without fear or favour. Although many of the recommendations of these committees have been broadly similar, they have not been accepted or implemented. In this context, the Second Administrative Reforms Commission (2006–08) noted:

> *'It is ironical that there has been no sincere attempt to restructure the Civil Service although more than six hundred Committees and Commissions have looked into different aspects of public administration in the country…The Indian reform effort has been unfailingly conservative, with limited impact…Civil service reform in India has neither enhanced the efficiency nor the accountability of the Civil Service in any meaningful manner.'*

In 1997, the Conference of Chief Ministers of States, convened by the Government of India to consider ways of improving performance and integrity of the public service, recommended that the existing rules and regulations should be amended within six months to enable exemplary prosecution and removal of corrupt officials and the weeding out of staff of doubtful integrity and that at the same time, a suitable mechanism should be worked out to reward employees who do good work. Since then, the Central Fifth Pay Commission (1997), the Geethakrishnan Commission on Expenditure Reforms (2001), the Surinder Nath Committee on Performance Evaluation (2003), the P.C. Hota Committee on Civil Service Reform (2004) and the Second Administrative Reforms Commission (2006–08) have all produced voluminous reports and recommendations on the subject.

The Hota Committee and the Santhanam Committee have recognized corruption as a major problem in the civil services; that much of the deterioration in the standards of probity and accountability within the civil services can be traced to the practice of issuing and acting on verbal instructions or oral orders which are not recorded. It should be made incumbent on every civil servant to formally record all such instructions/directions/ orders/suggestions pertaining to the discharge of his/her official duties which he/she receives, not only from his/her administrative superiors but also from political authorities, legislators, commercial and business interests and other persons/quarters having an interest or wielding influence.

The Santhanam Committee (1962) specifically recommended that '…there should be a system of keeping some sort of record of all interviews granted to accredited representatives…'. Rule 3(3) of the All India Services Rules 1968 specifically mandates that the direction 'of the official superior shall ordinarily be in writing. Where the issue of oral direction becomes unavoidable, the official superior shall confirm it in writing immediately thereafter.' This practice needs to be expanded and a written record kept of all orders, instructions, directions and suggestions from whichever quarters they emanate to ensure accountability in the functioning of civil servants.

Preserving the integrity, fearlessness and independence of a civil servant is an essential condition of the parliamentary system of government. While forming government policy is the legitimate task of a minister, a civil servant is expected to advise him/her freely, frankly and fearlessly at the stage of forming policy. The minister in turn should not interfere in purely service matters such as postings and transfers and should avoid any departures from the approved policies to accommodate individual cases as a result of political or other considerations.

At present, the system of transfers, postings, promotions, disciplinary and other personnel matters pertaining to the higher civil services are ad-hoc and non-transparent. Transfers are often used as instruments of reward and punishment, with officials being frequently transferred on the whims and caprices, as well as the personal needs, of local politicians and other vested interests. Officers, especially those in the All India Services serving in state governments, have no stability or security of tenure. Changes in government invariably lead to new rounds of transfers as the incoming group of political leaders seeks to reward supporters and put its 'own' staff in key positions. Moreover, the 'transfer industry' is backed by entrenched and powerful vested interests, as frequent transfers generate huge amounts of black money for corrupt officials and politicians, both directly and indirectly.

To give an idea of the number of transfers that take place relating to IAS officers in state governments, the figures relating to one state (Uttar Pradesh) are now indicated, based on RTI information. It should be noted that the position is roughly the same in most states, with minor differences. In Uttar Pradesh, which has an effective total of about 700 All India Service officers (IAS, IPS and Forest Service), the Mayawati regime effected 578 transfers in 1995, 777 in 1997, 970 in 2002 and 1,000 in 2007. The corresponding figures for the Mulayam Singh government, during the 18-month regime in 2008 were 321 IAS officers and 493 IPS officers. This paints the whole picture in its full tragedy for governance; assuming that half the number of officers completed 2-year tenures, the other half had an average of less than 6-months per posting; some probably as low as 3-months. Without referring to the personal inconvenience caused to these officers, imagine the adverse impact on the quality of governance. Ironically, the transfers would all have been ordered 'in public interest'. Before a field officer—a DM or SP or Deputy Conservator of Forest—can get minimum familiarity with his beat or territory, he is transferred out presumably a-la Durga Shakti Nagpal for coming in the way of a crony of the ruling party, or a mafia which is tangoing with the ruling power. This is the anatomy of failure of governance. No more commentary is required on the failure of our political executive to provide reasonable standards of governance.

A rational transfer policy should eliminate the 'transfer industry', do away with politicized transfers, curb the overall incidence of transfers, remove uncertainty and empower officers with a degree of security of tenure in every post and should be seen as being fair, objective and leading to career development. The key element and indeed, the only effective solution, is a guaranteed minimum and fixed tenure for officers of the higher civil services.

The Conference of Chief Ministers (1997) observed that frequent and arbitrary transfers of public servants affects the ability of the system to deliver services effectively to the people. It recommended the constitution of Civil Services Boards in different states presided over by the respective chief secretaries to assist the political executive and streamline the policy of transfers and promotions based on identifiable criteria. Subsequently, some states set up Civil Services or Establishment Boards with the Chief Secretary as the chairman and other senior officials of the state as members. However, as the Hota Committee observed, these boards set up by executive orders in different states failed to inspire confidence as, more often than not, they merely formalized the wishes of their chief ministers in matters of transfer of officials. Therefore, there is a need for establishing such independent, neutral Civil Services Boards, particularly for the states, which will be able to function without outside interference, keeping in view the paramount importance of preserving the integrity, fearlessness and independence of a civil servant. Direct political control or direction in the management of transfers, postings, promotions, inquiries, disciplinary proceedings, rewards and punishments has adversely affected the morale, capability, efficacy and morality of the civil services. These matters need to be de-politicized and entrusted to independent Civil Service Boards, which will closely monitor and ensure accountability at all stages, regulate transfers in a transparent and rational manner, protect honest civil servants, and identify and recommend punishments for those who betray public trust. This can best be achieved by including on the board retired civil servants and outside individuals of eminence and unimpeachable integrity. While the board will function in an advisory capacity to the chief minister, its recommendations should normally be binding; if they are not accepted, a detailed order should be recorded and presented to the concerned legislature.

The powers of transfers for all Class II officers should be with the head of department and not assumed, as is currently the case in many state governments, by secretariat departments acting at the behest of their ministers. The government should deal with transfers of only HODs (heads of departments) and additional HODs, or at the most of Class I officers. The government's role is policymaking and objective impact assessment and ensuring that the transfer policy as laid down is followed in the field offices. In addition to constituting an independent Civil Services Board, the policy should stipulate that transfers should not be ordered as punishment; if an employee is found remiss in his/her duties, he/she should be proceeded against departmentally.

The implementation of civil service reforms and instituting a rational and transparent policy on transfers will go a long way in insulating civil servants from wrongful and extra-legal pressures from the political establishment. In addition, an effort should be made to see that civil servants imbibe core values of integrity, objectivity, merit and excellence which form the basic framework of the permanent civil service.

Based on a PIL filed by 83 retired senior officers from different services, including myself, the Supreme Court in October 2013 gave recognition to the need for minimum tenures, for establishment of Civil Service Boards for recommending transfers and postings, as well as the need for recording of instructions, at the Centre as well as in State Governments. This major step stressing the commitment to the people of India, under Article 32 of the Constitution, enjoins the State to take certain measures to upgrade the quality of governance. With this, the scope of administrative reforms has moved into the judicial/constitutional arena; one hopes that the governments at the Centre and the States take it in the right perspective and proceed to implement the Aplex Court orders in letter and spirit.

Police Reforms

While the term 'administrative reforms' encompasses 'police reforms', it is necessary to mention that there are special features relating to this sector, which need the most urgent attention. Among the various departments directly dealing with the public at large, the police is the most ubiquitous, conspicuous and in a sense, of the highest importance in the context of maintaining a peaceful local environment. Arguably, the police also is the most corrupt department, feared and distrusted by citizens. It is always needed, but is seen as an extortionist, and a department with no concern for the facts of a matter, ready to manufacture its own version quite readily. This is also the force whose cooperation, subjugation, subservience and abject subordination which politicians, both at the field and secretariat levels, need most for their own purposes. Sadly no government at the Centre or in the states has devoted any meaningful attention to the reforms necessary in the police force—all attention has been on providing equipment, raising new forces etc.—all quantitative in nature, with no concern for improving quality that is so vitally essential.

The rot in the system is from the top to the bottom; you name the evil—politicization, corruption, deviation from norms—and this is the norm in every state, only the degree varies. Thus in many states, the chief minister makes it a key point to select an operational Director General (DG) of his own choice, who will play to his personal tune. Towards this, elaborate games are played to identify the most 'suitable' person, even if it means supersession of any number of competent and more able persons senior to the chosen one. The simple expedient of creating 'supernumerary' DG posts, of equal rank and pay, to provide 'berths' is used, most of them with no work to speak of, but designed to technically avoid the charge of supersession. These devices are used to accommodate the person identified by the political chief. One will note that with every change of government in every state, whether or not other incumbents are changed from their posts, the operational DG is invariably changed within days. In return the DG has to play 'ball' with the political chief.

All this relates to the highest levels in the state police force but let us look at the lowest levels, at the thana or the police station. The basic documentation in a police station is the 'General Diary' (GD), the first critical document in every case is the 'FIR'. It is an age-old problem that the General Diary, which is the 'log-book', is kept unfilled for days, and is suitably finally 'adjusted', to accommodate any version that 'requires' to be recorded. Thus, after a riot or a major local incident or a communal commotion, the GD is kept virgin for days and then filled up depending on the 'optimal' version that needs to be brought on record. Likewise, when a person comes in to lodge an FIR, this is not generally done routinely, particularly in rural areas; the FIR is informally 'auctioned'. It is not unusual that a case gets a 180-degree turn at its starting point. Very often it has happened that the lodger of the FIR is recorded as the 'accused' and the person actually charged initially becomes the accuser. These are deadly games routinely played at the thana level, nearly everywhere in India. The primary job of the district supervisory police officers, from the British days, has been to try and ensure the purity of the GD, and proper recording of FIRs—this is the fundamental building block of the police administration, of 'law and order'. The Superintendent of Police (SP) was required to do detailed inspection of every thana to ensure this. This is very similar to the erstwhile requirement that the Collector would inspect every tehsil in detail every year to verify the purity of land records, so vital for peaceful village life.

Alas, these fundamentals have now been totally forgotten. The SP has been marginalized with the postings of Station House Officers (SHOs)—thanedars—now being taken over by a computer in the chief minister's office, operated by a minion working under the direct supervision of the personal secretary to the chief minister, whose main function is to respond to every political impulse emanating from the field, demanding the transfer or reshuffle of an SHO. Thus, the quality of field police administration has been heavily compromised. This declining process has been continuously in operation for decades now. However, the deterioration is now complete and the local political boss, the MLA or his henchman has total and complete command over the functioning of the thana, over the GD and the FIR. No wonder there is near-total collapse of law and order in many parts of India.

Like elsewhere, solutions are possible, if the political will is there. Modern technology is now available, through computers, V-Sat, 3-G, 4-G connectivity and a whole lot of other infrastructure, to ensure that the GD is maintained continuously without break, and a back-up untamperable documentation is centrally available for verification. Likewise, there is no reason why the recording of FIRs with a back-up record cannot be organized through the computer in the thana. These are basic reforms which will transform the police administration, especially in local areas. Alas, nobody is interested in these fundamental shifts in improvement; much like the Lok Pal is not desired by politicians at the Centre, the local political goonda at the thana level will ensure that the computerization of the thana does not take place: who wants to point the gun at the 'golden goose'?

In the late 1990s, I had arranged for computerization of land records, on a pilot basis, in four districts in India—from memory two in Punjab and two in Madhya Pradesh. I had sanctioned that the entire expenditure will be borne by the Centre to get this experiment launched. Naturally there was local resistance from the tehsil staff. In one district, I recall that the computer operators who had to stay in the tehsil town to transcribe the records into the computer, got scared away by finding snakes in their bedrooms repeatedly, allegedly 'planted' by the local tehsildar! The point is that the local officialdom did not want this unwelcome change in their work, indeed their livelihood. Clearly the political leadership did not provide sufficient momentum to ensure the success of this initiative. I do not know whether in the last 20 years or so, land records have actually been computerized or not in most states—this is a fundamental requirement for improved village administration. India provides such services to any number of countries in the world, to provide a digital dimension to all local administrative records. It is ironic that we are unable to do so in our own country. The computerization of thanas is of even greater importance.

The same issues that have been covered earlier with respect to administrative reforms equally apply to the police sector. On an average, many SPs spend less than nine months in their districts. It will be absurd to expect them to perform with great efficiency when they are shifted so readily. Most of them are reluctant to 'fall foul' of the local political goons, or mafia, they look the other way, lest they get transferred overnight. Illegal and improper instructions, issued telephonically from local political henchmen, are the order of the day. Clearly the solutions of having an independent 'Management Board' for the services, security of tenure and amendments in service rules that require that every spoken 'orders' get recorded are key reforms which are absolutely essential. This has been the thrust of the pioneering PIL by Prakash Singh, an ex-DGP of Uttar Pradesh and of a Central Police Force. The apex court has ruled that these reforms need to take place and many states are in 'continuing contempt' of the apex court's orders. In short, police reforms are urgently required. It will be naive to expect improvement in law and order without major police reforms.

Appointments to statutory and constitutional bodies

The ability to appoint persons to high positions, as heads or members of constitutional/statutory bodies and other agencies has hitherto been the prerogative of the government. Appointments to the Election Commission, to the post of CAG or the CVC, as well as institutions like SEBI and Competition Commission contribute to the tone, temper and substance of administration. There is a growing perception, certainly not unfounded, that nominations to head these agencies are heavily loaded, to choose persons who are likely to at least collaborate, if not conspire, to further the interests of the government/party in power. The critical public interest in having neutral persons of high quality and ability to head these agencies is largely a relegated consideration.

In recent years, a Chief Election Commissioner joined the Rajya Sabha as a member of a political party within months of retirement. Another Election Commissioner who rose to become the Chief Election Commissioner had been 'named' by the Shah Commission. The selection of P.J.Thomas as CVC made a mockery of the requirements of legality, commonsense and intellectual integrity. In an earlier era, it was well known that a prime minister did her best and partly succeeded in packing the high courts and the apex court by her chosen nominees.

The situation is even worse in the state governments. The selection for critical posts like Chief Secretary and the Director General of Police are highly coloured exercises to favour chosen individuals who are certain to go well out of their way to conspire with the government in power, to further the latter's ends. It is now normal, standard and an almost invariable practice in nearly every state government, that only favourites will come to positions of significance.

It is little known that in the US every senior executive or judicial appointment has to be approved by the Senate, after a formal open and transparent hearing. The procedure involves a detailed 60-page questionnaire to be answered by the candidate, placed on public record, and questioned on every detail. Postings in India to constitutional and statutory positions are done in a hush-hush manner, often with cynical conspiratorial objectives and procedures. They need to be open, in the public domain and should meet all legitimate criticism. It will only be appropriate if selections to specified constitutional and statutory posts (like CAG, CVC, CEC and some others to be specified) are done only through a mechanism, resulting in unanimity, which includes consultation between the government and the opposition. Even for senior governmental posts in the Centre and in the states, like chief secretaries, DGPs or secretaries in the Centre, we now need sound, ethical, neutral management practices. Sadly we cannot trust our own governments anymore. If such reforms are not ushered in on its own initiative soon, these may have to be thrust upon the government.

14

WHO WANTS CORRUPTION ELIMINATED—EXCEPT THE CITIZEN?

A nation of sheep begets a government of wolves—Ed Murrow

Within a year of my retirement from the post of Cabinet Secretary, I moved to my own apartment in NOIDA. Those were the days when the mobile phone was not yet ubiquitous; I had a landline operated by BSNL, which had STD facility (domestic trunk-call facility). I had to get an International Subscriber Dialling (ISD) facility. I called the local telephone company office, somebody promptly came and spoke to me politely and got the application filled up along with the deposit required. Even though I waited for a week or ten days, the facility did not come through. When I called, somebody again turned up and said that I had not completed 'all' the formalities. I discovered that I was expected to pay a 'facilitation' charge, 'under the table'. I was told that the amount was one पेटी (one 'box'). Curious as I was to know what that meant, it turned out to be ₹10,000 in this context. I had been Cabinet Secretary to the Government of India; I had the option of calling the Telecom Secretary in the Government of India and requesting him to do the needful—in Indian conditions that may have been the prescribed course of action. However, in the circumstances, I felt it was prudent to pay the 'box' and close the chapter. In the event, the son of the telephone inspector was the courier who came to 'collect' the box. My need was great, my son was settling down in the US, and my first grandson had been born, and I had need for regular dialling facility to the US. There is no doubt that I would have got the connection fixed by 'pulling strings', that is, talking to higher authorities, and using 'influence'; which again could be seen as an unethical practice. However, if I had followed this route, I am sure that I would have had continuing operational problems with the phone connection, with regular 'break-downs' and great inconvenience.

Much later, one day I discovered a new bill showing arrears of ₹38,000 for my electricity meter, delivered at my door-step, which included a number of items, including non-fixation of various equipment etc. I took the phone and spoke to the Power Secretary in Lucknow and within a day an inspector turned up at my residence, 'verified' the facts, and the next day gave me a 'revised' bill of ₹11,000. This I paid and closed the matter. How many people in NOIDA have the ability to pick up the phone and speak to the Chief Secretary or the Power Secretary or the Industry Secretary or the Income-tax Commissioner or any of those authorities who wield power? My problem was sorted out in a day but imagine how long it would take an ordinary citizen to sort out this kind of a matter? Probably not too long as he would straightaway call the inspector, 'settle' the matter and go about his other activities. Long ago, sometime in the 1970s, I was in the residence of the then Power Secretary in Lucknow at a party, when the power supply broke down. The Power Secretary promptly called the Chairman, Electricity Board, and peremptorily ordered him to set the matter right—power was restored within 10 minutes. How many people in Uttar Pradesh can call the Chairman of the Board, when they don't get power? In Kanpur, Lucknow, Varanasi—the largest towns in Uttar Pradesh—there is a daily power cut of 10 hours. Can the residents there call the Board's Chairman or Power Secretary to restore power? In rural districts in Uttar Pradesh and in many other states, power is available only for 3–4 hours a day. Can an agriculturist call the chief minister or power minister on the phone, and peremptorily ask for immediate 'restoration' of power? Apparently all systems in India are available only to those who are influential—the others can like it or lump it—they do lump it!

A significant ethical question is involved—is the bribe giver and the bribe-taker equally culpable? Conventional wisdom is that it takes two hands to clap—there will be no bribe taken, if none is given. All of this is true but in practice can one treat the bribe-giver on the same footing as the bribe-taker? There can be no moral, ethical or legal way to condone the actions of the bribe-giver. But does the world consist entirely of bribe-givers and bribe-takers? Is there no role for governance, administration, a sanitized atmosphere for pre-empting bribes or providing an effective, swift, punitive retribution to bribe-takers and givers alike? Imagine the plight of a truck driver who has obtained a job in the Middle East, wanting in a hurry his International driving licence, or a passport as the case may be, without which his major career opportunity will go away. Imagine a student desperately wanting to stay in a particular town for higher education, which he cannot do unless he pays a 'capitation' fee for college entry, without which his whole career can be pre-emptively blighted. Imagine a philanthropist wanting to establish a high quality charity-oriented school or college or hospital, who has to obtain land for the same, which can be done only through a hefty bribe. Are these people committing crimes by paying bribes to get their legitimate objectives achieved? Can they be equated, on the same footing, with persons who demanded and received the illegal gratification? What they have done is clearly unethical and surely illegal, but are there credible extenuating circumstances? Can an outsider, who does not stand in the shoes of these people take the 'holier-than-thou' position that the bribe-giver is as much to blame, that circumstances are not relevant?

In the late 1960s, my father died in Chennai (then called Madras). He had spent most of his working life in Calcutta, and his income-tax returns were filed in the Calcutta circle. I had joined the IAS a few years earlier, and was posted as the District Magistrate in a district in east Uttar Pradesh. It fell on me to obtain 'probate' of his will in the Calcutta high court, complete the wealth tax/estate duty formalities in the income-tax office circle headquarters in Calcutta. As it happened, an income-tax commissioner, wife of a good friend of my late father was in that same office. The audit and finance chief of the company where my father worked in Calcutta also had enormous goodwill for him. All the paper work could be done very quickly. However, despite four or five visits, I could not get the final estate duty clearance and other relevant clearances, much as I tried repeatedly. Finally the income-tax commissioner, a personal well-wisher, advised me to be 'practical', and asked me to meet the supervisor of the estate duty department, so that the matter could be 'closed'. In the interim period of three or four months I had already made four or five trips between Ghazipur, Calcutta and Madras(the last to refer to the papers and produce 'clarifications' and 'copies'—all for the n-th time). She told me that this process could continue for the next few years, till I settled the matter with the office superintendent. These were the circumstances in which I paid a bribe of ₹50,000, to get the final release papers and clearances from the department. Clearly I had violated the law. What I had done was immoral, unethical, a senior officer of the administrative system in India had stooped to the level of violating an elementary law, but what was my option? Is it always the individuals who are to blame for violating the law? Should no responsibility be taken by the system for not creating conditions conducive to expeditious disposal of a citizen's requirements in a proper legitimate honourable manner? How can the system not correct itself but create conditions conducive for massive corruption, and yet blame the bribe-giver as much as the bribe-taker for violation of the law? In my case, every person in the income-tax/wealth tax/estate duty office in Calcutta, from the junior most Class IV employee to the Chief Commissioner, certainly the chairman of the Board and the finance minister, knew exactly what was happening—that no assessee can get his assessment completed without illegal gratification—and yet is it fair to blame each assessee for violating the law in the circumstances? This situation can be multiplied a million times in India, in every single office of the central and state governments, every block, thana and district office, every place where land is registered, licenses given, every point of interaction between a citizen and the state. Every citizen is liable to stand convicted of violation of the law. I cannot think of any businessman who can survive without bribing the electricity, telephone, excise, sales tax, income-tax or any other authority. Each one is a culprit; the bigger the businessman, the larger the crime.

The biggest business magnates in India are the biggest criminals—but hold your thought for a moment—do not convict them, before you convict every prime minister, every chief minister, every finance minister and every parliamentarian and every senior official of the central and state governments. Their crimes, which are often more of omission than of commission, are even larger than those of our businessmen and our citizens. The prime responsibility for making us a nation of criminals will vest with our political class not just for looting the country themselves, which is substantially true, but more for not doing enough to root out corruption at the points of government interaction.

Gunnar Myrdal, in his 'Asian drama' thesis of the 1960s prophesied that 'democracy cannot rein in corruption in India', as Asia is too 'culturally different'. His prognosis about India has turned out to be valid, even though his overall thesis of the inherent instability of Indian democracy has not been proved right, at least as yet! Whereas India is now ranked at a lowly 87 in the International Transparency Index, Hong Kong (13), Korea (39), UAE, Taiwan and Bhutan are all estimated to be much less corrupt than India. Thailand, China and Malaysia are ranked well above India, as are Brazil, South Africa etc. Clearly the problem is not so much cultural or even an issue relating to 'democracy' (Asian or Indian style), it is really India's failure to take appropriate structural, pre-emptive, corrective and punitive action. The Santanam Committee, as early as in the 1960s, had identified the main strands in the Indian corruption scene and had prescribed remedial measures. It is not a coincidence that nearly every major corrective proposed by Santanam has not been implemented till now. The Lok Pal or its equivalent, which was prescribed by Santanam in early 1960s is still not a reality 50 years later. Even after Anna Hazare's movement and other similar outpourings of recent anger, there is no clarity when this will happen. Left to our politicians, we may have to wait another 50 years or more.

***

I recall that decades back when I was working in the Leather Export Promotion Council, a brilliant man called Nagappan (who had studied only up to Class V), was the Chairman of the Council.

He was a leading exporter and had one of the best minds I have come across. One of his favourite sayings was that 'those who work in a honey packaging factory, would surely lick their fingers from time to time'. It was well recognized that officials at the lower level, dealing directly with the public—the patwari, the revenue collection amin, the constable in the thana—all would be appeased or propitiated with a tip or some token of gratitude by a citizen when his work was done. During Mughal times, the local satrap could do whatever he wanted and extract as much as he could, so long as he maintained control, paid tribute to the emperor and was loyal. The same applied to the entire hierarchy. The British brought in the concept of the higher civil services, un-bribable, totally dedicated to their task, who were like Plato's guardians charged with the responsibility of serving the public. They were paid a princely salary in the 19th century (the salary fixed by Cornwallis for a Commissioner in the early 1800s was ₹3,000 which continued for a hundred years). While intellectual dishonesty crept into the higher civil services from the time of independence, financial dishonesty used to be a total rarity in the Indian Administrative Services—the picture has sharply deteriorated in this respect in the past two decades.

Wherever you go, whichever agency you look into at the Centre or at the state level which deals with people's issues (as all do), you will find corruption ranging from very large to extremely large. Sometime in 2012, an amateur found out through his cell phone camera that 36 beat policemen, in different parts of the same town in Maharashtra, on the same day, were caught on camera taking bribes, on an average ranging from ₹200 to ₹500 and in one instance ₹4,000, from passing motorists, motorcyclists and others. Repeat this scenario in every small town, every village, every metro; repeat the search in every office everywhere in India—passport office, ration card office, driving license office; the block, the thana, the tehsil, the collectorate, the list can go on and on—the conclusion is inescapable that petty corruption at the field level is universal. Every District Magistrate, every Superintendent of Police, every field head of the department knows exactly how much and where the corruption is. If they are made responsible, accountable, with the fear of god put in them with their career at stake and interference eliminated, it is a safe bet that corruption levels will come down by 75 per cent (my loose estimate—don't ask me to prove it mathematically) in short order. Clearly everyone concerned is happy—nothing needs to be done—a citizen should learn to pay bribes, cheerfully and happily!

***

Corruption can be categorized in different ways, petty versus grand, transactional versus policy related, political versus administrative, centralized (mafia type) versus decentralized. A form of low level corruption, the equivalent of a 'tip' has existed in India and elsewhere from times immemorial. 'Baksheesh' as a word is still used in Germany and many other countries, as in India, to connote low level corruption, the word probably originating from Turkish. The concept of a bribe relates to when 'rent' is demanded as a right, for a legitimate service supposed to be rendered free of charge. Such corruption at the thana and tehsil levels has been known in India for centuries. With massive development funds flowing to rural areas in the post-independence era, large leakages ingeniously devised, blending with ascendancy of local politics, poor supervision and weak punitive action have encouraged rapid growth of this phenomenon. Thus, a policeman's job is coveted. If a new police recruit at the lowest level has to pay ₹2 or ₹3 lakh for being selected (the prevailing rates about ten years back), one can imagine that he would have to borrow the money from relatives and moneylenders at usurious rates. No wonder his compulsion to repay the loan force him into corrupt practices from the very day he enters the service. In the course of time his blood-thirst increases by the day as it advances to rapacious levels. My taxi driver told me once that his brother was in the short-list for employment as a guard in Delhi Metro and he was asked to make a payment of ₹1.5 lakh for final selection. The malaise has spread far and wide in the citizen-contact segments. The 2-G, Coalgate and other recent scams have abundantly illustrated how corruption is now a normal way of life in our political sector. Politics is now big business; heavy investments are made with a view to getting major returns. Just to illustrate how open the issue is, a Union minister (belonging to the Congress Party) in a television programme in November 2012 categorized the Congress chief of a major state as 'a mafia don—he is a don in mining, liquor and land'. Rajiv Gandhi as prime minister had once commented that only 16 per cent of development funds reach the intended beneficiary indicating the enormity of leakages and the extent of corruption with which a common citizen has to contend.

***

The 1960s and 1970s could be characterized as an era of shortages of cement, steel, heavy chemicals and nearly every item of industrial and common use. The license-permit raj which was the order of the day, allowed large scale rent-seeking by those in power during that period. It was thus in the early 1970s that L.N. Misra, the then commerce minister could openly run an assembly-line operation for issuing import licenses against payment of cash. He was ably assisted and supported by some members of the civil services. In Uttar Pradesh, for example, in the early 1970s, a small-scale industry minister ran a similar operation in his office with an application to be presented in one room for allotment of steel, cash representing the premium for the license to be paid in the next room and the permit to be collected in the adjoining room—in an extremely efficient operation, the total transaction taking not more than ten minutes! It was well known that a Director of Industries in Uttar Pradesh openly replicated the same practice, with the beneficiaries surrendering the permits to a 'consolidating' dalal (middleman/broker), sitting right in the directorate's compound, to bulk the permits into truck-or-rake-loads. The director could function openly with impunity since he ensured that 500 tonnes were reserved for the nominees of the chief minister every month—this was his 'protection money'. The unholy nexus between willing civil servants and politicians had its origins during this era—a major advance from the 'cutting-edge' low level corruption at the tehsil or block or thana levels suffered by a citizen, to institutionalization of transactional corruption.

That large family-owned business houses, relatively few in number, were able to influence policymaking in a significant manner, was well established by the mid-1960s. The advent of Dhirubhai Ambani on the industrial scene in India raised this to a new dimension. Nearly from scratch, within a few years, the Ambani group was able to build a large empire, mainly enabled by ensuring that an extremely friendly and beneficial policy atmosphere was continually created and improved at the occasion of each budget or import/export policy announcement, and in-between. The fine art of building a business empire not so much by work in the field but through a liaison network based in Delhi became established. In due course this included influencing Members of Parliament to lobby effectively in and out of Parliament and ensuring that key ministries in Delhi at the secretariat and political levels were populated by the nominees of a business house became normal practice. The Radia tapes give a clear insight into the way in which business houses apparently have a large say in appointments of ministers and officials, as well as general skulduggery in governance. In the 1990s it was not uncommon to hear of this or that chief minister amassing a fortune of ₹500 crore; by today's opulent standards, this may be low but the seeds were planted in the politico-administrative scene at the Centre and in the states during those days. It was also the era when Indira Gandhi wanted 'committed' civil servants. Initially the commitment referred to policy, then to the party and then to the minister concerned, with whom eventually the civil servant who would cooperate, moved on to become a collaborator, and anon a co-conspirator, sharing a part of the spoils. Politics rapidly became a new lucrative field for making money. Much like when a new petroleum field or gold mine opens up, people entered politics exclusively with the idea of making large fortunes.

Typical of the innovations used was the case of the 'business magic' wrought by the 'aam admi' Robert Vadra, when he earned a cool ₹50 crore, on zero investment in just a couple of months by facilitating the change in 'land use' from 'agriculture' to 'residential'. Many other innovations, each exceeding the earlier in brilliance have manifested themselves in the current century. To name only a few, 2-G and Coalgate are outstanding examples of mal-governance. It is surprising how much the government can lend itself to manipulation and abuse at the expense of the common man.

It needs to be understood that the active assistance and collaboration of a civil servant is imperative in this process of determined and reckless money making that a political executive has reduced itself to. Thus, officers are assessed with great care to see who will collaborate and eventually conspire and who will be squeamish and needs to be sidelined ruthlessly. Thus, the civil services was broken into three categories—the majority who would quietly implement orders without looking left and right, the relatively few who were totally upright and dared to express their views (and were consequently sidelined), and the chosen few who became partners wielding power and collaborating closely with the rulers.

A number of significant factors combined leading to the current debilitating levels of corruption in the country. Firstly, our Constitution makers did not imagine that human nature will manifest itself given the opportunity, that 'power corrupts'. A political executive, which realized its true position and strength in the system only from the 1970s, was not countered with any checks and balances and had unbridled authority without effective over-sight—the need for an effective 'Lok Pal' had not been visualized by Nehru, who imagined that all politicians following him would be of the same high nobility of purpose and imbued with a sense of public service.

The second major area relates to the failure of the IAS, the premier civil service of the country, to stand up united against the onslaught of the unenlightened self-interest of the political class. Without taking away in any manner from the great service rendered by the higher civil services in maintaining the unity and integrity of the country under very difficult circumstances—one shudders to think what could have happened to the country in the first three decades without the high quality civil service structure that we are blessed with—it is also a fact that the civil services allowed themselves to be infiltrated and dominated, and now silenced by the political class, who used all possible allurements for their ends. This process was also aided significantly by the Indira Gandhi diktat asking for a 'committed' civil servant. Another significant factor is the relative benign eye with which the judiciary at all levels has dealt with the issue of corruption. In general, exemplary and punitive impositions have not been sanctioned in swift proceedings on delinquent officials and politicians. Thus, Sukh Ram can roam free, changing political colours at will and thus, after 20 years of being charge-sheeted, the country still does not know if Lalu Yadav is a big crook or a great benefactor. All over the world, the main weapon against corruption is swift, exemplary, deterrent punishment. In India, while investigating and prosecuting agencies need to share a large part of the blame, our judiciary has not asserted itself enough to contribute to a clean system.

***

In summer 2013, it was reported that the railway minister of China Liu Zhiyu was convicted in a court of law for corruption. He was alleged to have amassed $10 million over a 25-year period. The punishment awarded was death. We now see as to how the Chinese take the issue of corruption seriously and could divine the linkages of this issue with the quality of development they have displayed. Apparently, it took only three months in China for the investigation and conclusion of the trial. The amount involved is roughly ₹60 crore, over a 25-year period—surely this would look trivial in the eyes of most of our politicians, many of whom probably spend as much in one election, to recover five-times as much during the following tenure of office. Our own railway minister, whose nephew was caught red-handed on a senior railway posting matter (squarely in the province of the railway minister) is not even an accused in the case—he will probably give evidence that nobody is guilty! Most self-respecting ministers in state governments would treat the amount of wealth amassed by the Chinese minister as piffling—recent central government scams have thrown up very large numbers. The Chinese event is a rude reminder to us as to how casual we are in dealing with such major governance issues.

There are other many equally important reasons. These include state control of major investigative agencies like the CBI, Enforcement Directorate and state vigilance directorates and the ineptitude of constitutional and statutory watchdog agencies like the CVC. We have recently witnessed what one person heading the CAG could do if he took his job seriously and realized that he was serving the people of India and not the government or political masters, and was bold and courageous in his investigations and his conclusions. It is a pity we have not seen too many examples of erstwhile civil servants, experienced and competent, who when given elevated responsibilities could shed their lapdog attitude and transcend and assume the full powers given to them by the Constitution or the statutes. T.N. Seshan showed the way in removing muscle power from the election scene, we need a new Seshan to rid our elections of money power.

There is no question that there is widespread corruption at the 'cutting edge' level. This has been endemic in India and has thrived through the Mughal times and also British times. This deep-rooted practice is a definite menace to society. It is the failure of the civil services class, the IAS and the other central services, that we have not been able to stamp out, or at least keep in-check, 'transactional' corruption. Classical excuses relate to political patronage, lack of political backing etc. etc. This 'routine' type of corruption needs to be distinguished from the kind of new post-independence corruption phenomenon where the business classes have abstracted licenses, approvals, changes in law and the like, and encouraged a wide variety of tampering with the regulatory structure for mutual reward between the businessmen on one side and the politician (supported by the bureaucrat) on the other, at the expense of the public. The tragedy is that with the 'opening of the economy' in the past two decades, the menace has grown to monstrous proportions.

Do we need a Lok Pal?

The Indian Constitution is a well thought out and wonderful piece of work. However, it has one yawning gap—there is no effective body to check and monitor the political class. Every other group of people in India has a disciplining mechanism, in addition to the umbrella cover provided by 'rule of law'. The founding fathers presumably thought that our politicians would be enlightened enough, and be so imbued in the spirit of public service, that they would not need a checking mechanism. This was major lack of foresight. Alas, power corrupts, absolute power corrupts absolutely; our ruling classes are now steeped in the height of venality thanks to this glaring blunder by our Constitution makers. The concept of Ombudsman or Lok Pal was to repair this gap. It would have been naive to expect the political class to willingly shoot themselves in the foot as has been proved by the deliberately dithering approach to the continually diluted Lok Pal Bill in the past 40 years. No Lok Pal Bill is likely to be passed for the next 40 years, if our supreme body, the Parliament, is left to finally decide the matter on its own. Thanks to the magic wrought by Anna Hazare, this was, for a while, being forced down the throat of the political class or at least we thought so earlier; but now we know the ability of our political leaders to hoodwink the country indefinitely.

Much has been written and spoken about 'unconstitutionality', a dangerous precedent and such-like descriptions of the Lok Pal concept. It may be recalled that ever since the Magna Charta of the 11th century, the British constitutional law has been subject to major changes at least ten times due to 'civil activism'. Then one heard the ridiculous comments by a senior minister that the proposed Lok Pal Bill will not change anything seriously. When criticized for this comment, his explanation was that the bill will not meet India's development needs like provision of primary education etc.—an even more absurd and uninformed comment. It is widely recognized that the level of corruption has a vital bearing on the quality of governance; corruption is an element in the development matrix and has linkages with every other element including poverty, income distribution, public health, education and the like. It is surprising that such an unenlightened comment could have come from an articulate, vocal and prominent member of the Cabinet.

The focus now has to shift to the contours of a possible Lok Pal Bill. We need to give ourselves a strong Lok Pal, with wide ranging powers, who will keep a close watch on the political class as well as on the senior bureaucracy, both at the Centre and in the states. It is equally imperative to ensure that the work of the Lok Pal will not come into conflict with the normal work of the judiciary. It must be remembered that despite all its faults and warts, the country owes the judiciary a deep debt of gratitude for upholding our Constitution and generally maintaining 'rule of law'. The judiciary's powers should not be whittled down, or compromised—that will not be in the national interest.

The best role that can be played by a Lok Pal is to entrust him with the task of swift, non-dilatory, impartial examination of prima facie information/evidence. He needs to have wide-ranging powers to do this and be enabled to act *suo motu*. Clearly the Lok Pal should not be allowed to become a large bureaucracy, an administrative dinosaur, whose head may not know what the tail is thinking or doing. This institution should be slim, have a specific role to play and should have the authority to call, as the occasion demands, on the services of any other government or quasi-government agency for information, advice or investigation. This should preclude the Lok Pal from being a 'corruption Czar', with the role to examine all actions by everybody in the country. Such a move would be counter-productive as it may create a parallel system which would impede the work of the legitimate government.

As has been mentioned, in the case of a civil servant, there is a well established procedure, requiring the person to stand down from office temporarily, pending investigation. This 'suspension' procedure is not deemed to be punishment or admission/declaration of 'guilt'. The official awaits the progress of the investigation, and is quickly 'reinstated' if he is exonerated at the investigation stage, or he is acquitted honourably after due process by the competent 'judicial body'. It is well established in the case of civil servants that 'suspension' is no punishment. A similar dispensation is currently not being applied in the case of the political executives, who are equally public servants. None has the 'fundamental right' to hold public office. The really effective role that the Lok Pal can play is to ask a public servant to step down from his office till he is cleared through due process in a court of law; this would be based on the assessment of the Lok Pal taking into account the first-cut evidence, preponderance of probability and other circumstances with respect to a politician or senior bureaucrat against whom allegations have been levelled. After all there will be more harm to society in allowing a delinquent public official to hold office till he is finally convicted after exhausting all appeals, than the occasional 'miscarriage' of denying public office to an innocent person. Besides I cannot think of any politician or minister or official in the past four decades that the country would have seriously missed if he had been denied public office!

It is not envisaged that the Lok Pal will be a weak office, with limited powers, responsibilities and jurisdiction. It is conceived as an extremely powerful agency, a super watchdog, a custodian of probity and a powerful umpire overseeing the ruling classes. It will be counter-productive to bring the Lok Pal's orders under the purview of the judiciary; his orders should be non-justiciable and would be deemed to constitute 'due process' for suspension of the political executive and higher bureaucracy, pending trial. The Lok Pal should also have unlimited powers to establish his own processes and procedures and to appoint special investigators or prosecutors in appropriate circumstances. He would have strong internal technological backup and powers to call on the services of any agency in the country. Similarly, his counterpart in the states, the Lok Ayuktas will have corresponding powers in the state, and would be under the umbrella of the Lok Pal.

For the Lok Pal institution to be effective, it is imperative that the main investigating agencies—the CBI, the ED, etc. at the Centre and vigilance directorates in the states—should be independent in their operations, and should not be controlled by the government. How this is to be organized is a matter of detail.

The institution of Lok Pal is not to be seen as the final solution to eliminate corruption in India. It would be the first, albeit the critical initial step, in the process. Electoral reforms, cleaning up the police system, tackling the black money issue etc. will all be part of an agenda, whose implementation has not even taken the first baby steps, due to lack of interest by the political executive. The Lok Pal could reverse this trend and eventually pave the way for superior governance.

***

If there is the will, corruption is one of the easiest areas to address and tackle in a relatively short period. Hong Kong, which was known as one of the most corrupt countries in the world was able to transform itself in short order—many other examples can be cited. All insiders know of the major areas where transactional and policy corruption flourish in the country at the central and state levels. If there is determined effort, if only the ruling classes resolve to root out corruption, the levels can be drastically reduced, if not totally eliminated. Sadly the ruling classes are the main beneficiaries, so it may be utopian to ask them to create a Damocles' sword to hang over their own heads. It is in this context that we need to see the Anna Hazare or Ramdev movements—not to dismiss them as unguided, 'undemocratic' forces to 'destabilize' the system. They are a public cry that a sinking ship should be brought back to even keel. If the call is not heeded and corruption levels increase, with corresponding deterioration of public interest, the end of our Republic may not be far away.

15

CAN COALITION GOVERNMENTS GIVE GOOD GOVERNANCE?

Together we shall overcome—popular saying

In recent months, much has been written about the compulsions of the so-called 'coalition dharma'. Besieged by a series of scams and corruption scandals, the Congress-led UPA-II government has sought refuge in the argument that the harsh realities of running a coalition government have necessitated unpalatable compromises and made toleration of corrupt practices within the government inevitable. Thus, for instance, Prime Minister Manmohan Singh attributed the appointment of A. Raja as telecom minister for the second time in 2009, despite evidence that he had flouted rules and acted unilaterally in allocating 2-G licenses, to the compulsions of 'coalition dharma'.

At one time, it was fashionable to attribute India's slow growth, as compared to China, to the fact that India was a democracy and could therefore not take decisions by diktat. We were told that being a democracy necessarily implied some sacrifice in terms of good governance and economic growth. However, one does not hear this argument being seriously advanced in the last two decades, after the Indian economy managed to achieve and sustain a high rate of growth.

One should not confuse between governing as part of a coalition and governing badly. The former describes the mechanics of government while the latter defines the quality of governance. Bad governance erodes the effectiveness of government policies and programmes, blunts the delivery systems of essential government services and public goods and leads to a break-down of accountability, probity and ultimately, the public trust without which no government can continue to function. At the end of the day, there cannot be any compromise with corruption, and any society or economy which seeks to rationalize or justify corruption on the basis of the compulsions of coalition dharma (or adharma) is embarking down a slippery slope which can only lead downwards in a vicious and ultimately self-fulfilling cycle.

The contention that coalition governments breed corruption, lead to bad governance and constrain growth is a variant of this now discredited argument and is equally spurious and without basis. The fact is that no party has enjoyed an absolute majority in the Lok Sabha since 1996. However, the Indian economy broke free from the shackles of the 'Hindu rate of growth' and climbed on to a high growth path after the economic reforms of 1993. Despite being governed by a series of coalition governments, India remained on this high growth path for two decades, becoming a key member of the BRIC grouping of emergent and aspirational economies and being seen as an important driving force of world economic growth as a whole.

***

The Deve Gowda and Gujral governments, from mid-1996 to early 1998, had short tenures as coalition arrangements between parties with widely differing perspectives. However, they were able to usher in far-reaching reforms, many of which are still playing out. Practically every reform in the past 15 years has had its origin and substantive advance in the period of these governments, especially the one presided over by Deve Gowda. I had the privilege of being the Cabinet Secretary during practically the entire period of these two governments; Satish Chandran was the Principal Secretary to Prime Minister Deve Gowda. Practically every major move during this period originated at the 'bureaucratic' level, had the full blessings of the political leadership (mainly the prime minister and the key ministers) and there was cohesion among the alliance partners that during the short period that they were in power, wide ranging reforms needed to be ushered in; this was also successfully achieved. While commentators in general have been, in a sense, contemptuous in their treatment of 'governance' during this period, an objective look will indicate the far-reaching nature of the positive moves taken during this period and the quality of governance that was given to the country. The following paragraphs briefly review the new directions initiated, and the results that were obtained. These are a matter of record, verified through contemporary documents of the period.

Right to Information Act

The Common Minimum Programme of the United Front (UF) government included a commitment to incorporate the Right to Information as a Fundamental Right in the Constitution. This was the first time that this proposal had been made at the government level and it signified a recognition by the government that the logic of globalization, economic liberalization and participatory democracy inevitably implied open access to information, knowledge and ideas as a means of empowering the common man.

This was the first time that the concept of Right to Information was brought up in the government, and pursued to the point where it almost became law. That it did not is only due to the fact that the government did not survive long enough to pass it. In pursuance of this objective, the central government set up a working group under the chairmanship of H.D. Shourie, a well known civil rights activist in January 1997, and mandated it to prepare the draft legislation on the Freedom of Information Act within a period of two months. Another eminent personality in the working group was Soli Sorabjee, a former Attorney General and legal luminary with a record of decades of campaigning for freedom of expression. The government signalled its seriousness of purpose and clear political will to move from an opaque and arbitrary system of governance to a new era of greater transparency, accountability and empowerment of the citizen.

During its brief tenure, the UF government managed to kick-start the process of making the Right to Information a legislative (even if not yet a fundamental) right. Predictably, the passing of a national level law proved to be a difficult and long drawn out task. In the event, the draft bill prepared by the Shourie Committee became the basis, albeit in an extremely diluted form, for the Freedom of Information Bill, 2000 which eventually became law under the Freedom of Information Act, 2002. This act was in turn repealed and replaced with the Right to Information Act, 2005, which is currently in force.

The activism of the central government with regard to the Right to Information Act also accelerated the process of enacting similar acts by a number of state governments. Thus, Goa first enacted a RTI Act in 1997, followed by Karnataka and Rajasthan in 2000, Delhi in 2001, Assam and Maharashtra in 2002, Madhya Pradesh in 2003 and Jammu and Kashmir in 2004.

Today, the RTI Act is recognized and widely used as a powerful instrument to exercise oversight and impose a degree of accountability on government decisions. It is not an exaggeration to say that RTI is the single most important instrumentality of ensuring, in the words of Abraham Lincoln, that a 'government of the people, by the people and for the people shall not perish from the earth.'

The Lok Pal Bill

The concept of the Lok Pal (ombudsman) was mooted by the Santanam Committee in 1962. However, it could not be pushed through, despite an effort made in the late 1970s by Shanti Bhushan. The next major effort was made during the Deve Gowda period.

Like the RTI Act, the passage of the Lok Pal Bill was a commitment made in the Common Minimum Programme of the UF government. This bill too had been in limbo for nearly three decades, with successive governments paying lip-service to the need for a Lok Pal to combat corruption in public life, but doing little to actually bring the bill on to the statute books.

The government, despite its minority status, prepared the draft of the Lok Pal Bill and made a serious attempt to get it passed in

Parliament. Deve Gowda had no hesitation in agreeing to the office of the prime minister coming under the jurisdiction of the Lok Pal.

The draft of the bill was discussed and finalized in a Cabinet meeting on 29 August 1996. At its next meeting on 9 September 1996, the Cabinet approved the bill. The Lok Pal Bill (along with bills on reservation for women, electoral reforms and Prasar Bharti Broadcasting) were listed for the budget session of February 1997. Unfortunately, the bill became a casualty of the political turmoil which saw the ouster of Prime Minister Deve Gowda in April 1997. The successor government headed by I.K. Gujral was not able to see through the passage of the bill.

Delhi Metro

One of the signal achievements of the coalition government was the clearance of Phase I of the Delhi Metro Rail Project in September 1996. Within a few months of taking over, the government was able to give the go-ahead to this major project, which had been hanging fire for over two decades. The materialization of the long-delayed yet much awaited Delhi Metro Rail Project was the result of a real and determined push by the government, despite strong opposition from the Ministry of Finance and other objections from several other ministries, including railways, surface transport and environment & forests. In another publication, I had written about the 'process' adopted for clearing the project—essentially this involved 'locking up' the secretaries of the concerned ministries in my conference room, providing them snacks and toilet facilities inside, and telling them that they will not be released till a final decision was taken. Not surprisingly, they were able to reach an agreement within two hours on a matter which had been subject to petty inter-departmental disputes for over a decade! Perhaps my inspiration was the method used in the Vatican by the cardinals for identifying the new Pope.

A key decision I took related to the appointment of Sreedharan as the Chief Executive of the Metro Corporation. Apart from turf wars between the various departments/agencies involved, the argument that he was 'over-age' was also trotted out to eliminate him. His appointment turned out to be a critical factor for the brilliant execution of the project and commencement of metro services in record time.

In the event the project started on the ground, with the mandate that within five years the first train should roll. The first metro train carrying passengers in Delhi started operations in October 2001, exactly on schedule. Ironically, as is normal in such matters, the inauguration was dominated by the leaders of the day of the central and state governments, with no reference to how the project came into being. As a footnote, it should be added that thanks to the success of the Delhi Metro, at least 20 metro systems are under construction in various cities and towns in India, as of summer 2013.

Petroleum

During its brief tenure, the coalition government was able to effect major, structural changes in the oil and gas sector; in fact it lay the foundations of the policy which is being followed even today. The announcement of the New Exploration and Licensing Policy (NELP) was a far-reaching reform which fundamentally changed the face of oil exploration in the country, infused substantial amounts of fresh capital into the industry and, over the longer term resulted in the discovery of major new oil fields by the private sector, thus reducing India's crippling dependence on oil and gas imports.

If my memory serves me right, the government was also able to find a formula to peg the prices of petroleum products, including petrol and diesel (probably only excluding kerosene and cooking gas), automatically indexing the pricing to London Crude. This significant decision, which takes into account the inevitability of linking market prices in India to crude prices was a major step forward in realistic pricing. I believe this significant advance was negated in 2004 by the then petroleum minister, who reduced petrol prices to take popular accolades when international crude prices temporarily dipped. We can now see the consequences of the political games being played nearly on a monthly basis, whenever gasoline prices are to be raised.

Telecommunications

Major advances were made in the telecom sector, which laid the base for the telecom revolution in the country in the next decade. BSNL and VSNL's monopoly were dismantled, and a set-up opened up in a big way for private players. The part privatization of VSNL was hailed internationally as the 'disinvestment of the year'. The internet was released from the monopoly of one government agency—one can see the results now, flowering in so many directions. This has also contributed to the rapid expansion of the Indian IT sector, with major new employment creation. Many new players were encouraged to bid for circles and to make massive investments. Unlike the 2-G spectrum scam ten years later, there was not a single complaint from any quarter about non-transparency or cronyism. The extraordinary developments in India in the telecom sector can be traced to the decisions taken by the Deve Gowda/Gujral governments.

The government sought to keep operational management of the sector at arm's length. The innovative device for this was the establishment of the Telecom Regulatory Authority of India as a statutory body with effect from 20 February 1997. Prior to this, the entire telecom sector (including telegraphy, phones, communication, radio, telex and fax) was regulated by the British-era Indian Telegraph Act, 1885 and the activities run as a department of the Government of India.

As an independent statutory body to oversee and regulate the telecommunications sector, TRAI's mission was to create and nurture conditions for the growth of telecommunications in the country in a manner and at a pace which would enable India to play a leading role in the emerging global information society. TRAI was expected to ensure a level playing field and conditions of fair competition among the private operators and between them and the PSUs, which were also brought within its remit.

The coalition government of the period recognized the need to have a rational policy framework for distribution of natural resources, in a manner which was practical, maximizing the benefits to the nation, keeping in mind the policy priorities of the government of the day. We saw in subsequent years how 2-G and Antrix-Devas sought to utilize scarce spectrum resources for private benefit, how Coalgate sought to use the crony capitalism route to impoverish the state while distributing largesse to selected private players and how mining licenses were distributed and other state resources treated as the private property of those in power. TRAI was the first major effort to bring arm's-length decision-making in the distribution of the state's assets.

Civil Aviation

The United Front governments led by Deve Gowda and I.K. Gujral recognized the importance of civil aviation for the development of business, trade and tourism and the role which it could play in bumping up the rate of growth of the economy as a whole. They also had a clear strategic vision for modernizing the sector through de-regulation and competition.

In January 1997, the Cabinet decided to permit up to 40 per cent foreign equity and up to 100 per cent NRI/OCB investment in domestic air service transport services. Barriers to entry and exit from the air transport sector were also removed, albeit with the caveat that preference was to be given to Indian Airlines. Although the United Front governments did not last long enough to see through the new policy, they did lay the foundations for the paradigm shift from government control and outright monopoly to de-regulation and private sector participation in the civil aviation sector.

The results are self-evident today. The domestic open skies policy has encouraged the entry of several new carriers and the arrival of the low cost airline model in India. Several private airlines like Jet Airways, Spice Jet, Indigo and Go Air have been successful in establishing themselves and have left the two public sector airlines far behind. Several new world class airports have been built in the metros as well as in non-metro cities; the public-private partnership (PPP) model has been successful in the long-overdue modernization of airports in Delhi, Mumbai and several other cities. The total fleet size of commercial airlines in India has grown exponentially and stood at 371 in February, 2013. Air connectivity between different parts of the country has improved significantly and air travel services for Tier II and Tier III cities has expanded and become more efficient.

In short, the seeds of change conceptualized by the United Front government and the concrete moves initiated have fructified and resulted in the growth of private airlines, increased competition and improved the number and quality of air services in the country.

Highways

The National Highway network, constituting less than 2 per cent of the roads in India, but carrying about 40 per cent of the total road traffic, was in urgent need of overhaul. Over 80 per cent of the highway network consisted of two-lane roads and a further 14 per cent was single-lane, with barely 5 per cent having been converted to four-lane highways. The Ministry of Surface Transport had identified a number of National Highways which needed to have their traffic-carrying capacity doubled over the next five years. The United Front government took a number of steps to provide incentives and encourage the private sector, both domestic and international, to invest in infrastructure development.

Under the new infrastructure policy, equity participation of up to 74 per cent was permitted for road and bridge construction in the case of foreign direct investment in infrastructure projects. As a further incentive, housing and other developmental activities were deemed to be integral parts of any highway project. In order to build confidence in investors and lenders in the early years of operation of the 'build-operate-transfer' system in India, in-principle approvals were accorded to proposals to provide a minimum 'traffic guarantee' to the concessionaires. Procedures for clearing projects were considerably simplified. A one-rupee cess on each litre of diesel was levied to form the corpus for a new highway fund. The ground work for enhancing the National Highway grid was well laid out during this period.

Taken together, these concessions helped to underline the importance which the government attached to the development of highway and port infrastructure and to incentivize the private sector to consider investing in this hitherto unattractive sector, where gestation periods were long and returns traditionally uncertain. This helped to set the stage for the rapid development of the National Highway network as a matter of national priority under the Vajpayee-led National Democratic Alliance (NDA) government.

Power Sector

A new power policy for the country was announced by the prime minister on 16 November 1996. Since power is a state subject, it tends to be heavily subsidized on the basis of social, political or electoral considerations. Outdated technology and poor maintenance result in huge transmission and distribution losses, which are sometimes as high as 50 per cent, as against the international norm of 10 per cent. Most State Electricity Boards are departmentally run and routinely suffer huge losses year after year without being held to account. State governments are generally reluctant to either raise power tariffs or restrict subsidies. It is therefore not surprising that successive governments have been unable to reform their State Electricity Boards or cope with the increasing demands for power generation in a growing economy.

In October 1996, the Centre announced that state governments would be allowed to clear power projects of all sizes and costs without having to come to the Central Electricity Authority (CEA) for clearance, a major departure from the earlier policy. By a notification on 10 April 1997, the union government delegated to the state governments the authority to issue environmental clearances to certain categories of thermal power plants, after holding public hearings with all the concerned parties and stakeholders.

The government also decided to unbundle power transmission from power generation and distribution and allow transmission to be treated as a distinct commercial activity. This was an important initiative to facilitate the issue of separate, 'stand-alone' licenses to private transmission companies. Power transmission was opened for private investment by a Cabinet decision in January 1997.

It should be added that the central and state Power Regulatory Authorities, whose primary task was to fix tariffs without political considerations, were established during the period. However, due to intense politics in this area, the concept of an independent regulator has not been as successful in this field, as it has been in the telecom field, though it has brought some rationality in decision-making processes. The nation has miles to go before it can reach a satisfactory power supply position.

Nation-Building

The phrase 'unity in diversity' has been used to describe India's social and cultural ethos so frequently that it has become a truism and is often taken for granted. While the idea does have its origins in ancient Indian scripture—the famous *Vasudhaiva Kutumbakam* or the whole world is one single family of the *Mahopanishad*—its rediscovery and enthronement as an over-arching political concept owes much to the brilliance, eloquence and charisma of Jawaharlal Nehru.

Yet, as we have discovered, the unity of India is by no means a historically given fact, but is, on the contrary, a distant objective to be constantly sought and striven for. Tribals, Dalits, the poor and the dispossessed (recently dismissed, collectively and cynically, as 'mango people living in a banana Republic') all attest to the reality of the many 'other Indias' whose diversity translates, not into the happy harmony and unity of the Nehruvian myth, but rather into the disaffection, alienation, hatred and insurgency of Naipaul's 'million mutinies'. Today it is no longer possible to assert with confidence that every Indian feels himself to be a part and parcel of the Indian experiment in nation-building; that India runs in his blood and is inscribed in his DNA.

John F. Kennedy's *ich bin ein Berliner* in 1963 and Ronald Reagan's 'Mr. Gorbachev, tear down this wall' in 1987, have rightly gone down in history as examples of effective symbolism and communication. In their own much more modest ways, both Deve Gowda and I. K. Gujral instinctively understood the importance of symbolism in politics. Deve Gowda's knowledge of Hindi was rudimentary, but he tried to learn the language, famously delivering his 1996 Independence Day speech in transliterated Hindi, reading from an English script. However, instead of being appreciated, he was ridiculed and derided.

Jammu and Kashmir

In 1996 the prime minister visited the Kashmir Valley, the first time in nearly ten years, which was followed up with two more visits in succession. This tempo was kept up by I.K. Gujral who within a fortnight of taking over, made his first visit outside Delhi, to Kashmir. In July 1996 the government announced a $ 715 million rail project to connect Baramulla in the Kashmir Valley with Jammu and the rest of the country. This project was later declared as a national project and was thereby assured of committed funding (readers will recall the photo opportunity used by the prime minister of the day and party chief in summer 2013, to inaugurate a bridge, which was part of the project announced in 1996—naturally again there was no reference to the origin of the project). A major road project—the revival of the historic Mughal Road—and acceleration of two hydroelectric projects were also announced. The 480 MW, Uri hydroelectric project has since been built and commissioned, despite extremely adverse circumstances of insurgency, at a cost of ₹3,300 crore in the remote Baramulla district, close to the line of control,

In another radical departure from the existing practice, ambassadors of various countries, foreign journalists and office bearers of important international NGOs were permitted to visit the Valley, in order to counter the propaganda that there were gross violations of human rights in Kashmir.

The close attention paid to normalizing the evolving situation and reviving the political and democratic process in Jammu and Kashmir (J&K) culminated in the holding of elections to the Legislative Assembly in the state in September 1996. The National Conference, as the single biggest party in J&K, had hitherto demanded the restoration of the pre-1953 status for the state and had refused to participate in the elections to the Parliament; the prime minister spoke to Farooq Abdullah and persuaded him to participate in the Assembly elections. Farooq Abdullah's agreement to participate in the Assembly elections came less than a month before the first phase of the elections and it transformed the political situation in the state.

Ultimately, elections to the 87 seat Assembly were held in four phases in September 1996. A large number of candidates, 1,029 in all, or an average of 12 contestants per constituency, contested the polls, braving death threats from militants, and an average polling of nearly 54 per cent was recorded. Both the local and international press acknowledged that the polls, held after a decade, were by and large fair and peaceful.

The credit for re-establishing the democratic process in the state goes to the coalition government of the day.

Uttarakhand

By the 1990s, the demand for separate statehood, dating back to 1957, had achieved almost unanimous acceptance among both the local population and the national political parties. The state Legislative Assembly of Uttar Pradesh passed government-sponsored motions demanding the creation of Uttarakhand state in August 1991 and again in August 1996.

The critical intervention was made by Prime Minister Deve Gowda in his Independence Day speech on 15 August 1996, when he conceded the long pending demand of the people of Uttarakhand for a separate state and announced that a bill would shortly be introduced for this purpose. While the announcement was by no means altruistic, being timed just before the Uttar Pradesh Assembly elections in September-October 1996, the political momentum in favour of a separate state of Uttarakhand essentially became unstoppable after the United Front government took the bull by the horns and endorsed the demand for the new state.

I should add here that I had joined the post of Cabinet Secretary very early in August; I would have strongly advised a re-think on this issue. I believe that quality of governance is size-neutral; small states need not necessarily mean that they are better administered; indeed in Indian conditions, there could be inverse relationship between direct attention to detail by the political executive and the outcome. The jury is out on the performance of Uttarakhand, Jharkhand and

Chhattisgarh; the Telengana/Seemandra genie may not be so easily rebottled. Reckless permission to break-up states, mainly on political considerations, could lead sooner or later to 'Balkanization' of India. These are my personal views. However, the fact is that the formal genesis of Uttarakhand came about this way.

North-Eastern States

After suffering decades of neglect and exploitation, the seven North Eastern states, the 'step-children of Mother India' have become sullen and alienated. Various groups have been formed and are involved in insurgency in these states. In this troubled and complex scenario, the short-lived United Front government was able to engage with the problems of the states as a matter of priority. The central government had recognized the need to pay special attention to infrastructure development in the North East.

The first concrete economic and financial package for the region was announced in October 1996. The ₹6,100 crore package was ear-marked for several specific projects, including the fourth rail-cum-road bridge over the Brahmaputra at Bogibeel, upgradation of the Guwahati airport, developing industrial growth centres, road projects, railways, hydel power, drinking water supply schemes and health care programmes. The creation of the department and later the Ministry of Development of the North East (DONER) owes its origin to this period. The announcement was made in Guwahati by the prime minister after a week-long visit to all the seven states of the North East.

Unlike the present scenario, when the North Eastern states merit passing attention only when elections are round the corner, the United Front government did make a sincere effort to study the problems of the region in depth and lay the foundations of a long-term strategy of governance, development, inclusiveness and integration.

India-China Border Agreement

35 years after the border war with China, a pact was entered into between India and China (29 November 1996) on mutual troop

withdrawal and a pledge that 'neither side shall use its military capability against the other'—the first time both countries agreed to abjure force on the border, since 1962. This was the culmination of earlier steps taken by the previous government, particularly in 1993, for preparing an understanding relating to the Indo-China border. The 1996 border agreement was accompanied by other measures, intended to give momentum to India-China economic relations. After the border disaster of the 60s, this clearly was a breakthrough intended to pave the way for a solution to the pesky border problem with China; the issue was put in cold storage thereafter. It would be recalled in this context that the border issues are again in prominence in 2013; sadly this strategic issue has been reduced to political knee-jerk response and reaction mode in a pre-election year. The point is that the coalition government saw the strategic importance of settling the border with China and took the first concrete steps in this regard; there was the recognition that if China and India learn to cooperate on major international issues (keeping their respective special interests and concerns aside), their collective weight in international affairs can be formidable, for the mutual interest of both countries. Only in October 2013 has a new agreement signed between India and China, which incidentally does not take the relationship, including delineation of border, any further.

Women's Reservation Bill

History will record that the Women's Reservation Bill was first moved in the Lok Sabha by the Deve Gowda government. The bill was discussed in the Cabinet meeting on 28 August 1996 and thereafter introduced in the Lok Sabha as the 81st Constitutional Amendment Bill, as it then was, on 9 September 1996. Discussions on the bill were blocked on various technical grounds in a pattern which was to become familiar in later years. A subsequent attempt to get the bill passed by I. K. Gujral, who succeeded Deve Gowda as prime minister, met the same fate.

The Women's Reservation Bill was passed by the Rajya Sabha as the Constitution (108th Amendment) Bill, on 9 March 2010.

As of now, the Lok Sabha has yet to vote on the bill and there is little expectation that the bill will be enacted in the foreseeable future.

Nuclear Testing

After the nuclear Pokhran test by Indira Gandhi's regime, there was a clear need to re-verify and update the nuclear armaments status. I had worked very closely with Satish Chandran to persuade Deve Gowda to permit a third test, to validate all computer assumptions. Initially Deve Gowda was horrified, afraid to touch the issue with a barge pole; he was persuaded to agree in the overall interests of our defence-preparedness. As it happened, before the start-up process could begin, he lost his position due to the politics of the day, and was succeeded by Gujral, who was a dyed-in-the-wool pacifist. He was terrified at the thought of a nuclear experiment from our side and peremptorily dismissed the idea. It took three months of gentle persuasion, to convince him of the major utility of this line of action. As irony would have it, he lost his job within three days of agreeing to this proposal. It was thus that in the 'Top Secret' list of ten-top-priority items pending before the next government, I had listed this as item number 4 before the new Prime Minister Vajpayee. In the event, Pokhran-II took place weeks into the new government—I had retired a month or so prior to that.

Issues of Governance

A mention needs to be made of the Conference of Chief Ministers on Effective and Responsive Administration held in May 1997 under the aegis of Prime Minister I. K. Gujral. The conference recognized the urgent need to ensure a responsive, accountable, transparent and people-friendly administration. It also approved an action plan for an effective and responsive government at the Centre and in the states, while explicitly acknowledging that political will to implement the plan was both necessary and essential.

While this kind of jargon is not uncommon in government meetings, what was remarkable was the precision and detail in the elements of the action plan adopted at the end of the conference and the agreement by all the chief ministers that their states would work for the implementation of the action plan, after making appropriate allowances for variations in local circumstances. The contrast with the present situation, where many chief ministers routinely boycott meetings convened by the central government, is self-evident.

To give a few examples, the conference decided that the central and state governments will formulate Citizens' Charters specifying standards of service and time limits for delivery, avenues of grievance redressal and a provision for independent scrutiny with the involvement of citizen and consumer groups. In the age of e-governance, this is an idea which is now beginning to gain traction in many states.

Devolution of powers and resources to elected local bodies in rural and urban areas was another element of the action plan, which later fructified in the 73rd and 74th Amendments to the Constitution recognizing Panchayats and Local Administrative Bodies as a third level of administration.

The conference acknowledged that secrecy and lack of openness in government promotes corruption in official dealings and is inimical to accountable and democratic governance. To counter this, the chief ministers recommended e-governance and the availability of open information on essential services and approvals including land records, passports, investigation of offences, administration of justice, tax collection and administration, issue of permits and licences etc. Some advance has been made, but we have a long way to go as we are nowhere near the standards reached in a number of other countries; note that this is one clear route to reduce transactional corruption.

As the principal instrument for the implementation of government policies and programmes, it is a *sine qua non* of good governance that a honest civil servant be protected from politically motivated harassment and be allowed to do his work without outside interference. In this context, the conference recognized the need for objective and transparent decisions on postings, promotions and transfers of officials, particularly those working in key areas and resolved that institutional arrangements would be evolved to ensure stability of tenure and de-politicized postings at all levels.

Remarkably, the conference of chief ministers, essentially a conclave of politicians, explicitly recognized that the 'politician-civil servant criminal nexus' was an evil which needed to be dealt with 'ruthlessly'. It will be recalled that the 1993 report of the N. N. Vohra Committee, which exposed the existence of a deep nexus between political personalities, public servants and crime syndicates, has still to see the light of day. The malaise that Vohra identified has become worse a hundred-fold in the next two decades. In contrast, the conference of chief ministers recognized the need to check the politicization of the civil services and sought the cleansing of civil services at all levels, adherence to ethical standards, commitment to basic principles of the Constitution and a clear understanding of the relationship regulating politicians and civil servants.

Even more significantly, the action plan set clear time limits for implementation. Thus, the entire process of making approvals, sanctions and issue of permits simpler, transparent and single-window-based was to be adopted as a priority agenda and implemented over the next one year. Legislation to make Freedom of Information a statutory right of all citizens, along with appropriate amendments to the Official Secrets Act, 1923 were to be introduced in Parliament 'before the end of 1997'. The existing procedures for departmental enquiries and vigilance proceedings against government employees were to be revamped within three months. Further, existing rules and regulations were to be amended within six months so as to enable exemplary prosecution and removal of corrupt officials and the weeding out of staff of doubtful integrity. At the same time, suitable mechanisms were to be worked out to reward employees who do good work.

I have dealt at some length with this remarkable political initiative to improve governance, perhaps the only one of its kind in the history of independent India. While there are any number of studies on public administration and many committees and commissions have been appointed, both by the central and state governments to study and make recommendations on improving the civil services and the delivery of public goods and services, follow-up and implementation have always been weak or non-existent and proved to be the Achilles heel of successive governments. While what needs to be done has always been relatively well known, there has been little political will for establishing systems which will promote efficiency, impartiality, accountability and transparency.

In this context, the 1997 conference of chief ministers was a forum where elected politicians rather than selected bureaucrats or experts, endorsed a time-bound agenda of substantive reforms. It is perhaps not an exaggeration to state that, if this agenda had been implemented within the indicated timeframe, there would have been a substantial improvement in the quality of governance and in turn of the quality of life in India today.

***

In these paragraphs, an attempt has been made in brief to highlight the far-reaching moves made during a brief period of a coalition government, between mid-1996 to early 1998, led by two prime ministers; the minority government had clearly no major clout in Parliament, but owed its existence to a stalemate between the two major parties. Even the coalition consisted of more than 12 regional and smaller parties and yet, there was remarkable coordination among themselves, a credible consultation mechanism within the political machinery of these parties, as well as an interface between the political forces of the coalition and the executive, both political and permanent. In a highly cooperative atmosphere, each major political or administrative measure got the blessings of the coordination group headed by Late Harkishan Surjeet of the CPM; thereafter there would be no interference in the process of implementation.

In retrospect, the key to the 'achievements' of the coalition governments of 1996–98 rested on their having agreed on a Common Minimum Programme, constructive meetings every week among the political parties under the chairmanship of Harkishan Surjeet and very positive and dynamic leadership provided by Deve Gowda initially, followed by Gujral. There was clear recognition that political support and clearing policies was with the coalition partners and thereafter, all implementation was totally left to the senior bureaucracy to supervise, and follow through on the decisions. Thus, there was clear division of labour between the coalition parties, the ministers and the senior bureaucracy.

One index of the quality of achievements is reflected by the fact that despite the major changes effected in so many vital sectors, there has not been a single major complaint or allegation of favouritism or crony capitalism during that period. For example, in the defence sector, which is notorious for allegations and 'deals', during the period of Mulayam Singh as defence minister there was not a single finger raised or suggestion of impropriety mooted.

***

I had the privilege of being the Cabinet Secretary during this period. I worked closely with Late Satish Chandran, who was Principal Secretary to Deve Gowda during that period—a man of vision and understanding; as well as with N.N. Vohra, an extremely able civil servant, who worked with Gujral in the same capacity. I had the full support and trust of both prime ministers. Decisions which now take months of dilly-dallying could be pushed through in days. Let me share some personal memories of that period.

I recall a very senior official, of the rank of secretary, who was caught in a misdemeanour and asked to resign the same night, under a special provision of the Constitution where an official can be removed in national interest, without detailed process. This happened with no publicity whatever. I also recall at least two files that I called from different ministries, and in my capacity as secretary to all departments, wrote strong notes opposing the final decision of the minister concerned, had the PM (who is deemed to be minister for all departments) supporting my view, to get the department's minister over-ruled, on his own file. I also recall that during that period, very strict policy was followed that secretaries and joint secretaries would be posted to ministries based on certain parameters, which included that they would not be favourites or desired partners of the ministers concerned. Alas this policy was terminated soon thereafter and one can see the consequences in 2-G and so many other recent instances. Besides, a sharp eye on the activities of staff officers of ministers was kept to ensure a clean image—delicately but firmly, at least two were asked to be relieved.

With the change in the Gujral government, Brajesh Mishra, the new Principal Secretary to prime minister took charge, who changed the ethos of relationships at the top in the bureaucracy. Freedom was suddenly given, sponsored by him, to various ministers to run their 'fiefdoms' as emperors. The sharp decline in administrative standards since then can possibly be traced to this. The role of the Principal Secretary to the prime minister, as also that of the Cabinet Secretary in ensuring quality of governance is of vital importance. Brajesh Mishra, who had little knowledge of mainstream Indian administration, took charge of the administrative apparatus; willy-nilly acting as a political head, he sidelined the Cabinet Secretary and functioned as a political chief of administration, rather than as an administrative aide of the chief executive. For whatever reason, Vajpayee had effectively ceded all control over the operational governance system to Mishra, confining his attention to large, purely political issues. With the high promise and quality of most of the ministers, as well as the stature of Vajpayee, the government could have performed much better, if the back-stopping arrangements were better organized. This gap could possibly be traced to one single factor—that Brajesh Mishra, who had no real qualification to do so, had full control over the operational apparatus and possibly could not give it effective direction.

I need to refer to the image of Deve Gowda, who was literally 'caught napping'—frequently the press would ridicule him as the sleepy prime minister, who could not keep his eyes open in meetings. Having seen him at very close quarters, I know the reality. Deve Gowda was alert all the time, was listening to everything going on. When he seemed to dose off, it was a kind of a signal that he was bored—which was often—and that he did not think much of what was being said.

16
DO WE RECOGNIZE THE GLORY OF OUR CLASSICAL ARTS?

A man with no music in his soul is fit for treason, spoils and stratagems—Shakespeare

Having spent my early childhood in an ashram in the deep south of India, the only sound heard in the house was of bhajans and stotras, of Lalitha Sahasranama, *Arunachala Shiva* (in Tamil, composed by Ramana Maharishi). Every day from 4 to 10 am and from 5 to 8 pm, these were sung by the assembled devotees, each using his or her own unique notes, ragas and special effects. The overall effect may not have been cacophonic, but cannot be described as harmonic music, except by the most ardent devotee steeped in divine inspiration. The only other 'music' heard there was the veena, as the instrument symbolizing goddess Saraswati, the patron of knowledge. Young ladies in the ashram were encouraged to practice the veena; the results were not too different from that heard of the bhajans! Television had not arrived and the radio was used only for cricket commentaries. I still remember listening, ball-by-ball, to the thrilling commentary of the 1948 Leeds Ashes tests, as a 10-year old, when Bradman and Morris, on a 5th-day pitch, scored 404 runs in one day to snatch a historic victory for Australia. The Ipod and Ipad were not known, essentially we were completely innocent of any contact with classical music.

It was only in 1952, when I was about 14-years-old that I got to hear classical music in Kolkata (then known as Calcutta). The occasion was the annual Sadarang Conference of classical Hindustani music in Esplanade. My father had received a complimentary pass to the hall, and having 'shown his face' there, handed over the pass to me around 10 pm promising to send the car back for me in an hour to take me home. I had no idea what I was getting into. The only items listed for the night's programme was a vocal performance by the duo Nazakat and Salamat Ali Khan, brothers from Pakistan, followed by a then new-comer Gangubai Hangal. I had planned to spend half-an-hour there, but bewitched as I was by the sound of Hindustani classical, I went home at 5 am with much regret that the programme did not continue. I recall that the Pakistani brothers sang only two ragas in about four hours; Gangubai Hangal, only one raga for much of her performance, with some bhajans and lighter songs in the final half-hour. Contrast this with the one-hour shows of classical music today on television and radio when the artist displays his expertise through eight or ten ragas; or of a regular concert where ten ragas are sung in two hours, apart from a number of tukdas and bhajans. I was hooked, and would go to every possible concert that I could manage to during the next four years in Kolkata.

My first contact with Carnatic music was in Kolkata sometime probably around 1956. My father in his capacity as the President of the Tamil Sangam of Calcutta had invited 'Flute Mahalingam' for an evening performance in an open-air enclosure, somewhere near Dhakuria Lakes. The performance was to start around 7 pm. We awaited the arrival of the flute genius; around 8.30 pm the buzz went around that Mahalingam who had arrived that morning from Chennai by train (from a then prohibition area), was holed up in his hotel room, barely conscious, with an open bottle nearly empty by his side. Apparently my father along with his co-organizers went to great lengths to 'revive' him, which took much time. Meanwhile they had to periodically go to the podium to invent excuses for the delay in the arrival of the maestro. Around 11.30 he did arrive, escorted (nearly carried) by three office bearers to the stage, where he had difficulty in identifying his own flute and recognizing the accompanists. Anyhow he started his performance, and as word spread that the great man was performing, people started pouring out of their houses in the predominantly south-Indian neighbourhood; the pandal was full by midnight. Normally Carnatic classical performances finish by 10 pm at the latest. This one started around midnight but then we were privy to the most glorious five hours of divine Carnatic music that anyone can ever listen to. Mahalingam, only half-conscious, unaware of the crowd in the pandal, kept us in raptures till 5 am. I could never imagine that anything in the world could be as exalted and uplifting as the quality of music that was delivered by him.

However, my first real contact with Carnatic classical music was in Ghazipur (in east Uttar Pradesh), where I was Collector. Kalyan Baksi, who joined me as probationer trainee in the IAS, had brought for me a gift when he returned after the Pooja holidays—the *ragamalika 'Bhavaiyami'* by M.S. Subbalakshmi, summarizing the *Ramayana* in six wonderful musical stanzas in different ragas along with *Shrirangapura Vihara* on the other side of the HMV gramophone record. Only those who have heard this in their younger days can remember the thrill and discovery of high quality music. With this I was hooked to Carnatic music.

One then listened to the greats of music—Ariyakudi, Semmangudi, the plebian GNB, MLV and so many others—I became an aficionado. I even started criticizing, commenting and analyzing, especially, indeed only, when I sensed that my companion didn't know much of music! I would even name the ragas (mostly wrongly I guess) and display a sense of superiority. The reality is one does not need to technically understand or recognize the ragas or the notes, or the combinations—all that is required is that you lose yourself in the magic of the music, and enjoy it. In later years, I discovered that M.S. as a Carnatic musician was not all that great, many others including some I have named earlier were far superior singers, with better voices, more lilting, and with greater command over their art, indeed more satisfying. M.S., hitting the high notes, would become irritatingly 'nasal'—she was outstanding in Tamil, Sanskrit, Telegu and Hindi bhajans, mainly because of the *bhavana* and simulated 'devotion' that she injected into her bhajans; her *Vishnu Sahasranaam* and *Lalitha Sahasranaam* are immortal works.

It is debatable whether purely as an artist she deserved the Bharat Ratna more than other great exponents of Carnatic music. The fact is she had the right combination—political backing by Rajaji, support of the media (Kalki), the aura of emerging from a 'dancing girl' family to marry into 'respectable' high society, coupled with high quality talent—these got her the highest award. One has seen the same phenomenon in so many other walks of life. It is not always the best exponent or the best practitioner who bags the highest prize, it is a combination of circumstances, support and backing, right connections, coupled with talent.

***

During my posting in Chennai I took the occasion to travel by car extensively in south India and once spent half-a-day at Tiruvarur. Those familiar with Carnatic music would know that the three 'greats' of classical music—the Trinity—Tyagaraja, Muthuswamy Dikshitar and Syama Shastri—all were born in Tiruvarur, a small temple town about 40 miles from Tanjore. They all lived in houses within a 100 yards of each other in the same small town. They were born within 15 years of each other in different households, in the late-18/early-19 centuries. This most remarkable fact has not been commented upon or explained adequately, as to how this extraordinary coincidence could take place. The situation could be likened to say, Beethoven, Mozart, Strauss and Verdi being born within a mile of each other, within a 20 to 30 years period. The extraordinary coincidence in the case of the Carnatic greats has not been explained anywhere. There is no record of a common ancestor, nor of a common teacher or guru who was in contact with their families. Which common gene was shared by these three divinely gifted people? Is it possible that much the same way that *Amrit* leaked out and fell at different spots of our blessed land, some special divine spark was present in Tiruvarur, and came into contact just with these three people over a 40-year period? Was there a supernatural/outer space intervention? If you recognize the magical quality of the music of these three greats, you cannot over-rule the theory of divine intervention—music injected into them from outer space emanating from a higher civilization?

There is a record of Muthuswamy Dixitar leaving the village early, and moving on to Varanasi with his guru. Dixitar, those days, visited every major north-Indian temple—Pashupatinath, Kedarnath, Badrinath and so many others and left immortal compositions in praise of each divine manifestation in these places. His brand of Carnatic music also got highly enriched by induction of a number of Hindustani ragas, which now have got blended into the Carnatic style. There is the story of Muthuswamy's visit to a Christian function organized by the Collector, where he got enthralled with the harmony inherent in the western classical style. On that occasion, his melodic performance of Carnatic music, greatly appreciated by the British audience got him the gift of a violin—the first time violin became part of Carnatic music. Today every vocal performance in Tamil Nadu has a violinist accompanist, even solo violin Carnatic music performances are not uncommon.

***

The 'season' in Chennai is a major annual event, from about 15 December to 4 or 5 January. Everyone who is anyone in the world of Carnatic music has to perform in one of the 40 or 50 sabhas—the more the invitations, the higher his rank. This is like the Wimbledon in Carnatic music, in fact much more than that; it is all grand slams rolled into one. Musicians are rated by where they perform, and at what time of the day. The Music Academy is the most sacred temple for Carnatic music. Membership of this hallowed institution is more difficult to obtain than of the Delhi Gymkhana or Delhi Golf Club. The waiting list is for more than 50 years and the joke is that as soon as a child is born, the application for his child—to come 25 years later—is already made, well before the father starts going to school! The Music Academy is a grand institution; its management committee reads like the who-is-who in Chennai. My good friend Ambi Srinivasan, a man of many accomplishments in business and other fields, would rightly consider his membership in the management committee of the Music Academy of much significance.

A visit to the Music Academy any season evening will get you to see the cream of the Brahmin community in Chennai. Everyone who should be there will be there. The average age of the audience is about 65 years, many are in wheelchairs, with a large sprinkling of second or third generation NRIs in their teens and early 20s; aristocratic, eagle-nosed, and the equivalents of the dowager-duchess are also a common sight. In the cafeteria, one can meet famous Tamilian Brahmin greats of the past five decades. The equivalent of 'strawberry and cream' is served in the form of *keeravadai* and 'filter coffee'. Inside the hall, the regulars, male and female, looking like well-bred vultures, enjoy the music, scratching their bald heads to the 'tala'. With music steeped in their blood, they can recognize the raga even before the artist opens his mouth. They have seen it all from the days of Chowdiah to Maharajapuram to Madurai Mani to L. Subramanian, and frown at impertinent improvisations or variations. Suddenly there is spontaneous applause at an innovation, which gets accepted as the new norm. This is the Mecca of Carnatic music. At the first sound of a minor *apaswara* (false note), there is a collective sigh, barely heard, of acute disapproval; there is a gasp of approval at an imaginative and tasteful variation.

In one recent performance, the brilliant young Abhishek Raghuram, grandson of the legendary percussionist Palghat Raghu, made his classical vocal debut. He wowed the knowledgeable audience with his classical style, embellished with wonderful variations; clearly a maestro of the future. Alas he blotted his copy-book by extending his performance by as much as ten minutes beyond the period allotted to him by the 'Academy's authorities', incurring their 'displeasure'. One wonders if he would be denied future assignments at the academy for this grave blunder, thus jeopardizing his career.

With the renaissance of classical music, thanks to the internet, youtube, Ipad and Ipod, there is a great revival, with practitioners all over the world innovating, enjoying themselves and reliving the greatness of their tradition. Thus, in at least 50 towns in the US, and an equal number in Europe, and elsewhere in the world there are sabhas and associations devoted to classical music—many exclusively to Carnatic or Hindustani—some to a combination of the two. Thus, from at least six suburbs of San Francisco, practitioners of Carnatic music, who hardly know India, arrive in Chennai for the season and have their formal public performances. Unknown as they are, they hire the hall, pay for the accompanists and get their friends, relatives invited for the performance. It is not unusual for a budding 'artist' to spend say ₹20 lakh for this 'experience'; there is great thrill in rediscovering one's heritage.

Another special feature of the 'season' is the lecdem—lecture demonstration for the benefit of the innocent—that is held in a number of sabhas in the mornings. Usually an exponent talks of history, special features and attributes of a raga, or of a style, or of a method of rendering this aspect of the art or the other. There are usually two kinds of audiences—the young teenagers, both Tamilian as well as Caucasian or other foreigners, generally from the US, Europe or Japan, coming to learn or participate in an arty forum; also very old ladies and gentlemen from Mylapore, coming along to relive their past, and to see if there are new innovations or interpretations of what they already know. The tiffin is usually of high quality, often superior to the quality of the lecdem!

***

I once presided over the *Bharatanatyam Arangetram* (debut) of a young danseuse in Delhi, where the *natwanar* (teacher) was a Canadian lady, herself an artist of repute. The chief guest was the famous danseuse Geeta Chandran. In my short speech, I spoke of my great enjoyment of the performance (which was only partly true) and mentioned that this was despite my total previous ignorance of the grandeur of this art form. Geeta, in her comments, rightly chided me saying that I should be ashamed of my ignorance of this art form. She also rightly said that every Indian should make the effort to understand the very great cultural treasure that we have inherited.

In every part of India there is a great tradition of classical music—from Kerala to Karnataka to Maharashtra to Bengal to Manipur—there is equally a grand tradition of classical dances. One wonders if there is any other country in the world so blessed with such treasures of fine art experiences and their practitioners to be found everywhere.

Wherever you go in the US you can turn on the television or the radio to listen to a classical music performance; there are 24-hour dedicated channels for Mozart or Beethoven or other classical greats.

It is a tragedy that when we turn on our television sets, we do not have access to 24-hour performances of classical music or dances. With Doordarshan and All India Radio having great archives, a treasure-house of performances over the years by all-time greats, the cost of mounting these television channels or radio stations will be miniscule. Alas one does not see our culture ministry or I&B ministry encouraging, through government or private channels, attempts to give pleasure to millions by broadcast of these performances; equally preserving the greatness of our tradition. Perhaps, much like our traditional knowledge relating to yoga or ayurveda or other distillations of our 5000-year old culture, the continuation, revival, innovation and improvement in our classical art forms will be left to Indians in the US and Europe, as well as to foreigners who recognize the greatness in these art forms, and bring new energy and enthusiasm to maintain and revive them.

17

CRICKET IS RELIGION—OTHERS DON'T EXIST?

Mute Miltons abound in our remotest areas

The Indian tennis legend Ramanathan Krishnan once told me this story. This was Calcutta in the 1950s, when it was the national tennis capital—Indian tennis was then 'ruled' by Ganesh Dey. Krishnan told me that whenever a major tournament was held anywhere in India, one could invariably see that the chief local organizer, within a couple of months would buy a plot of land and a new building would come up there. Dey had achieved a coup in getting Bergellin, the great Bjorn Borg's coach, as well as the famous tennis player Sven Davidson to play some matches in Calcutta —he had thrown a party to celebrate the event. Krishnan recounted that as Dey stood up to make his short speech 'I thank you from the bottom of my heart'… suddenly realizing that 'foreigners' were there, he added … 'and from my wife's bottom'…. This story has wide currency in sport circles, being placed in the context of different occasions at different times. Krishnan says he was present at the time of the original. Since those days, Indian tennis has been captured as the personal property of the 'Khanna' family—every sport in India belongs to one family or the other. This is not surprising in a country where our national politics has belonged to one family for the past six decades.

Krishnan, a close relative of mine, while a highly private and reticent individual, is a great raconteur. He has travelled widely on tennis circuits and has a fund of tennis-related stories, which can stand up in any company of jokes. Thus, for instance, one relating to a national tournament in Amritsar, where Krishnan was partnered by Akhtar Ali, a nationally ranked player in a doubles match against a local team. Their opponents were two Sikhs, who looked like twins to them, wearing the same kind of dress as well as same coloured turbans. Krishnan and Akhtar won the first set easily. Suddenly Akhtar mentioned to Krishnan that only one of the opponents was serving on all the service games, not alternating as per the rules. So they decided to slow down the game, lost a couple of games to see whether the opponents were actually alternating the service. Soon they discovered that Akhtar was right. At the next change-over, Krishnan gently asked one of the players as to why he was not serving during his turn and got the matter-of-fact answer: 'I have a sore shoulder, am unable to raise it'. When Krishnan politely mentioned that this was against the rules, the Amritsar player quite aggressively said that he had obtained the 'referee's approval!' When the referee was asked if that was true, he did confirm that he had given his concurrence! Having settled this important rule issue satisfactorily, the doubles match continued with Krishnan and Akhtar emerging as winners. Looking back on my own career in the Civil Services, while I do find the story very funny, this kind of an event actually happens nearly every day in administration. Rules are flouted openly, without an apology, and approval by a higher authority is cited as the justification. In essence this is what allegedly Robert Vadra did in Haryana, but made a profit of about ₹50 crore; our poor Punjab doubles team merely lost the match! In any case, any sportsman would enjoy this episode.

In 1961, when I was a student at the Imperial College in London, Krishnan reached the semi-finals at Wimbledon, one of the two times he did so. I was then staying in a students' hostel, sparsely furnished, with toilets at the end of each corridor. As an amateur, the lifestyle of a world class tennis player those days meant that he had to count every penny. Krishnan spent that fortnight in our hostel in an adjoining room—no room service, no masseur, the spartan life of a student, while competing in a physical sport at the world class level! I need to add one more memory passed on to me by Krishnan. During Wimbledon time in June-July, the then Prime Minister Jawaharlal Nehru would visit London nearly every year in summer. Krishnan proudly remembers at least two occasions when Nehru invited him for breakfast, somewhere in Kensington where he was staying. Indira Gandhi, who later became India's prime minister, acted as house keeper. Krishnan recalls that Indira had especially arranged for dosas and would personally go to the kitchen to bring them to the table to serve the visitor. Imagine the scene—would anybody in power or in a ruling family at the state or in the Centre, do anything similar today?

To come to a more serious point, in 1959 Ramanathan Krishnan was ranked third in the world in tennis. He had reached the semi-finals at Wimbledon twice in his career. No Indian has ever gone beyond the quarter-final stage. Clearly he was head and shoulders above any Indian tennis player of any time, and one of the very few from India ever ranked at the highest levels in any field sport, in world rankings. By contrast, the next best tennis players, Vijay Amritraj and Ramesh Krishnan had best rankings of 16 and 23 respectively. Leander Paes and Bhupathi have won a number of grand slam championships, which is highly illusory glory—Leander Paes' best world ranking has been 73 in singles and that of Bhupathi 217—much like empty drums making the most noise, they make the most waves. Sadly it is the likes of Paes and Bhupathi who put up the most tantrums and exhibit poor behaviour. India is not even in the world group in the Davis Cup; probably we are now as low in the tennis world as in soccer, athletics or in so many other field sports. Recall that that was the amateur era; Indian players with half Krishnan's talent are now professionals, in totally different income leagues. The point to note is that Krishnan is a genuine legend in the field of tennis, who raised India's prestige in the sports arena all over the world. The country just does not know how to remember, honour and felicitate the greats of the past.

***

One winter in the 1980s, when I made an overnight stop at Frankfurt, and went for a morning walk on the snow covered roads, I reached a nearby park. There was an imposing statue of a handsome man right in the middle of the park. I was curious about his identity—was it Adenauer? Kohl? Beethoven? I found an unfamiliar name with the legend in German inscribed underneath. I asked a passerby to translate for me. The statue was of the curator of the park, who had held the position for over 30 years. Can one imagine any park in India dedicated to or commemorating or celebrating anyone except a political leader, a prime minister or a chief minister or another person who has been a parasite on our society? In Mumbai you can see the Wankhede stadium, you can visit Chinnaswamy stadium in Bangalore or you can visit the MA Chidambaram stadium in Chennai. You won't find a Merchant or Umrigar stadium in Mumbai, or a Dravid stadium in Bangalore. The most that you will find is a Shiv Lal Yadav 'stand' in Hyderabad or a Gavaskar stand in Mumbai. You certainly will not find a 'Krishnan tennis stadium', though a 'Khanna stadium' can be found easily. The only exception I can think of is the K.D. Singh Babu stadium in Lucknow—I wonder how this aberration occurred! In New York, you can go to Arthur Ashe stadium, in Paris to Yannick Noah arena, in Rome to Pietrangeli stadium and in Madrid to the Manolo Santana stadium. Surely nothing to commemorate Ramesh Krishnan or Vijay Amritraj or Paes in India. Rod Laver arena or Margaret Court arena in Australia are natural but any arena or stadium in India has to be named after an administrator, who instead of contributing to the game, has been a parasite and a beneficiary. Vishwanathan Anand, who has brought more laurels in the international sport arena than any other Indian is hardly known or remembered or commemorated in India. Is it surprising that we have no standing or position in international sports worth a mention?

Whenever India plays an international event, particularly in cricket, it is televised and widely seen. But in other sports, the coverage of our football or hockey or badminton or any other sport, unless it is an international event, is nearly non-existent. Indian television shows the English Football league—New Castle United versus Stoke city. Who except V.S. Naipaul or Nirad Chaudhuri (Nirad who?) knows in India where Stoke City is. We cannot see Kanpur versus Bangalore football, as no such event exists. This is the dish handed out to us by our daily television sports channels, when on those rare occasions no international cricket match is available to be broadcast. I recall many years back, All India Radio would fill up its sports quota of two minutes during the peak-hour national news, referring to Ivanovich losing in the second round in an obscure tennis tournament in Dubai—I wonder if those interested could be counted on the fingers of one hand. In August 2013, the major sports news reported by our television channels as 'breaking news', and repeated for a few days, was that Somdev Dev Varman had 'qualified' to play in the US Tennis Open. Yes indeed, he had been allowed to be a participant; he had not won the tournament!

***

Clive conquered the country but it was Macaulay who conquered the spirit of India. He was responsible for cricket replacing Hinduism as the main religion in India! My first contact with the religion, or way of life called cricket, started from my early school days in Tanjore. I really cannot trace the inspiration for the same. My uncle, Swaminathan who grew up with me and who later played for the Chennai University and the Indian Air Force teams was the first to take up the game. A neighbour T.M. Durai was an accomplished player. Somehow, from the age of about 9 years or so one got hooked to this game. One of my earliest memories is of playing cricket with neighbourhood boys in the Tanjore suburb where I lived, in the non-descript maidan with make-shift implements was this poor boy, from a neighbouring house, going into his pocket between overs to get a small bite of the dosa which was lodged there, and which constituted his evening 'tea'.

Soon our playing conditions improved in the maidan, actual stumps (on one side, with change-over) and cork balls at least, if not cricket balls were ushered in and there was minimum rolling of the pitch to reduce the dimensions of the pits. With one pair of dirty, smelly, half-torn pads—one for the left leg of each batsman—the quality of our cricketing conditions sharply improved over the next year or so. I still have a memory of a senior lawyer in Tanjore district *katcheri*—court for you—who was a cricket aficionado, who would join us late in the afternoon, just at dusk, after his day in the courts. He would arrive in his 'Singer' motor car, still in his official costume—shirt sleeves, black jacket, tie, heavy turban and dhoti worn in the traditional style (not the flippant wrap-around), with long white socks and black shoes. Imagine a person today wearing this kind of dress in public or even in private! He would take off his turban and jacket; he was very keen to bowl, not so much to bat. He had a vial containing snuff placed in his shirt front-pocket so while beginning an over, and again half-way through that over, he would dig into his pocket, pick up a liberal pinch and inhale it deeply; clearly that would impart much spin to his off-breaks. He would pitch the ball well outside the off-stump and make it turn, with a whirring movement past the leg-stump; I do not know if the rule limiting two-men back-of-square-leg existed those days, as he would have three leg-slips. In short he was a delightful person to learn cricket from. After dark, we would sit around the stumps and he would regale us with delicious stories, some off-colour I guess, which I couldn't fully comprehend. I have many memories of Chari-sir.

The other lasting memory is of a cricket match organized in our maidan, between two teams, one headed by the District Collector. We then had the glorious spectacle of the Collector, a strapping six-foot-plus Scotsman, whose name —McLaughlin I still remember; the first Caucasian I had ever set eyes on—who was a good head taller than anyone around him, and was the cynosure of all eyes. He even had, what we all believed was a 'sandalwood' bat—the highest quality wood that we had heard of. He had a large canvas duffel bag, long and wide as a coffin, to carry his 'gear', which included the abdomen guard which we had never heard of earlier. He even changed into 'buckskin' shoes with steel sprigs. In short, he took our breath away, in so many ways. I do not recall any great cricketing performance displayed by him on the field; the visit by such a great man to our maidan was sufficient memory for a lifetime!

Another memory from school is, while I was in the final year, playing a match representing my class against the full school team, scoring 80 or so not out. The games master Alexander, on his own declared the innings closed even while I was the class captain—he did not want a new ground record established, particularly by a slip of a tiny boy, who was not even in the reckoning to represent the school team; he assessed that he would be criticized for this lapse. Elsewhere, I have already mentioned about listening to the radio commentary, till late in the evening, with heavy static and the flowery language of John Arlott, along with was it Brian Johnston, barely comprehensible, the landmark partnership between Bradman and Morris in the immortal Leeds test of 1948.

***

It was natural that my passion for cricket got me into the ambit of the Excelsiors Club in Calcutta, predominantly a sports organization run by and for south Indians of the south Calcutta lake area—basically 'Madrasis'. I started attending the nets from the first year in college, discovered that I had good hand-eye coordination, was tried out as the 'second' wicket-keeper, and soon sealed my spot as the 'first' wicket-keeper. In the course of four years, the Excelsiors Club did fairly well and in my final year we got promoted to the first division, where we had the opportunity to play the best teams in Bengal—Mohan Bagan, East Bengal, Sporting Union (Pankaj Roy and P. Sen), Rajasthan (Dattu Phatkar)—names familiar to old timers—am I already that old? Perhaps I did contribute a little, with a number of 50s, and generally one or two centuries on an average each season. One recalls the privilege of playing in the Eden Gardens a number of times, and once scoring 50-odd runs there. With my preoccupation with Club cricket, I never took the trouble of going to the nets in St. Xavier's College, where I would likely have found a place in the college team. For two years, I was in the Calcutta University 17, though I never got a chance to play in the first-11 mainly because Gopal Chakravorty was the 'first' wicket-keeper and did not have the grace to allow the second wicket-keeper any chance for a look in (Dhoni and Kartik!). Among my pleasant cricket memories from Calcutta is a newspaper cutting from the *Statesman* headed 'Ramanan and Goswami score centuries'. Goswami is that incomparable legendary sportsman who was the illustrious captain of Indian football, captained Bengal cricket for many years, represented Calcutta University in tennis and also played first division hockey. He would have excelled in any sport—a most versatile sportsman.

***

Calcutta used to be a sports loving city, with well organized facilities for football, cricket and hockey among others. In the respective seasons, league encounters between the various teams, divided into divisions, well planned and organized was the feature of the sports scene in the 1950s. Excelsiors was in the third division league of football (the fourth division was the lowest), and played hockey in the third division, the lowest division in the tournament. I played inside left in football, though I do not recall any significant performance. I probably did enough to hold my place in the team, possibly due to lack of enough rivals! It was much the same for hockey also.

Calcutta of course was madly in love with the game of football—probably the love affair with this game has cooled off a little in recent years, I am not sure. Mohan Bagan and East Bengal were the leading lights in this game and their twice-a-season meetings in their respective grounds were treated as warfare by the Calcuttans. Victory or defeat in each match was analysed to the finest detail, the culprits, the heroes and the traitors were lifted to heavens or torn to pieces in addas in every tea house. 'Jolly' Kittu, who hailed from Tanjore played for East Bengal. I knew him from our hometown, and he used to come to our house in Calcutta a couple of times each season for dinner. I used to get an annual season pass to the East Bengal ground, which was used nearly without fail. A venerable gentleman called Bhattacharya, who was a member of the legendary Mohan Bagan team of 1911, which beat a British team in a historic encounter to win the IFC Shield (Mohan Bagan players barefooted and IFC players in leather football shoes) was a clerk in my father's office. He was good enough every year to give me an annual season pass to the Mohan Bagan grounds (perhaps the habit of cadging, taking undue advantage of situations and circumstances started early for me, well before I joined the IAS!). Most football season evenings would be spent watching matches in the maidan, with the adda to follow.

I need to mention one memory. Before the major soccer matches, there used to be long queues to obtain daily tickets, limited in number. It was not unusual for a sizeable number of people starting to queue up after dinner the previous day. On match day, the serpentine line would go winding for hundreds of yards. Suddenly one would see a charge by the mounted police at an arbitrarily chosen spot, fairly close to the ticket counter, breaking and disbanding the queue and scattering those waiting patiently, ostensibly to handle some minor local skirmish. However, more often than not, the charge was meant to dislodge the queue, allow the 30 or 40 newcomers accompanying a tout to get a favourable place in the queue, clearly for a 'consideration'. Surely the police platoon on horseback was on the take! One saw these 'games' being played even at a young age, for shall we say 'business reasons'. One has had the misfortune to see much the same kind of games, in totally different circumstances, being played in our administrative spheres. A. Raja's 'performance' in telecom merely followed a long tradition well known and practiced in all spheres of Indian life!

***

One other memory, not directly sports-related, but in the context of a baseball match that I saw in the Chicago Cubs stadium in Chicago, probably in 1968, about which I had written elsewhere. Between innings, at the general toilet area, the person at the urinal next to me spoke to me earnestly, surely about the state of the match, in a language which I didn't understand—almost certainly Spanish. I take it that he must have identified me as a Mexican. When I did not respond, he looked at me contemptuously, distinctly and gutturally uttered the word 'gringo' and went away. I could not fathom what he was saying; I interpreted his comment as a pejorative reference to the size of my private parts! It was much later that I came to know the meaning of the word, and realized that he had no such ignoble thoughts and was merely expressing his irritation that I was not a fellow Latino.

This brings me to the stand-up toilet bowls in India in hotels, airports, restrooms or clubs and other public places. Presumably the positioning of the bowls, particularly the height at which they are placed is geared to European or American standards. An average Indian male is probably a good six inches shorter in height and has to contend forever with a bowl placed much higher than his groin. The result as can be imagined, is indeed unpleasantly experienced by most while going to such places—an unhealthy potentially infective physical contact of one's extreme—the 'business end'—with the edge of the bowl, or an unseemly spill-over on to the front of one's trousers. Clearly our stand-up toilet bowl makers did not apply their minds to the specifications of Indian male physiognomy! Some further research may be required in this regard.

Old timers, who have followed American baseball, may recall the famous grand slam home run by Carlton Fisk in Fenway Park, playing for the Boston Red Sox against Cincinnati Reds in the sixth game of the 1975 World Series. The image of Fisk sprinting to First Base, willing the ball to stay in by waving his hands, is immortal in baseball lore. This is remembered as a classic in baseball, with a swirling wind swinging the ball inches into fair territory, just ensuring that the Boston team would play the 7th and final match of the series, which alas they lost. I happened to be sitting in Fenway Park, watching the ball fly through. Whenever I narrate this story at a party in the US, I become the centre of discussion, a hero of sorts for a few moments, as this great event in baseball is remembered.

Still on baseball, Pete Rose, first baseman for Cincinnati Reds, and already a legend, already in the hall of fame of baseball, played for Cincinnati in that match referred to. A couple of years later, I read with dismay that he had been discovered cheating, caught 'spot-fixing' with television evidence available of his signalled communications with the bookies. It only took a couple of weeks, probably less, for him to be thrown out in disgrace, dethroned from the hall of fame, all his records (of which there were many glorious ones) wiped out from the statistics of the game and unceremoniously and contemptuously discarded to the dustbin. I do not remember if there was any prosecution or incarceration. In the context of the BCCI-IPL spot-fixing brouhaha of 2013, it is worth remembering that eternal vigilance is required to maintain the purity of the game. It is very easy to destroy reputations built over decades; ultimately public confidence in the probity of the game is the only sure way to attract and entertain people.

***

Except in cricket, India is not recognized in terms of any field sport internationally, though some advance has been made in badminton in recent years. We were the home of hockey in the 1930s and 1940s, with the legendary Dhyan Chand and K.D. Singh Babu, compared with the likes of Bradman. Since then, the game has caught on elsewhere and these days we struggle even to get to qualify for the Olympics. In other lesser hockey tournaments, in general India finds itself struggling not to end up last in the field—the Koreas, Malaysias, New Zealands and the Argentinas have left us far behind. There seem no prospects of an early revival.

There are two key factors why sports have not flourished in India, and reached anywhere close to international standards, even standards in many neighbouring countries and the region. Firstly, the poverty levels in India are so high that a very large proportion (many estimate it at 70+ per cent) has no preoccupation except to forage for basic food for survival. Lacking in nutrition and micronutrients, a growing young person is ill-equipped to participate in competitive sports. There is no time for any recreation or sports activities. Secondly, there are no organized sports facilities in most schools with respect to any of the recognized sports, at the village/town levels. As one drives by the highway or goes by train, one can see young boys playing with rudimentary equipment in wayside fields and in make-shift grounds with primitive facilities. Even in urban and semi-urban areas, the primary and secondary schools are so short of space that they can barely accommodate the classrooms; and there is no provision for a playground. In many urban primary schools, the authorities specify a large neighbouring privately-owned garden or public park as the 'playground' for the school to fulfil the compulsory 'requirement' of providing playground-space dedicated to school children. This is patently false certification, indulged in by nearly every school, private or public and verified as correct by municipal authorities. It is astonishing how patent large-scale falsehood can prevail in an endemic fashion with no penalty attached, all concerned being fully aware of the mass untruth—a national character flaw? This is somewhat akin to the large-scale betting and fixing involved in international cricket; all authorities concerned are aware of its extent and prevalence, even though many may not directly indulge or participate in it.

Many decades back, as the District Magistrate in a remote east Uttar Pradesh district, I had dedicated a small portion of the garden attached to my residential bungalow to be converted to a cricket practice area with nets and a 'rolled' pitch. All the 30 or so young boys who started coming for practice had no clue about the basics of cricket—the concept of bowling, as opposed to throwing was unfamiliar to them; the idea of a straight bat was unknown and hitting was naturally cross-batted, baseball style. To cut a long story short, within a couple of months, many of them became reasonably good bowlers as well as batsmen and also learnt the basics of fielding, Within two months a Ghazipur district team was formed, we were able to play matches in Mohammedabad and also with local teams in Ballia, Varanasi, Jaunpur etc. Years after I left Ghazipur, I came to know that of the boys who started their nets in the Collector's compound, six or so played for Gorakhpur or Lucknow University, and at least one played for UP state. The conclusion is inescapable that there is enormous talent, of every variety, in every district, including the remotest and most backward in India. It is only lack of opportunity and availability of basic facilities that has prevented the potential talent from blossoming. In another context, I have referred to the VidyaGyan School system, which conducts the same experimentation in the primary/secondary education field. There is enough empirical evidence available to indicate that the raw undeveloped talent in our remotest areas is potentially as good as the best available in the country. Providing opportunities is the main obstacle because of which we have not become a 'developed' nation during the past seven decades.

In India, state support to sports is generally seen to mean creating stadia and large urban facilities. These are third-order requirements; the first order is generating large-scale participation of the younger population in sporting activities across the nation so that a sizeable pool of talented young boys and girls can be identified, for which a separate mechanism of first-round filtering needs to be established at local levels. Jeev Milkha Singh says 'build more driving ranges, not golf courses'. Thereafter a basic formal coaching system, say at the tehsil, block/small town level needs to be in place to train budding potential. Those who excel in these facilities, and show promise, are then ready for playing at the university/state/national levels, for whom the large stadia and urban facilities are necessary. At present we short-circuit the procedure and take the easy route, and expect to identify quality at the top-most levels as if it will turn up routinely and magically. As in other walks of life, we wish to build 20-storey buildings, without a foundation; we wish to have excellence in higher education, while a large proportion of young children are illiterate; many 'graduates' cannot compose one sensible coherent sentence to express their thoughts. This same syndrome of focusing on form without any concern for substance, thirsting for success without any effort, afflicts our sports arena also. This is the significant reason why we have failed to make a mark in international sports.

***

Cricket is a primary example of a sport dominated by politicians in India. Nearly every chief minister, or a senior political leader in a state is a member of the cricket's governing council, BCCI. Since money, power and prestige are associated with high office in cricket, this relationship is inevitable. The power elite use their political clout for positions in the sports administration body and use the sports body to assist their political careers. This is a fine art in which high specialization has been achieved. The ruling motto is that once you reach the top echelons, 'you scratch my back, I will scratch yours'—a crony approach to day-to-day management and handling of major issues becomes a working model. Usually the sports body's administration is a mutual-support group. If the sport incidentally benefits, well and good, otherwise it is just bad! It is not surprising that whenever major allegations of betting, fixing and sleaze surface, these are soon 'handled', controlled, managed and whitewashed. Then it is business as usual, till the next crisis. There is a striking parallel between management of our cricket board and our politics.

The situation is not too different with respect to other sports like tennis or football or badminton and the like, except that India does not have the same pre-eminent international position in these sports as it has in cricket. As you analyse each of these, you will find that the chief of the federation or association is always a politician; if the political party to which he belongs loses power, he will soon be 'eased out' and will be replaced by a politician from the current ruling class. The chief executive usually holds office for upwards of ten or 15 or 20 years, and has a bunch of cronies representing the state associations to vote him back to power year after year. He ensures that they are rewarded suitably with diversion of government funds, or foreign trips or for organizing 'lucrative' tournaments. It is a self-perpetuating, self-benefitting, self-interest group. One will invariably find this pattern in nearly every sport in India. All the funds given for the 'development' of a particular sport are used mostly for foreign travel by office bearers and similar purposes for their benefit. The interest of the sport or sportsmen is of little concern to anyone. The Indian Olympic Association (IOA), the apex field sports body, is a prime example in India of manipulators controlling sports, with no concern for the interests of the sportsmen—indeed they couldn't care less if Indians cannot participate in the Olympics, so long as they remain in power; they are really 'politicians' not sports administrators. It is obvious that groups of self-appointed crooks, who use the national politics of the day for their benefit, will ensure that no law prescribing number of terms, age limits, etc. will ever come into existence. Do you expect the Parliament and the politicians to pass a 'Lok Pal' law which will effectively curtail the untrammelled powers of the political class, across parties, and their exploitation of their position and power!

* * *

Amidst all my sports activities in college in Calcutta in the 1950s, I could find time to play table tennis. I did this in nearly all my spare time; I fancied that I was a 'good' player. Once at the South India Club, my friend introduced me to his guest, a right-handed player, with whom he had a couple of games. The guest barely beat my friend. I deemed myself a superior player to my friend; when the guest offered to play with me, and that too left-handed, clearly it was 'easy meat'. We even entered into a bet, the wager probably a sleeve of balls. In the event, the 'guest' beat me, indeed thrashed me 21 to 2 and 21 to 1. It just turned out that he was the then national champion Chandrasekhar, a left-handed player, who was playing with my friend right-handed for fun! Moral of the story—don't bet unless you are sure to win.

I will not start any 'golf stories', as that may require another book! I will confine myself with one incident at the Delhi Golf Course, relating to my late friend Dhruv Seth. Actually he was better known as Sushma Seth's husband, rather than by his own name. This is not uncommon—how often do we refer to Mrs Singh's husband, or Mrs Ishwaran's husband, much like Mrs Margaret Thatcher's husband—what's his first name? Diverting further, at the annual Byron Nelson Golf Tournament somewhere in Texas, the prize for the winner is distributed by the 'widow' of Byron Nelson—the male chauvinistic attitude is implicit even in the US. Why doesn't anyone refer to the 'widower' of so-and-so lady? But even if this were to be done, we are so steeped in our male dominated psyche, that he will be called 'widower' of Mrs Smith!

Coming back to Sushma Seth's husband, on hole number 15, a dog-leg left, his drive from the tee took a big duck-hook and was swinging well to the left and would have even crossed the adjacent fairway of hole 14, when an unfortunate bird came into the ball's way. We heard a crunchy noise; the ball came to rest in the middle of our fairway, so did the dead body of the bird. Sushma Seth's husband made a par in that hole, the only one of the day! I wonder if he remembered to thank the bird that sacrificed its life to enable him this 'birdied' glory.

Now that golf stories have started, I need to add just one more, this from Air Marshal Dhawan in Lucknow, recounting a round he played in a course near Cairo, sometime in the 1970s on a par-3 hole. The tee shot got embedded on a palm-tree—Dhawan had no choice except to clamber on to the tree, play the shot from a semi-reclining position and sure enough it went into the hole for a 'birdie'—as remarkable an incident as is possible, except that one could not get any corroboration or eye-witness to confirm the miracle. Many golfing and fishing stories are of this kind!

18

THOSE CAREFREE SCHOOL AND COLLEGE DAYS

The days of our youth are the days of our glory ... Lord Byron

In this chapter, I go back to my school, college and early days. It is not uncommon, I suppose, for an old man to hark back to old memories so I may be given the indulgence. While I have picked incidents from my early life, I wanted to give a picture of what school and college days were like over 50 or 60 years back—probably not too different from what they are today, so a younger reader may make a comparison.

I did primary schooling in National High School in Calcutta, a predominantly Tamil organization, with practically all students being Madrasis, as anyone south of the Vindhyas was called in Calcutta those days. These were tumultuous days in the mid-1940s, a couple of years prior to independence. Though I did not know these details, it was also the time when Suhrawardy as the Chief Minister of Bengal deliberately did not allow the police to curb a series of major riots instigated by Muslims. When the massive Hindu backlash started, the armed police came down very heavily. At any rate these were troubled times in Calcutta, when my parents decided that I should go to Tanjore for further schooling and to live with my grandmother in the ashram which she was presiding over. Janaky Matha was a devotee of Ramana Maharishi of Tiruvannamalai and herself had a large following those days, indeed even now, four decades after she is gone. At any rate, I recall one Class IV Hindi examination in the school, where I had no clue what the question paper asked me to do; I merely wrote ('एक, दो, तीन, … … दस') the first ten numbers in Hindi; the only Hindi that I knew! The advice to beauty-contestants says, 'if you do not know the answer to the question, smile and give the answer to any question that you know'—an art perfected by politicians.

In the ashram in Tanjore, we had the benefit of the visit of a 'tuition master'—Sivarama Iyer. Pronounced quickly in Tamil, it had the potential to sound a little vulgar, making a reference to pubic hair—a method of referring to him that we preferred rather than calling him 'master'! He became the 'tuition master' for our generation of young children and covered at least six or seven of us in the ashram. He was one of the teachers in the Viraraghava High School, where he used his 'influence' to get me enrolled in first form—sixth form being school-final—effectively a double jump or even triple jump, without any transfer certificate or academic credentials that I could lay claim to. I do not recall any serious coaching by him or lessons that he taught us. However, he was extremely effective in getting us to pass each term examination and annual examination in the school. His method was elementarily simple; on the morning of each test, he would ask me to answer a limited number of very specific questions/exercises, chide me, abuse me, criticize me, but make sure that I would correctly answer those questions. Surprise, surprise, at the test the same day in the school by some magic, identical questions given to me by Sivarama Iyer would appear; one was well-equipped to perform reasonably well enough to pass! With this simple but effective expedient, I was able to move from first form to fifth form (I was to learn much later that the essence of the technique employed by my tuition master is regularly applied in administration—favourites and cronies manage to get on to the 'inside-lane', licenses and other scarce items are distributed with unerring accuracy to favoured individuals, using well-defined techniques). I was puny compared to the others in my class and was nicknamed 'new boy'—(*pudu paiyan*)—an appellation I carried through six years of schooling.

They say that once you learn to ride a bicycle, you will never lose the balance. Even after a gap of many years, one can ride a cycle. I am not sure if I can do that now, but I remember the time when I was learning the art. The cycle was a little too big for me and I would tentatively push it forward, move one leg on to the pedal, and try to vault on to the seat. One morning as I was trying the exercise, Master came in on his bicycle, and observed me. His comment: 'Why are you trying to impregnate the bicycle—can't you find an animal or another person?!' Coming to think of it, bicycling is good exercise, non-polluting, inexpensive. In most cities today, you can reach your destination faster on a non-motorized bicycle than in a motor car. Even today, large numbers of people go to work in China, Japan and even in places like Amsterdam, by bicycle. Did we make a strategic blunder in India by encouraging motor cars in place of the bicycle to ape western models, when more efficient, less expensive domestic models were available? Was it the first of many policy blunders—was Mahatma Gandhi right or wrong?

The footpath from our home/ashram to the school took us across the railway line, across a culvert over the Kaveri canal, through a dried up lake from the times of the Maratha kings, on to the main town and then the school itself. Up to third form (corresponding to Grade VIII), the school was located in Mangala Vilas, which used to be the harem of the Maratha kings. The school was located close to the Big Temple, a major landmark in temple architecture, created by the Cholas not far from Saraswati Mahal, which houses one of the best libraries of old literature in India with many authentic ancient manuscripts in Sanskrit and Tamil, now under the loving care of the descendents of Maratha kings.

Every morning, we started the two mile (3 km) walk to the school; the leader of the pack was my uncle, and two older children of ashram inmates, devotees of Janaki Matha. Every third or fourth day, one of these three would make up their minds not to go to school that day—my views didn't count—so near the waist-high sub-canal we would take off our clothes, have a long dip in the water, have our lunch from the 'tiffin-box' lovingly packed at home, have a nap in the shade, and get back home in the late afternoon. Under penalty of serious unspecified punishment, I was directed by my uncle and his cohorts not to mention the manner that studies were undertaken that day. In the culvert on the main canal, which was about 15 yards across, there was the parapet wall, probably six inches thick. On a dare, I would undertake the perilous walk along the parapet wall, about 30 feet above water level, with the swirling canal water below, often with fairly strong winds blowing in that open area, with no knowledge of swimming; in retrospect, a risk which was unbelievably absurd, inexplicably stupid where there was no return, probability of failure not too low and punishment for failure the severest possible. One shudders even now at the near-suicidal risks taken—perhaps it was the age!

Sanskrit was my second language in school, English being the first, the medium of instruction was Tamil though. I did study six years of Sanskrit, essentially following Bhandarkar's Grammar. My memory is that the teacher tried to do a good job; but at the end of six years, I am not sure I really got to know the language enough to pursue studies of our scriptures and other great literature without help. I was and am unable to do these important things, defeating the basic purpose of learning a language. Clearly the pedagogy in teaching Sanskrit was abysmally poor those days—I wonder if it has improved. A language taught exclusively through grammar will take a long time to reach the mind of the student. Much later, I learnt German and French through newer techniques, the essence of the teaching is to start with simple short stories and to proceed increasing in complexity. In three months, I probably learnt more of these two languages, than in six years of Sanskrit. The only lasting benefit of my second language in school is that Sanskrit words are not unfamiliar to me, I can look at the root (*dhatu*) and divine its meaning, explore its derivatives. In picking up Hindi from scratch many years later, my limited Sanskrit was a major key in facilitating the process. The other clear benefit was that I could follow, even though not too accurately, great Sanskrit literature, like the *Gita* or the *Vishnu* or *Lalitha Sahasranaams* (well known prayer verses) where I could get a good picture of what was being stated.

Sometime in 2013, the Union Public Service Commission (UPSC) issued a notice making some changes in the curriculum relating to the preliminary and regular examinations for the IAS and allied services; these mainly related to removing an 'Indian language' from the requirements as a subject. In other words it would have been possible for a person with no knowledge of any Indian language (except English of course) to appear in the exam and do well enough to make it to the merit list. Astoundingly, this was announced only in February or so of that year, with the prelims to start three months thereafter. UPSC, which is a sound, conservative and responsible agency ought to have given at least two to three years' notice to the candidates, considering that many prepare for years for appearing in these examinations. Be that as it may, a major controversy arose as to the wisdom of dropping all Indian languages (except English) as a possible compulsory subject, for the series of exams. I appeared extensively on television channels to press one major point—any senior official, who during his life time will work largely in a state government and also in rural areas will need to have a strong working knowledge of at least one Indian language. With the underlying cultural backdrop connecting the various states with disparate languages, customs etc., the knowledge of any Indian language will facilitate very considerably the ability to learn another Indian language. Exclusive knowledge of English language will not adequately prepare anyone to understand the cultural underpinnings of social life in any state—language is an important window to the culture and society in any part of India. With the dispensation proposed by UPSC, it could have enabled one with no knowledge of any purely Indian language to enter the higher civil services. This would diminish his ability to learn the language and culture of the state to which he is assigned. In my own case, my knowledge of Sanskrit enabled me to understand the culture, ethos as well as the language in Uttar Pradesh—Hindi. In retrospect, even if I had no knowledge of Sanskrit, even with my Tamil, it would have been possible for me to have learnt Hindi. Astonishingly, despite major superficial differences, the culture, trains of thought and ethos of society in Uttar Pradesh are not different from that in Tamil Nadu. In the event, UPSC rightly shelved the proposals and reverted to the status quo—sensibly so.

    Scholars say that Sanskrit is a 'perfect' language. Thoughts and ideas can be expressed very precisely in that language, more probably than in any other. There is such a treasure house of knowledge and experience in our *Vedas, Shastras, Puranas, Upanishads* and other records of a 5000-year-old flourishing civilization. Indeed, Bharat has witnessed all that is possible to experience over the millennia. This is embodied in our great literature; there is an awareness in the western world of the magnitude and value of these treasures. However, we have lost the key to these treasures by ignoring the study of Sanskrit language. While 'modernizing', we have thrown away our golden past.

***

The ashram had an extremely pious environment. Permanent residents, headed by Janaki Matha, my grandmother, included about ten family members, along with another six or seven families, devotees of Matha. In addition, nearly every day another ten or 12 devotees landed up to be in the ashram, to have darshan of Matha and to participate in the daily routine, which included about five hours each in the morning and in the evening of bhajans and stotras, sung in chorus, by all present in the prayer hall. Matha had time to supervise the management of the ashram and was assisted by old relatives, who were permanent residents. Sometime in the late mornings or early afternoons, or even in the night after dinner, my grandmother would ask me to read for her, in Tamil, *Gyaneshwari*, the commentary on the *Bhagwat Gita* by Sant Gyaneshwar. Originally this was rendered by Gyaneshwar in South Maharashtra, centuries back in Marathi, as a series of lectures. Somehow, through the remarkable Indian oral tradition, Gyaneshwari got recorded—at some stage it must have been translated into Tamil. It is great literature, and lays bare the wonders of the *Gita* in the simplest possible terms for the reader. Much later I tried to get an English version of Gyaneshwari; searching high and low. I failed till I went to the United Nations bookshop in the Fort area in Mumbai, where I found a copy sponsored by UNESCO, as part of their 'heritage literature' series. It is astonishing how we are unable to recognize the pearls, treasures, wisdom and heritage which is amidst us, and is available just for the asking and taking. It is left to a foreigner from 5,000 miles away to comprehend the greatness enshrined in our literature, and package it for larger consumption.

I wonder if Indian psychologists have analysed this failure; clearly the observant Caucasian is able to identify the greatness in India's past and adapt it or at least appreciate it. Perhaps we need a foreign psychologist to tell us what is wrong with us!

***

I often wonder how I cleared my high school examinations, the 'school final' in 1952, conducted by the secondary school board. At least till fifth form, I had no clue as to what was happening in the classrooms. While I didn't resent the other classes, the only one I really enjoyed was the thrice-a-week arts class. The teacher who understood student-psychology would spend the entire time telling us rollicking stories. We had no need for any art paper or easel or pencils—it was story time! Some spark from somewhere must have entered me as I finally managed to stand second from my school in the school final examination—a great surprise to me, most of all.

Many years later, I had to go to Varanasi to give a lecture at the Banaras Hindu University (BHU). My younger brother who had passed out from BHU sometime in the early 1960s earnestly asked me to make sure that I visited *Sankat Mochan* Hanuman Mandir (temple), located just outside the BHU main gate. He asked me to pray for him there, which I did during that visit to Banaras. When I asked him as to why he insisted on my visiting this particular Hanuman Temple, he replied that the way he studied engineering at BHU, there was just no way he could get his degree. He attributes the degree exclusively to the devout prayers to Hanumanji at Sankat Mochan Mandir—he can think of no other explanation. I do not know who my Hanumanji was in Tanjore—perhaps it was the piousness of the ashram that my prayers were answered, indeed even when the requests not articulated!

***

When I finished the school final in 1952, Madras University had a prescribed minimum age of 15 years at time of entry for the intermediate course (two years intermediate + two years degree). Since, thanks to the kindness of my Master Sivarama Iyer, I fell short of this by about two years, I had to move to Calcutta, which did not have a prescribed minimum age for college, to join the St. Xavier's College. It was quite traumatic to move from Tamil medium instruction to all classes conducted in the English medium. My 'new boy' status continued, though in a different vein. There were many reminders in the first few months that I needed to 'adjust' to continue onwards.

For example, in the very first month, in the English 'tutorial', Fr. Vernon, of Irish extract, asked the class of 25 or so to write an essay on 'Soliloquy of a broom', during the class session. The next week's tutorial session was devoted to an analysis of the students' efforts, and suggestions for improvement. Fr. Vernon pointed out the 20 most 'glaring' mistakes, without mentioning the culprit's name—like Abou Ben Adam, my name led all the rest—I 'bagged' 16 out of the class's 20 howlers. The very next week, the subject of the essay was 'the Child is the Father of the Man'—I did slightly better—only 12 of the glaring errors of the top 20 were attributed to me. While Fr. Vernon sneeringly looked at me in the class, which treatment to be fair to him he gave to everyone even-handedly, or even-eyedly shall we say, he did not openly let me down—merely calling me separately to let me know that I needed to 'improve'!

The first two semesters went in a blur—I had little knowledge of what was going on around me—I was focusing more on the use of English language in the treatment of physics, chemistry and mathematics. Bailon D' Sa our maths professor spoke elegant English, and enthralled us with his diction and fluidity. He would let it be known to the class of his latest contribution to some mathematical journal on the subject 'some new problems of topology', adding to one's inferiority complex. Roy Chowdhary the algebra teacher would tell us 'A Bharies as B, B Bharies as C, so A Bharies as C'; Ghosh, the chemistry professor would refer to 'mars gash'; Professor Dhar of English fired my imagination with his own rendition of Keats: 'haard melodies are swit, those unhaard are switter (sic)'. With such massive English language complications to contend with, it was a diffident and unhappy camper indeed who entered the hallowed portals of St. Xavier's every morning and left it in the afternoon a frustrated young man, who appeared to be doomed without a future.

Naturally, the first quarterly exam results were abysmally poor, but not unexpected; so much so, I did not even share them with my father. Without remembering it now, I guess I persisted, did not give up, was not willing to accept defeat. One day, at the end of two semesters, I suddenly saw my physics marks were 76 per cent—I could not believe it. I was absolutely certain that the physics teacher had been careless while correcting the second quarter papers. I waited for a full two-days for the bombshell to drop, that is, his informing me of the mistake committed and revising my marks to 26 per cent or so which I expected. As it sunk in that my marks were genuinely earned, the college experience dramatically improved, and went on to a new plane.

***

We had many stalwarts in the faculty of the college. P. Lal, in the English faculty was a nationally famous poet, his work appearing regularly in national newspapers—the college was agog when he was even invited 'abroad' to a conference of poets somewhere. Vishwanathan, who was quite portly in his 30s as he was then, was already an author, and an important figure on the Bengali stage, with much recognition. He even acted in lead roles in a number of Bengali films, even though he was in the English faculty in the college. These great teachers were able to fire one's imagination— Jean Anoulih's *Five Characters in Search of an Author*, or *the King is Dead—Long Live the King* were examples of extra reading, outside the prescribed syllabus, spurred due to an association with these fine teachers. At one stage I even had the temerity to challenge them to a dictation-spelling contest, of a piece I had learnt from a relative; the actual sentence read: 'a harassed cobbler and an embarrassed pedlar sitting on a cemetery wall eating Britannia biscuits made of desiccated coconuts went into unparalleled ecstasy at the symmetry of a lady's ankles.' I tried this out on P. Lal and Vishwanathan; to my eternal delight, they both made at least five spelling mistakes each—this probably was the high point of my college course in St. Xavier's. If it also punctured a little of the high esteem (admittedly much of it justified) that they held of themselves, all the better!

You may like to try it out with someone who is pleased with himself about his command of the English language.

Among the other memories of college days could be mentioned the need to visit the private rooms of Fr. Goreux, who was probably in his 50s at that time. He was our mathematics professor and in his younger days had been in the group headed by Einstein somewhere in Germany or France. He smoked cigars incessantly. Once you opened the door to his room, a fragrant delicious aroma would hit you, giving much pleasure; an incentive for me to visit him often, find excuses to get there to experience the feeling. I suspect I became an inveterate smoker in later years mainly because of a subconscious addiction to tobacco which started at that time and manifested itself a few years later. Goreux would solemnly define mathematics as 'something that entered the notebook of the student from the notebook of the teacher, without entering the head of either!' I bet a majority of the students and teachers in colleges would agree. Talking of tobacco, in later years when I became a chain smoker, I wanted to 'kick the habit'; I took to pipe smoking to reduce tobacco intake. Visiting New York City on some assignment, I recall walking along Fifth Avenue, entering a high quality smoking-pipe store and lovingly examining the specimens on display. There was one 'full-week set'—7 pieces, one for each day shaped differently, that took my fancy. I drew the attention of the salesman, who looked like a Wall Street banker, and asked him for the price. His reply: 'Sir, if you ask for the price, you can't afford it!'

**

One word on the second language issue. Since I could not touch Hindi or Bengali as second language for the intermediate course (Sanskrit was not offered in St. Xavier's College), I chose Tamil even though I did not study it as a language in school. Though this was not taught in the college, we were allowed to write the exam. The course itself was not too complicated or difficult, with not much stress on grammar etc. The main syllabus consisted of Kamban's *Ramayana*, written about 1,000 years back, in Tamil, in particular *Ayodhya Khand*. By and large it followed the Valmiki text—while Valmiki treated Rama as 'an ideal man' (आदर्श पुरुष), Kamban looked at Rama as an avatar (अवतार) (incarnation of god). Kamban's *Ramayana* is renowned for its poetic imagination, and is a recognized masterpiece in Tamil literature. During the two summer holidays that I had, I devoted a large part to study this text, where my teacher was a brilliant young man—Matha Das—a devotee of Janaky Matha in the ashram. He was a genuine Tamil scholar, himself a poet of repute and was able to inculcate in me great love, curiosity and interest in Tamil literature. In one of his long verse poems, celebrating his Guru Janaky Matha I still recall the quality of his poetic imagery; referring to her as a Jeevan Mukta (attainment of nirvana while still living in this world and doing the routine chores, otherwise possibly also called Sahaja Yoga), he described her in fluid Tamil as '*Tamarai elai mel tanneerey, thayir mel vennai thani wazhvey*'—her life was like a drop of water on a lotus leaf, a lump of butter swimming on the buttermilk'—one of spiritual detachment in life.

What I treated as a chore, in terms of learning Kamban, Matha Das converted to a pursuit of great pleasure. I looked forward to the two-hour post-lunch session when he would go through the text stanza-by-stanza with me, and bring out the finer points of the composition. Today, nearly 60 years later, I can recite verbatim a number of stanzas from Kamban's *Ayodhya Khand* with as much pleasure as I got the first time I understood it—for example, describing the defeat of the asuras who had come to disrupt the yagyna (sacrificial penance) of the great sage Vishwamitra. Rama frightened them so much that they ran away in great rapidity, '*one in front of the other*' (not one behind the other, that is, he routed them, creating chaos); I could give 50 instances of Kamban's genius. Describing Rama's entry into Mithila, Sita's town, Kamban talks of the starry-eyed young girls looking at Rama striding the streets—those who saw Rama's shoulders could not take their eyes off, so enthralling was it—the same for those who saw Rama's hands, and so on—was there one person in Mithila who could see Rama whole?—so beautiful was he! Among the regrets in my life, one is that I could not find the time or energy to read Kamban's *Ramayana* in full or more of Tamil literature, which is replete with great ideas and expressions. In Tamil, *Katratu Kaimannalavu, Kalladadu Ulagalavu*—What you know is like a fistful of sand, what you don't know is as big as the universe.

***

The two years in the University of Calcutta, in the Department of Applied Mathematics went by in a whirl. It is astonishing how our post-graduate courses, even one in an institution as renowned as Calcutta University focused on rote-learning. Even at that high level of the subject, it was treated as mechanical conveyance of some solved problems from the teacher to the student; Goreaux was right—it was a mere matter of notes passing from the teacher to the student, neither having to apply his mind. The professors, unlike the ones that I saw in St. Xavier's College, were completely demotivated, treated the lectures as chores to be performed. In a monotone continuous lecture, with no animation, energy, or application of mind, they would cover the day's prescribed quota of 'dispensing' knowledge. It was all so mechanical, so routinized, that neither the student nor the teacher was interested. I recall that the statistics professor would deal with abstruse and complicated statistical applications, without laying the ground work—a comprehension of the basics of the various distributions, particularly the Gaussian distribution. The focus was on going into the higher reaches, without bothering to see if there was a foundation. Is this typical Indian mentality? Always building the upper floors without laying a foundation? Our professor on particle dynamics had a great reputation—he had studied at Gottingen University in Germany—much that he talked about was Greek and Latin or rather Deutsch to us. Only the professor who taught us 'fluid mechanics' tried to lay a foundation; each class was interesting. This is the practice that I saw being observed at Harvard University, where I spent a year obtaining a Master's degree—the beginning of each course would intensely focus on the basics and fundamentals for the first two weeks or so; the professor would ensure that everyone was on board, before embarking on the journey for the higher reaches. Incidentally, this failure to carry the class is a basic reason why our primary education system has failed in India. There is no pedagogy to speak of, but more of this elsewhere. In short, I have no serious academic memories of my M.Sc. course in Calcutta. The time was essentially spent on cricket, sports and every movie that came to town. It was not difficult to pass with high grades, only a very poor student could have failed!

***

Perhaps a couple of words would be in order about the year or so that I spent at the Imperial College in London, during which time I also prepared for the IAS examination. I had studied the 'Schlichting's theorem' in my M.Sc. course so it was a great surprise to see the great man—old, bearded Professor Schlichting himself actually teaching us at the Imperial College of Science in London the next year—a venerable old man, who took the course, and started from the beginning, to hold the class together through the semester. How many students can recall studying a theorem in whichever class they are in, and go on to meet the author of the theorem in an academic atmosphere!—I presume this happens regularly at the research stage, but surely not too often at levels below.

There are so many events and incidents that I am tempted to recount but here are just a few, briefly. I spent a year at the Indian YMCA Hostel in Fitzroy Square, off Tottenham Court Road, presided over by the patriarch Malaiperuman, a character in his own right. He identified me after a few months as the appropriate person to be the leader of the students' union. It was thus that every month or so I would preside over a meeting, where special guests were invited. I had the honour to sit next to Vijayalakshmi Pandit, then High Commissioner to UK. On another occasion, our guest-in-chief was Harold Macmillan, the then PM of UK. I still have a photograph of the welcome address given by me, wearing the only good shirt and the only suit, charcoal grey, that was my possession—for variety I would interchange between the two neckties that I had.

Incidentally within days of the Macmillan visit, I was going by the 'Tube'—metro to you—and who entered the compartment but the prime minister himself. He was carrying his own umbrella and briefcase, was accompanied by just one person, presumably a secret agent, who stood at a reasonable distance. All those in the compartment quickly recognized that the prime minister was amidst them—after a quick look up, they went back to their newspapers.

The PM stood through the three or four stations till he alighted, with not a second look from anyone. Can one imagine such a scene in India, today or at any time? I once saw the Chief Minister of Uttarakhand travelling in his convoy of more than 100 vehicles near Karanprayag, with all traffic on the other side stopped for more than 45 minutes. No VVIP worth his name can be seen in public without 30 or 40 dancing black-cats. One wonders if the security agents accompany them to the toilets also in their own houses! Admitting that the security situation all over the world has deteriorated sharply in recent decades, the kind of worship that we do of VVIPs in India is surely obscene. The other day a friend resident in a Swiss town related a real life story of going to a coffee shop with his brother visiting from India somewhere in Switzerland. They struck a conversation with a stranger, who seemed friendly and had goodwill for India. Only after the coffee, when he was leaving, did the stranger introduce himself as the President of Switzerland. My friend couldn't believe it so he went to Google and ascertained that it was true. I spent six years in Geneva in the 1980s and to this day I do not know the name or face of the president or the finance minister of Switzerland at that time. Surely, the more developed a country is, the less ostentatious their leaders—empty drums make the most noise. To those who don't believe this story, there is the video on YouTube, in August 2013, of the Swiss president of the day visiting China on an official trip, being shown collecting his own suitcase from the baggage belt and pushing the trolley to his car. President Truman of the US was known to have retired with absolutely no property, except a small house inherited by his wife. He drove home in his own car driving himself away from the White House as he retired, not accompanied by anyone. He personally went and purchased his rail or bus tickets for his post-retirement travel. Compare this with the opulent demands of President Pratibha Patil, who acquired vast land through dubious means to construct, at huge official cost, a post-retirement 'humble' residence. Clearly, the poorer the country, the more pompous the official.

During that period, I 'prepared' for the IAS examination—basically on the insistence of my father. The special feature of the examination is that a candidate has to prepare at least two subjects, one each at the graduate and post-graduate levels in addition to the fields he studied in, in his undergraduate course. This is the built-in feature to ensure that the entrants to the service should have the ability to come up to a reasonable level of grasp in a subject unfamiliar to them in a short time. It was autumn 1960—I was in London, appearing for the IAS exams (London, and possibly New York, were centres those days, since discontinued). My preparedness for the exams was extremely limited, perhaps confined to reading the notes from K.S. Iyer's Postal Tutorial coaching in the 'electorals'. The preparations were so tardy that I had not even studied the format for the general knowledge or English essay papers. So much so, that when the seven subjects to choose from for the 'essay' were revealed to me in the exam hall, I had a shock. I was totally ignorant of any information or background or experience on any of the topics prescribed. After looking turn by turn at each of the topics for a full half an hour, noting with a side-wise glance that all the others had furiously launched their attack on their chosen subject, I finally decided to take a plunge on the topic 'The Moon—fact and fancy' probably dictated by the fact that I knew some facts about the moon from my astronomy paper in the higher mathematics course! Anyway, I composed whatever I could improvise on this esoteric subject over the next hour or so and completed my task a good half an hour before the closing bell—thoroughly frustrated, angry with myself for not having prepared properly, and generally in a state of disgust. As I was leaving the venue, the chatter of the others who wrote the exam that day with me (including Moni Malhoutra, J.P. Singh and Vinod Grover—whom I did not know at that time), filled the stairway with learned references to Voltaire, Bertrand Russell, Bentham (referred to with panache as Benzhham) which added to my distress.

I summoned the will to go to the next day's exam, probably on English language and grammar. I was having breakfast at what I thought was 8 am at the YMCA Hostel, prior to taking the underground to the venue at India House in Aldwych. I half heard someone at the next breakfast table, about the winter time change, that it was past 9 am—the clock had been taken forward by an hour at mid-night. I left the breakfast half eaten, sprinted to the metro station, and was perspiring in the train when it broke down in the tunnel, in the middle of nowhere due to some failure in the system—the first and only time this happened during the nine months that I was in London that year—perhaps the time change had something to do with. As I raced from the station to India House, I reached there panting, bedraggled and in an awful physical and mental state when I met my guardian angel in the form of K.P.S. Menon, First Secretary in the Indian Mission. He took one look at me, understood my predicament, and told me that he would give me an extra hour beyond the official closing time and asked me to take 10 minutes to compose myself before sitting down for the paper.

At the end of the compulsory round of exams, I judged that I had done terribly, and it was futile to persist with the process of completing the other subject papers. I send a postal aerogram to my father who was based in Calcutta, briefly informing him that I intended to stop the process of completing the papers, and promptly forgot about it. There was a gap of 12 days between the compulsory and my subject papers. About a week later, I got a phone call from Calcutta—it was my father imploring me to go through the papers to the best of my ability for 'his sake'. I completed the process, more to oblige him than with any real expectations. In the event it is very likely that the English essay examiner may have got disgusted with reading repeatedly about 'men being born free', Immanuel Kant and the like, and found an amateurish attack on the moon to be a refreshing change. Clearly he was in a liberal mood, that I got very high marks for that paper, among the highest awarded to an essay!—one cannot account for tastes!

One of those who appeared in the IAS exam with me in London was Ravi Dayal, from a distinguished family, who was in Oxford on a Rhodes scholarship. He was quite brilliant—needless to say he was in the top bracket in the written examinations and was an automatic to be called for the interviews, held in Delhi in January/February 1961. The previous summer he had spent his holidays in Moradabad, where his elder brother Virendra Dayal was the District Planning Officer. Senior Dayal was deeply immersed in his field work, went to every block in the scorching heat and was trying to push through the current ideas of 'democratic decentralization'—

bringing the involvement of the local village bodies in development administration. During Ravi's IAS interview, this fact somehow cropped up. A board member asked Ravi about his experiences in the villages and blocks of a district. Ravi Dayal replied roughly in the following manner: 'It was beastly hot, I went to one place and had enough; the rest of the time I spent in Moradabad town, I was in the air-cooled room, curled up with some good books.' He received zero marks in the interview quota—the board judged that his 'attitude' was not appropriate—a Rhodes scholar was found 'unfit' for the service! I believe that the rules have now been changed, there are no minimum marks in an interview. As one comes across officers all over the country today, the key issue is one of attitude and approach—a feeling that one is serving the public. Compassion, I would rate as the number one requirement in an IAS officer; note that they already have high IQ, demonstrated through the examination route.

***

Again some Sankatmochan Hanuman must have been in-charge of my personal affairs, I passed with sufficiently high rank—which after 35 years made me the senior-most in the service, eligible for selection to the post of Cabinet Secretary.

On joining the IAS after the competitive examinations held in September-October 1960, I was to join the National Academy of Administration at Mussoorie in summer. It was wonderful to be in the academic atmosphere with not much responsibility or work to do, except be present for the various lectures. In retrospect one understands how ineffective the career preparation was at the academy—the real training started only when one joined the district a year later. However, lectures and lecturers were there to be endured. The real point of the academy was to bring people from all over India together, many of whom had not been exposed to the language, culture, food and other personal habits from other parts of India. Thus, probationers from the deepest south of India could meet, understand, and find a common denominator with, say, their counterparts from North East India. Besides probationers were, more often than not, allocated to non-home states, and got a taste of their future workmates by meeting their counterparts from the allotted states at the academy. The overall atmosphere was one of holiday—the impending reality of field work had not yet sunk in. The real benefit of the academy, and I believe that this is the major gain, and an important one, is for young officers destined to hold senior positions in Indian administration to get to know how strong the common elements were among themselves, despite the large variations in their language, origins, social backgrounds etc. One got to know the great diversity, and the underlying unity that is India. The other benefice, a major one is the bondage created at Mussoorie, the networks that facilitated transaction of government business over a 40-year period. Surely the architects of the IAS had understood the potential that the academy had in readying the probationers to start their careers in their respective states.

During the first weeks at the academy, many weekends were spent in Delhi, as groups of probationers would go 'to town', for distraction from the serious studies! I recall, in middle August, as we were returning by the overnight train from Delhi, about eight of us were in a first class compartment of the Mussoorie Express, all with valid reservations—I was sleeping in an upper berth. Sometime in the middle of the night, it could have been at Muzaffarnagar, a large number of locals, burly Jats, forced themselves into the compartment—probably they were going to the next town for the village bazaar or on a group visit for something. They woke up the probationers, and three or four sat down in each of the lower berths, nearly occupying the full area. When there was not enough room, I remember one of them shaking me rudely, and asking me to sit up, to make room for two or three more in my upper berth. When I remonstrated, and gesticulated shouting something about reservations, two of them bodily lifted me from the upper berth, took me to the window on the other side (those days there were no steel bars on windows), threw me on the platform and returned to the berth, a job well done. Suddenly the train started moving, I ran to the main door, hanging there for a while till a fellow probationer opened the door for me and brought me back in. I should add that the visitors were not unkind to me, they offered me sitting space in my own upper berth, not mentioning a word. That probably was the moment when I finally understood that I was back in India—London was 6,000 miles away!

The lecturers were of poor quality. For instance, the history professor would talk of 'the main crops in that area are rice, wheat, sorghum and paddy...' Professor Ramaswamy, the economics professor, entertained us with many stories, including an injunction to the boys in private conversations, to make sure that they had intimate encounters with eunuchs before their marriage, as a necessary preparatory step—an advice I did not take, I do not know how many others did. It is also not known to me what corresponding advice he gave to the female probationers in the batch. A memorable quote from Ramaswamy: 'Karl Marx, sitting in his ivory tower, contemplating humanity ...' the rest was irrelevant.

One story relating to Ramaswamy is relevant, as it pointed to an essential administrative feature that I would see repeatedly in my service period. The 1961 batch was divided into four groups, and each group was sent on 'Bharat darshan' to one part of India to get a feel for local conditions all over the country. Ramaswamy was our 'batch leader' with his wife staying back in Mussoorie. This was winter time which saw heavy snow in Mussoorie going up to 5 feet deposits on the roads. Someone in our batch, I am not sure who but I have a strong suspicion, sent a telegram to the academy in Mussoorie that Ramaswamy had died of a heart attack—as cruel and heartless an act as is possible, which cannot be described as any kind of joke. The reaction in Mussoorie, particularly in Ramaswamy's household can be imagined; because of the heavy snow, telephonic communication could not be made. The batch received a frantic message for details of Ramaswamy's death, and asking for further steps. In his inimitable nonchalant style, Ramaswamy himself telegraphically replied 'All well in batch IV—Ramaswamy'. I am unhappy to say there was no proper inquiry to identify the culprit who played the prank, if it can be called that. Surely he should have been identified, and his services terminated without fuss. Recall that no cause or reason needs to be given for termination of the services of a probationer, Article 311 does not apply.

One other bright period during the Mussoorie academy course was the 'army' attachment for two weeks. I opted for the high altitude group based at Tangdar, not far from Muzaffarabad, a few miles from the line of control overlooking the PoK border. This was sometime in November when winter had settled in. Our small group of 10 was attached to 6/5 Gurkhas, commanded by Colonel Bakshi and part of a brigade headquartered there. This was an experience to remember—even the road trip to Tangdar, driving from Srinagar, was exciting. The army vehicles moved on chained tyres; there was one valley to be crossed, where the possibility of an avalanche was ever present. One had to cross that on foot, only in the night, single file, walking not in unison or rhythm, in absolute silence, to minimize the chances of an avalanche being triggered. The daily routine in the camp was designed to 'teach these civilian bastards a lesson', so the day would start at 3 am, since the main drive should be done before day-break with so much snow around. On reaching the road-head to approach the picket, the climb would start up the hill—a painful, prolonged, agonizing trudge it would be. In the last 500 yards or so, a sturdy young Gurkha soldier (short as I am, he was a good foot shorter than I was), grabbed me by the shoulder and practically ran up the slope over the fresh snow and with huge relief, the army outpost on the ridge was reached, around 2 or 2.30 pm. The hot *chai*, heavily laced with sugar and cream, tasted heavenly. After an hour there, espying the Pakistani picket across the valley by binoculars and exchanging stories about the encounters and firing in the past years, the return journey would start. This would last only an hour, as much of it was done sliding down on the snow at a fair clip; the only concern was not to go down so hard so as to crash on to a projecting stone ledge; then on to the waiting truck. Sharp at 7.30 pm, the assembly would take place at the brigade mess and at 7.45 pm Brigadier Varma (probably from the famous Ravi Varma family, belonging to the old Travancore Raja's army, which merged with the Indian Army after independence), the Brigade Commander would arrive, order the first bottle of Old Smuggler opened—the first drink for everybody would be on the brigadier. A bottle those days cost ₹8 in the mess; the brigadier who probably did nothing the whole day would stand and drink at the bar—nobody could sit down while the brigadier was on his feet. Around 11.30, when the brigadier had downed his 4 or 5 drinks, dinner would be served and then we would return to our camp beds only to get up at 2 am, have a quick shave with the hot water also meant for our morning tea, and be ready for visiting the next picket that day. This was the exciting daily routine. On the odd days when we had 'free' evenings, a 'teen-patti'—'flash' cards session—would be organized by the local officers, along with some forest contractors with heavy betting—at least it seemed very heavy to us at that time—with a daily transaction of about ₹400 each, which was our monthly salary those days. One could see even then the great 'generosity' shown by forest contractors to the local army officers—they showed no compunction to us IAS boys, who were fleeced mercilessly. The ten days went by very fast. We could get a clear picture of the harshness and barrenness of the very difficult life of the soldiers and their officers in these extreme conditions. The programme was designed to give the 'soft' civilians a glimpse into the harsh living conditions of our armed forces in our border areas—it was successful in achieving its purpose.

AT THE END

This was 15 August 1947, I was 9-years-old, in a neighbourhood primary school where I was enrolled for a brief while in Tanjore. We assembled in the small courtyard, the 60 or so small children, with the headmaster unfurling the National Flag for the first time, in what I recollect was a formal and impressive ceremony—I get a lump in my throat whenever I remember the occasion. Toffees were distributed—I recall one lemon-drop and one orange-drop for each child; for 66 years I could recall distinctly the wonderfully sweet taste in my mouth, as I revisited the moment. But, I must confess, that in the past few years a tinge of bitterness has got added on to the taste. Suddenly I start getting worried: Is the country going on the right track? Is it just an old man's nostalgia, looking back at the good things, not seeing the great developments going on around him or is there some substance to the increasingly gnawing worries that are getting to me about the country's stability and future?

India is at the cross-roads. We have the choice to continue with vote bank politics, the widespread endemic corruption and our preoccupation with petty politics in our governance. We equally have the choice to take a major jump to bridge the gaps and move towards a high quality society. Sadly our electorate has not yet matured to be able to see through the venal, disruptive and selfish elements that wish to control the levers of power and thus influence the quality of our governance. We merely need to reach the highway—an element of luck is required, that a new leader emerges to break a new path. Fortunately, he need not do too much—make sure that our policies are reoriented properly, and minimum administrative standards are met to deliver results. Our people are strong enough to take the ball and run.

This book is a cry of anguish; it is also a call for reforms. Some essential critical steps that need to be taken urgently are referred to in the various chapters. However, all reforms constitute a continuum. Clearly the list of measures mentioned is not exhaustive, does not cover all elements where urgent changes are required; nor has the argumentation been detailed and supported with full data. Differing opinions are possible on each of the reform suggestions. However, each item has to be looked at in-depth, and a clear view taken about the way forward. Governance is 5 per cent policy and 95 per cent implementation. Good implementation of sensible policies is the need of the hour. This is not rocket science—basic commonsense is what is required. Above all governance is only as good as the people who govern us.

At the end, all we need is a new beginning; there is enormous inherent strength in the citizen, who has been suppressed, just not given the chance. In this democracy, the system and governance has so far been geared to suit the requirements of the ruling classes. All the citizen needs is the opportunity, provided the basics to find his feet, and allowed to flower—this he will do in quick time. Two-thirds of this century surely then will belong to India.